CELEBRATIONS OF GOD'S

SACRAMENTS

Joseph Martos

W9-AHT-241

Harcourt
Religion Publishers

Our Mission

The primary mission of Harcourt Religion Publishers is to provide the Catholic and Christian educational markets with the highest quality catechetical print and media resources. The content of these resources reflects the best insights of current theology, methodology, and pedagogical research. The resources are practical and easy to use, designed to meet expressed market needs, and written to reflect the teachings of the Catholic Church.

Nihil Obstat
Rev. Richard L. Schaefer

Imprimatur
✠ Most Rev. Jerome Hanus OSB
Archbishop of Dubuque
January 1, 2002
Feast of Saint Joseph Mary Tomasi, patron saint of liturgy

The Nihil Obstat and Imprimatur are official declarations that a book or pamphlet is free of doctrinal or moral error. No implication is contained therein that anyone who granted the Nihil Obstat and Imprimatur agree with the contents, opinions, or statements expressed.

Scripture Unless otherwise noted: The Scripture quotations contained herein are from the New Revised Standard Version Bible: Catholic Edition copyright © 1993 and 1989, by the Division of Christian Education of the National Council of the Churches of Christ in the U.S.A. Used by permission. All rights reserved.

Excerpts from the English translation of *Rite of Marriage* © 1969, International Committee on English in the Liturgy, Inc. (ICEL); excerpts from the English translation of *Rite of Baptism for Children* © 1969, ICEL; excerpts from the English translation of *Rite of Holy Week* © 1972, ICEL; excerpts from the English translation of *The Roman Missal* © 1973, ICEL; excerpts from the English translation of *Rite of Penance* © 1974, ICEL; excerpts from the English translation of *Pastoral Care of the Sick* © 1982, ICEL; excerpts from the English translation of *Rite of Christian Initiation of Adults* © 1985, ICEL. All rights reserved.

Photo Credits appear on page vii.

Printed in the United States of America

ISBN 0-15-901106-X

10 9 8 7

Contents

Sacraments and Divine Life 37

4   Baptism: Immersion in God's Life 65

5 Confirmation: Affirmation of God's Life 89

6 Eucharist: Celebration of God's Life 121

Introduction

The telephone rings impatiently. The excited voice on the other end announces, "It's a girl! She's beautiful! We're calling her Nicole Marie. Everyone's fine. Gotta go. More calls to make. Pass the word. Hey, I'm a dad! Bye." A call to celebrate.

Our lives are lived from celebration to celebration. But what is a celebration? It is a way to observe, remember, and communicate things that are

really significant in our lives. Is it always a party? No. But it is always connected with something important, and it always involves other people. We are social beings with definite needs. We need other people in our lives in order to be happy, and to be happy forever we need to let God into our lives. Our relationship with others and with God is the heart of the sacraments. Sacraments celebrate significant events in our lives in a special way. They touch our human journey and connect it to our journey with God.

We are born into a family, a culture, a society. Baptism celebrates our entrance into the Church, either as infants or later in life as converts. We are welcomed into a new family, a spiritual family, a community of faith. As we are nurtured and as we mature within our human family, we are given additional responsibilities, and our ideas and skills are valued. Confirmation recognizes, deepens, and celebrates our Christian life, strengthened by the Holy Spirit. Families provide physical and emotional nourishment with food and love. Eucharistic worship offers us great spiritual nourishment—Jesus himself. The Eucharist celebrates the shared life of the Catholic community that gathers weekly (or even more frequently) around the altar to be in communion with Christ and with one another.

Relationships are meant to bring out the best in us. Sometimes we fail and we need help. The Sacrament of Reconciliation celebrates the embrace of a loving God and of a supportive community that wants us to be the best persons that we can be. Anointing of the Sick is also a sacrament of support, touching the lives of those who are very ill or elderly. It is a healing sign of God's spiritual strength in times of physical weakness.

Families are begun and blessed in the Sacrament of Matrimony. Couples profess their love for and dedication to each other before a community that supports their journey together. In a similar way, through the Sacrament of Holy Orders, the community welcomes the bishops, priests, and deacons who have responded to the call to dedicate themselves to the service of God and the Church.

Besides giving us support and affirmation in our journey through life, the sacraments also celebrate our unity with other Christians who walk that journey with us. They connect us with a wonderful tradition of people growing in their relationship with God and others. In one form or another, the sacraments reach back to the days of the earliest Christians, they are woven into the Church's history, and they stretch around the world today, touching the lives of Christians just like us. (Most Christian Churches that do not call themselves Catholic have sacraments, although most of them have not kept the traditional seven.) The sacraments celebrate the important moments in our lives and the mysteries of our faith.

From ancient times until today, the sacraments have been a special bond of unity among Catholic Christians. These traditional Church ceremonies are signs of their unity with God and with one another, as well as with the Church centered in Rome. Whether we live in Europe or Asia, North or South America, Africa or Australia, Catholics the world over retain these sacraments as signs of what we believe in and as symbols of how we are to live as Christians. The sacraments affirm the unity of Catholics in a worldwide religious communion, and they symbolically unite the significant moments of a Christian life within a single perspective. That perspective moves from birth through all the passages of our lives, blessed and supported within the community of the Church through its sacramental celebrations.

Scripture

[On the day of Pentecost, Peter addressed the crowd,] "Fellow Israelites, I may say to you confidently of our ancestor David that he both died and was buried, and his tomb is with us to this day. Since he was a prophet, he knew that God had sworn with an oath to him that he would put one of his descendants on his throne. . . . This Jesus God raised up, and of that all of us are witnesses. Being therefore exalted at the right hand of God, and having received from the Father the promise of the Holy Spirit, he has poured out this that you both see and hear. . . . Therefore let the entire house of Israel know with certainty that God has made him both Lord and Messiah. . . ."

ACTS 2:29–30, 32, 36

Prayer

O give thanks to the LORD, call on his name,
make known his deeds among the peoples.
Sing to him, sing praises to him;
tell of all his wonderful works.
Glory in his holy name;
let the hearts of those who seek the LORD rejoice.
Seek the LORD and his strength;
seek his presence continually.
Remember the wonderful works he has done,
his miracles, and the judgments he uttered. . . .

PSALM 105:1–5

Rooted in History and Culture

Roots

Roots are very important to people. Some of us grew up in the same city or town where we were born, but many of us have moved with our family to a new place. A few of us may have moved many times. Still, we usually like to keep in contact with where we came from. We are curious about our old neighborhood, the house we used to live in, even our former school. We usually try to keep in touch with our grandparents, even if they live far away. For those of us whose parents are divorced, we usually want to maintain our connection with the parent with whom we are not living.

Moving deeper and farther back in time, most of us want to know about our family history and our ethnic backgrounds. We may not speak the language that our immigrant grandparents did (or great-grandparents or great-great . . .), but, as Italians or Poles or Hispanics, we find another part of who we are in the customs and traditions of our ancestors. Those of us who are citizens or residents of the United States identify with the history of our country. Our relatives may not have fought in the Revolution, but we find part of what we are in the stories of colonial times. What we inherit from our past is called **tradition.** All of us, whether we realize it or not, are the inheritors of many traditions—family, ethnic, national, and religious, to name a few.

Activity

Select one of your family traditions (for example, the way your family celebrates a certain holiday, or where you go on summer vacation) and write a short essay about it. Tell what you have gotten out of that tradition and why you intend or don't intend to pass it on to your own children.

tradition what is handed on or passed down from one generation to the next

Research

Find out about your roots.

1. Ask your parents or grandparents about where your family came from, how they came to this country or to this part of the country. Write down your findings or share them with the class—with photographs, if you have them.

2. Bring to class something (photo, souvenir, old toy, for example) that connects you with your past. Explain what that connection is.

3. On your own or with your parents, make a list of family traditions. Describe some of them to the class and explain why they are important.

Journal

Reflect and journal on the following things in your background. Choose the ones that you identify as having the greatest impact on you.

- Extended family (parents, grandparents, great-grandparents, uncles and aunts, cousins, and so on)
- Place of origin (city, town, or region in the U.S. or beyond it)
- Ethnic, cultural, or racial background
- (North, Central, South) American heritage
- Religious tradition

Catholics today benefit from family, ethnic, and religious traditions.

Catholic Tradition

Activity

Find your birth certificate, Baptism certificate, Confirmation certificate, First Communion certificate, and photographs or memorabilia from those events. Make a scrapbook or create another suitable way to preserve and display these items for yourself and future generations.

Tradition the passing on of beliefs and customs from generation to generation; the living transmission of the gospel message in the Church

---

liturgy a formal act of religious worship; a religious ceremony or ritual; a church service; the Church's celebration of the Paschal mystery

---

sacrament broadly, any sign or symbol of a sacred reality; a Christian ritual that celebrates or signifies a sacred mystery

---

Tradition is very important for Catholics. Whether we grow up as Catholics or join the Church later in our lives, we become part of a community of believers with a tradition that is two millennia long. Our religious tradition has always included the Sacred Scriptures. In fact, it was in the early Church that the New Testament was written and the Jewish Scriptures were adopted as our Old Testament. We have always had a tradition of reading and responding to God as revealed in the Scriptures.

Our tradition has always also included a liturgical and sacramental life. Catholic worship from ancient times has been called a **liturgy,** from the Greek words meaning "work of the people" or "service in the name of the people." It is the Christian people's work, our vocation, to praise and thank God for the gifts of life and salvation given to us through the death and resurrection of Jesus Christ. And Catholics have always done this.

In our liturgy, therefore, and in our **sacraments,** we discover our connection with God, with one another, and with our historical roots. For Catholics those roots go all the way back to the time of Jesus and the apostles, and they weave through the centuries drawing nourishment from the many cultures through which they passed. In their outward appearance, the Catholic sacraments have blossomed in a variety of forms, depending on the cultures that nourished them. For this reason, the sacraments have sometimes changed dramatically in appearance, the way that plants and flowers have evolved to adapt to changing environments.

> ## WHAT THE CATECHISM SAYS
>
> When we celebrate the sacraments today, we proclaim the faith we have received from the apostles. Our communal liturgical prayer reflects our faith in Jesus and the Church's great tradition.
>
> See the *Catechism of the Catholic Church*, #1124.

Salvador Dali's representation of the Last Supper captures both meal and sacrifice. What signs and symbols do you see in this painting? What do they represent?

Early Informal Practices

During the very first decades of Christianity, the apostles were still alive and the faith was spreading rapidly. If we look in the New Testament, we see that the apostles baptized new converts in water and prayed over them to receive the Holy Spirit. They shared the sacred Bread and Wine, remembering the Lord's Last Supper. They appointed leaders in the communities they started, and they gave instructions to pray for and anoint the sick.

We also see, however, that the sacraments in those days were very informal. Neither Jesus nor the apostles gave detailed instructions about how the Christian rituals should be performed. A good deal was left up to the inspiration of the moment and the creativity of the leaders in each community. This was quite appropriate when communities were small enough to meet in people's homes and express their faith spontaneously. Today we associate religious ritual with special vestments and utensils. In the early days, however, everyone came dressed in their ordinary clothes, including the pastor. They used their everyday plates and cups, and they used the bread and wine that were customary in their culture. Baptisms were done in nearby lakes and streams.

The basic ingredients of the rituals were rather informally borrowed from the culture of the times as well. Bread and wine were used by Jesus, but he used them because they were common foods in Palestine and because they were always part of special Jewish meals. (The Eucharist might look somewhat different if Jesus had been born in China!) Baptism in water, anointing with oil, and touching people while saying a prayer or blessing were also found in the Mediterranean world where Christianity grew up. The Jewish people gave these rituals new meaning in light of God's covenant with them. The early Church, in turn, borrowed these familiar symbols and gave them further new meanings.

Within a few decades the Christian faith was firmly rooted in most of the cities around the Mediterranean Sea. From Israel in the east to Spain in the west, from Egypt in the south to Italy and Greece in the north, the same sacraments could be found in every Christian community. Although the ceremonies were not quite as informal as at the beginning, they still showed a good deal of variation from one community to the next.

SCRIPTURE

The following Scripture passages illustrate the spontaneity and informality of Baptism during the first decades of Christianity.

DisCussioN

In the large group, discuss the following questions:

1. Would you like the sacraments to be less formal today? Explain.

2. What might happen if there were no rules regarding sacramental celebrations?

The official said to Philip, "Tell me, was the prophet talking about himself or about someone else?" So Philip began at this place in the Scriptures and explained the good news about Jesus.

As they were going along the road, they came to a place where there was some water. The official said, "Look! Here is some water. Why can't I be baptized?" He ordered the chariot to stop. Then they both went down into the water, and Philip baptized him.

Acts 8:34–38 (CEV)

While Peter was still speaking, the Holy Spirit fell upon all who heard the word. The circumcised believers who had come with Peter were astounded that the gift of the Holy Spirit had been poured out even on the Gentiles, for they heard them speaking in tongues and extolling God. Then Peter said, "Can anyone withhold the water for baptizing these people who have received the Holy Spirit just as we have?" So he ordered them to be baptized in the name of Jesus Christ. Then they invited him to stay for several days.

Acts 10:44–48

Review Questions

1. What is liturgy?

2. In the broad sense, what is a sacrament? In the Christian sense?

3. How did celebrations of the sacraments in the early Church differ from how they are celebrated now?

Sacraments and Mysteries

Discussion

In a small group, discuss the following questions:

1. We could say that love and friendship are spiritual realities. What are some other spiritual realities? (Make a list of these.)

2. For each spiritual reality you listed, what might be its opposite and negative spiritual reality?

3. How do you benefit from or suffer because of these spiritual realities?

mystery   something that is real but hidden from view; a spiritual or intangible reality known through experience but only partially understood

Journal

Have you ever had something that you would call a religious experience, or have you ever met someone who did? How would you describe that experience? What were some effects of that experience?

For about two centuries, it seems, Christians had no general name for their religious rites. Instead, they referred to each ritual by its own proper name: Baptism, the Lord's Supper (an early name for Eucharist), the Laying on of Hands (conferring a blessing or an ordination), and so on.

Around the year 200, a Christian writer named Tertullian wrote about religious conversion and defended the Church, which was being misunderstood and sometimes persecuted. He tried to explain to the Roman authorities that the followers of Jesus were indeed religious, even though they refused to worship the emperor or participate in other Roman religious rituals. In this work, Tertullian likened Christian Baptism to the *sacramentum* or pledge of fidelity made by Roman soldiers, for through it Christians promised fidelity and devotion to Jesus. Christians should not be considered irreligious, Tertullian argued, just because they did not practice the Roman sacraments; for the truth was, that they had their own special sacraments. Tertullian's work is the first known Christian document in which the broad term *sacrament* was applied to a Christian religious ritual.

Around the same time that Tertullian was writing in Latin near Rome, other Christians were writing about the Church's rituals in other parts of the Roman Empire. Borrowing from the Greek religion, their general name for a religious ceremony was *mysterion*. That word, however, also meant "something hidden or unseen." Eventually, the word **mystery** was adopted by Latin authors who used it to designate the special meaning or unseen reality that is celebrated in a sacramental ritual. In this way, Christians in the Roman Church came to speak of sacraments as visible signs that refer to spiritual realities or mysteries.

Eventually Christians could speak of Eucharist as a sacrament of Christ's presence, Baptism as a sacrament of God's acceptance, Confirmation as a sacrament of the Spirit's power, Reconciliation as a sacrament of God's forgiveness, and so on. This insight into the relationship between the two words—the insight that sacraments are signs of mysteries—gave the Church a way to speak theologically about its special rituals.

TERTULLIAN

Tertullian (c. 160–225) came from northern Africa to Rome, perhaps to practice law. As an adult, he became a Christian and eventually a priest. An excellent thinker and writer, conversant in Latin and Greek, Tertullian became a great defender of Christianity. He wrote in support of Christianity against Roman non-Christian beliefs and practices and against heresies that arose within the Church. He was thus especially influential on the Church in the West and helped to bring a distinct Latin aura to it. Tertullian encouraged high moral standards and a prayerful spirit among Christians. In his later years, he joined the Montanists, a group that stressed such rigid morality that the majority of Christians regarded them as heretics. Nevertheless, Tertullian's writings had a significant impact on how Catholics talk about the sacraments.

Communal Celebrations

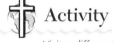

Activity

Visit a different Catholic church from the one you usually attend. Try to find one that is noticeably different from the church in your own parish. Take note of the differences in architecture and art work. If possible, attend a liturgy there and notice the similarities to and differences from what you are used to. Discuss what you have learned.

As far-flung communities around the ancient world celebrated the Christian mysteries, sacraments in the second and third centuries took on a more communal flavor. Each local church had its own distinctive way of expressing the Christian faith, using the basic sacramental elements inherited from the time of the apostles. Some used the laying on of hands to symbolize the giving of the Holy Spirit, others preferred anointing. Some used holy water in their ministry to the sick, others used blessed oil. Although all used readings from the Bible in their liturgies, each church picked the readings it wanted to use and added its own prayers.

Parallels to these communal traditions can be found in parishes today. Even though the main elements of the sacraments have become more standardized than they were in the early centuries (the result of later developments), there is a fair amount of variation. Most parishes baptize by pouring a small amount of water on the head, but some now practice immersion in a baptismal pool, the way it was done in the early days. Some parishes offer communal anointing services for the sick, while others have only private anointings. And each parish has its own preferences in liturgical art and music, giving a stamp of individuality and local culture to Catholic worship wherever it is found.

Discussion

In the large group, discuss the following questions:

1. Have you ever attended Mass or another religious ceremony in another country? In another state? Describe how it was like and different from liturgy in your own parish.

2. Looking back on that experience, what can you learn from it?

Ceremonial Liturgies

When Christianity became the favored religion of the Roman government, Sunday was made a public day of rest (until then it had been just another working day), and Christians were allowed to use the court buildings, called *basilicas,* for their weekly worship. Later, basilicas were built exclusively for religious use, and this cultural style of architecture, with its rounded arches and domed roof, was often copied for cathedrals. Such large meeting places made it possible for Christians to worship together in larger numbers than ever before.

As a result, in the fourth century, the Christian sacraments became much more ceremonial. Long processions, chanting choirs, candles and incense, embroidered vestments and gold altar vessels became the order of the day. And since other activities were often strictly limited on Sunday, liturgies grew to three and even four hours in length!

We get a marvelous "time capsule" view of what these ancient liturgies looked like if we attend an **Eastern Rite** service that is still performed in this traditional way. Many **Orthodox Churches** also preserve the distinctly Greek and Middle Eastern flavor of this early period, although their services today are often shorter than they were in the past.

We also see a reflection of the pageantry which came into Christian worship during this period in papal and episcopal Masses. Whether he is in St. Peter's Basilica in Rome or on a visit to a Catholic community somewhere around the world, the pope's Masses are filled with ceremony and are attended by large crowds. And in the Sacraments of Confirmation and Holy Orders presided over by a bishop, the liturgies are always elaborate and impressive.

Eastern Rite a Catholic Church whose liturgical traditions are very ancient and different from the Roman or Latin Rite and whose origins are in Eastern Europe or the Middle East

Orthodox Church a Church whose liturgical traditions are very ancient, but which is not in full unity with the Catholic Church (The Catholic and Orthodox Churches split from each other in the eleventh century.)

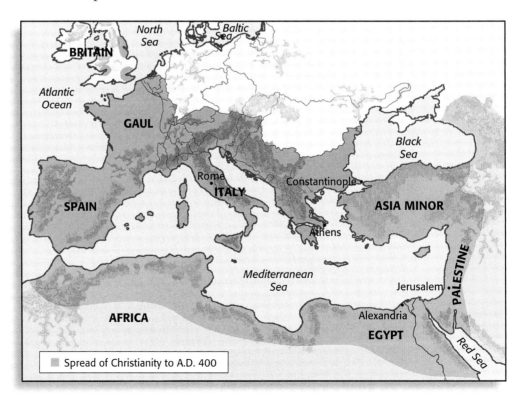

In which of the Christian areas on this map are there strong Christian centers today? Where would you find Orthodox Churches? Where would you find Eastern Rite Churches?

If there is an Eastern Rite or Orthodox church near where you live, visit it with a group of classmates and your teacher. (You can find them in the Yellow Pages under "Churches.") Telephone the pastor and ask if you might meet with him and visit his church as part of a class learning activity. Take note of what you learn, and discuss your experience in a written or oral report. (If you attend a liturgy at an Orthodox church, please do not go up to receive Communion. Only members of the Orthodox Church are allowed to receive Communion at their Eucharistic liturgy.)

Church buildings and ceremonies are similar in Greek Orthodox and Eastern Rite Churches.

After the collapse of the Roman Empire late in the fifth century, the celebration style of the sacraments became much simpler. Cities and monasteries may still have had the resources for elaborate liturgies, but in most places the ceremonies were cut to the bare minimum. Unfortunately, loose Church discipline in the late Middle Ages allowed some members of the clergy, who wanted to take advantage of the people's lack of understanding, to get away with what amounted to spiritual crimes. Parish sacraments were cut down to the bare minimum until they almost seemed like magic tricks performed on invisible souls. Bishops' liturgies, at the other extreme, became, at times, royal spectacles geared to heighten the prestige of the "princes of the Church," as the bishops were called. Clearly the situation called for a remedy.

WHAT THE CATECHISM SAYS

Eastern and Western traditions in Confirmation differ on when the sacrament is celebrated. In the early centuries of the Church, Baptism and Confirmation were celebrated together—a "double sacrament." The anointing with chrism after Baptism was understood as the confirmation or completion of Baptism. In the West the churches wanted this anointing to be done by the bishop. Due to the growth of Christianity, the bishop soon was unable to preside at all Baptisms. Therefore, the post-baptismal anointing, or celebration of Confirmation, was delayed until a time when the bishop could preside.

In the East the churches continued to celebrate this anointing at the time of Baptism, with the priest as presider for both sacraments. With the inclusion of Eucharist at this ceremony, the Church in the East celebrates to this day all the Sacraments of Christian Initiation at one liturgy. At the Easter Vigil in the West, adults and children who have reached the age of reason usually follow the same custom and celebrate Baptism, Confirmation, and Eucharist.

See the *Catechism of the Catholic Church*, #s 1290–1292.

Rooted in History and Culture

Uniform Rituals

canon law the Church's code of laws

missal book containing the ritual of the Mass

sacramentary a book of rules and prayers for the proper performance of Church rituals

Discussion

In a small group, discuss the following questions:

1. Have you ever attended Sunday worship or another church service (for example, a wedding or funeral) in a Protestant church? Describe what it was like.

2. Looking back on it, what can you learn from this experience?

Activity

If there is a Catholic church that has occasional Masses in Latin near where you live, visit it with a group of your classmates and your teacher. (Alternatively, find a videotaped presentation of the Latin—sometimes called Tridentine—Mass; check your parish library and the diocesan media center.) Note the similarities to and differences from the Mass that you usually attend. Describe those similarities and differences.

Sadly, the remedy for the abuses of the Middle Ages did not come until after Christian Europe divided between the Protestants in the North who decided to take reform into their own hands and the Catholics in the South who remained faithful to the pope. But at last a reform-minded pope took action in the tumultuous sixteenth century. Pope Paul III called a general council of the Church to take a serious look at the celebration of the sacraments and other clerical practices.

The Council of Trent (1545–1563) tightened the reins of control by the Church in Rome on sacramental practices and halted the abusive liberties that were being taken by free-wheeling clerics. Bishops were held accountable for what went on in their dioceses, and a new regimen of seminary training was made mandatory for priests. Parts of **canon law** were rewritten, and a new **missal** and **sacramentary** were introduced. All clergy were expressly forbidden to depart from these liturgical books without explicit permission from Rome.

For the first time in history there was a uniform style of sacramental practice throughout the Catholic world. In time every word and gesture of the priest was controlled, down to the smallest detail. Even the cut of vestments and the style of Church music were strictly regulated. This liturgical uniformity lasted about four hundred years, until the middle of the twentieth century. The effects of it can still be felt in the way Catholic parishes are sometimes content to do things the same way they have always done them. There are also Catholics who resist and fight every time a change is introduced. Even though the revised rites for the Mass and the other sacraments honor the Eastern Rites and permit local adaptations in the Latin or Roman Rite, they still contain a central core that is the same for all Catholics around the world.

WHAT THE CATECHISM SAYS

The ability of the Church to adapt its sacramental celebrations to differing times and places is most apparent in the changing forms of the Sacrament of Penance through the centuries. From a time of public penance and sometimes only one such opportunity in a person's lifetime, the Church moved gradually to private and frequent celebrations of its sacrament of forgiveness. For a time books of penances dictated specific penances for specific sins. Today most parishes celebrate communal Reconciliation services during Advent and Lent, services that include an opportunity for private confession of sins and individual absolution. Whatever its form, the sacrament always included contrition, confession, and satisfaction on the part of the penitent and, on God's part, forgiveness through the Church. This topic will be explored further in the chapter on the Sacrament of Reconciliation.

See the *Catechism of the Catholic Church*, #s 1447–1448.

"One though many"—the Catholic Church is known for its unity in diversity. This is most evident and celebrated in the liturgy.

Renewed Development

The most recent liturgical revisions came as a consequence of another general council of the Church, the Second Vatican Council, also known as Vatican II (1963–1965). The liturgical commission established by the council returned to the roots of the Catholic liturgy in the early centuries of Christianity. This return to liturgical roots was made possible by scholarship that uncovered those roots in Scripture and other early Christian writings. The liturgical commission set about the task of replanting those roots around the world. The result has been the emergence of more variety and diversity in the celebration of the Church's sacraments.

At the beginning of this chapter, we saw that part of the genius of the Catholic tradition has been its ability to draw strength from every culture in which the Church found itself. In the past, the Church's sacramental life was nourished by the many cultures through which it passed in its long Mediterranean and European history. But the Catholic Church is no longer just a Mediterranean Church or a European Church. Today it is a worldwide Church, drawing new life from non-Western cultures, just as it did from Western culture. There is one great difference, however: In the past, the Church's sacraments were nourished by successive cultures, one after another; today they are being nourished by a variety of cultures all at the same time.

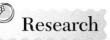

Research

Look on the Internet for information about the Second Vatican Council (Vatican II). Write or talk about what you learned about the impact of that event on the Catholic Church.

The Church is still one Church, but we are also a culturally diverse Church. Though the basic rites are the same for all Catholics around the world, the ways in which those rites are implemented are now as beautifully different as the cultures in which they are performed. An African Mass contains the same words as a Mass in Europe, but the liturgical celebration will be as different as the cultures are different. Baptisms and Confirmations in Asia and Australia both follow the instructions issued by the Vatican, but they may also follow those instructions in exotically different ways.

In the United States, those fortunate enough to live in a large city with diverse ethnic groups may catch a glimpse of this diversity when attending a Black Gospel Mass or a Mariachi Mass or an Oriental Mass. Each celebration reflects in its own unique way the pluralism of contemporary North American society. Yet each also shows, if we take the time to reflect on it, the unity in diversity which is the historical heritage of our Catholic tradition and our means of communicating and celebrating the mystery of Christ.

HISTORICAL CONNECTION: LATIN AND MYSTERY

Draw a simple time chart of Christian history, dividing it into the Apostolic Age (first century), the Early Church (second through sixth centuries), the Middle Ages (seventh through fourteenth centuries), the Renaissance (fifteenth and sixteenth centuries), and the Modern Era (seventeenth to the twenty-first century). In each section of the time chart (You may decide on some variations regarding the centuries of each era.), draw or paste pictures that represent the people or culture of that period.

The collapse of the Roman Empire was caused by the invasion of Germanic tribes from northern Europe. Even after these people were converted to Christianity, few of them could really understand the liturgy. In the West the Mass and sacraments were celebrated in Latin, the written language of the day, but most people spoke only their own tribal language or local dialect.

The simple rituals performed by priests in a strange language took on a very mystical air in this medieval setting. Listeners could only guess the meaning of prayers said in hushed tones. Water was poured, oil was smeared, ashes were applied, hands were laid, and blessings were given while people stood by, silently watching. What the priest was doing and what was happening in the sacraments seemed very mysterious.

Older people who can recall the quiet Latin Masses before Vatican II might remember the sense of mystery that surrounded them. Baptism and Confirmation, Penance and Extreme Unction were also sacramental times when something strangely wonderful seemed to be happening. Today much of the strangeness has been dispelled by the fact that the words of the rite are spoken aloud in our own language, thus fostering our understanding of what is being said in the sacramental rites. Every now and then we may still experience the religious wonder that is part of our medieval heritage, or the religious wonder might be experienced without the sense of strangeness.

Research

Ask older members of your family or parish what it was like to attend Mass when it was in Latin. Especially ask if they felt the Latin liturgy conveyed a greater sense of mystery than the liturgy in English does. Relate what you have learned.

Review Questions

1. Why is the term *mystery* used when talking about sacraments?

2. What are some of the ways that sacramental celebrations changed over the centuries?

3. What did the Council of Trent accomplish by introducing a new missal and sacramentary?

4. How do sacramental celebrations in the East differ from those in the West?

5. What did the Second Vatican Council accomplish in liturgy by going back to our historical roots?

Summary

Catholic worship is like a tree that has deep roots in the soil of the past, a tree whose trunk has grown through a succession of cultures for almost two thousand years and whose branches are today flowering in a variety of fashions. One way to connect with our Catholic roots is to learn about the history of the sacraments and see how they were formerly celebrated. Even though today there is a good deal of variety in liturgical celebrations, the sacraments point to mysteries that are the same in every time and every place and every culture.

Chapter One

Scripture

When the day of Pentecost had come, they were all together in one place. And suddenly from heaven there came a sound like the rush of a violent wind, and it filled the entire house where they were sitting. Divided tongues, as of fire, appeared among them, and a tongue rested on each of them. All of them were filled with the Holy Spirit and began to speak in other languages, as the Spirit gave them ability.

Now there were devout Jews from every nation under heaven living in Jerusalem. And at this sound the crowd gathered and was bewildered, because each one heard them speaking in the native language of each. Amazed and astonished, they asked, "Are not all these who are speaking Galileans? And how is it that we hear, each of us, in our own native language?"

ACTS 2:1–7

Prayer

Let the same mind be in you that was in Christ Jesus,
who, though he was in the form of God
    did not regard equality with God
    as something to be exploited,
but emptied himself,
    taking the form of a slave,
    being born in human likeness.
And being found in human form,
    he humbled himself
    and became obedient to the point of death—
    even to death on a cross.
Therefore God also highly exalted him
    and gave him the name
    that is above every name,
so that at the name of Jesus,
    every knee should bend,
    in heaven and on earth and under the earth,
and every tongue should confess
    that Jesus Christ is Lord,
    to the glory of God the Father.

PHILIPPIANS 2:5–11

Scripture

The day was drawing to a close, and the twelve came to him and said, "Send the crowd away, so that they may go into the surrounding villages and countryside, to lodge and get provisions; for we are here in a deserted place." But he said to them, "You give them something to eat." They said, "We have no more than five loaves and two fish—unless we are to go and buy food for all these people." For there were about five thousand men. And he said to his disciples, "Make them sit down in groups of about fifty each." They did so and made them all sit down. And taking the five loaves and the two fish, he looked up to heaven, and blessed and broke them, and gave them to the disciples to set before the crowd. And all ate and were filled. What was left over was gathered up, twelve baskets of broken pieces.

LUKE 9:12–17

Prayer

Praise the LORD, O Jerusalem!
    Praise your God, O Zion!
For he strengthens the bars of your gates;
    he blesses your children within you.
He grants peace within your borders;
    he fills you with the finest of wheat.
He sends out his command to the earth;
    his word runs swiftly. . . .
He has not dealt thus with any other nation. . . .
    Praise the LORD!

PSALM 147:12–15, 20

Symbols of God

CHAPTER OVERVIEW

Symbolic Actions

symbol something visible or tangible that reminds us of and is able to put us in touch with a reality that is invisible and intangible but still real; something that communicates effective emotional or spiritual meaning

symbolic action an action that says more than words can express, that communicates what is in the heart and what we want someone to know

Have you ever given a gift to someone in order to say "You're special to me" in a way that said it better than words alone could? Your gift symbolized what you wanted to say, and it keeps on saying it every time your friend looks at or uses your gift. It says both "You're special to me" and all the other things you feel but for which you cannot find words.

Have you ever stayed with a friend who needed you, just to be there with him or her until the crisis had passed? The gift of your presence symbolized the care and concern you have for your friend, and it did that in a way which words of consolation alone cannot express. By "acting out" your care and concern, you communicate them much better than by saying them in words. You give a gift or help friends express the love you have for them. Looking at it the other way around, when someone gives you a gift or lends a helping hand, you get a sense of the way the person cares about you. Even though you can never literally get inside the mind and heart of the other person, **symbols** bridge the gap between the two of you and reveal what is in your hearts.

We have seen that in every age, in every culture, the Church has performed sacramental actions. Why? Why don't Catholics just read the Scriptures, learn the lessons that they teach, and put them into practice? Why do they insist on ritualizing or "acting out" what the Bible teaches? Why are Catholics concerned with putting into "body language" things that might seem to be just as easily said in words? The answer is that **symbolic actions** often say more to us than mere words can express. Sometimes words alone cannot express everything we would like to say. Sometimes symbolic actions, such as the giving of a gift or the giving of personal time and attention, are the best or an additional way to communicate what we want to express and reveal to others.

In the story of Tobit, two people each have half of a document. When the pieces are put together, Tobias receives the money he was sent to retrieve. The word symbol *originally meant "to throw or put together."*

Jean Charles Cazin, "Tobias and the Angel."

Chapter Two

DisCUSsioN

In a small group, discuss the following questions:

1. What are some of the ways that you symbolically express who you are (the clothes you wear, the organizations you belong to, the things you do, and so on) and through which other people get an idea of who you are?

2. What are some of the things you observe about other people that symbolize who they are and tell you about them?

Activity

If symbols are concrete signs of unseen realities (think of signs of spring), find pictures or photographs that symbolize realities that really cannot be pictured because they are intangible or spiritual. Good examples, introduced briefly in the last chapter, include human qualities such as friendship, honesty, and loyalty. Explain your collection, saying what each image represents to you.

DisCUSsioN

In the large group, discuss the following questions:

1. What are some conventional symbols that people wear (badges, uniforms, and so on) that tell you who they are?

2. When you see a symbol (for example, a police badge), in what ways do you perceive the person wearing it differently?

3. What are some of the kinds of things that symbols convey about people? Repeat this exercise using different types of clothing or insignia.

4. Are feelings real? Can they be seen? Explain.

5. How do we know what others are feeling?

6. How do we express our feelings to others?

7. Are values real? Why or why not?

8. Are morals real? Give reasons to support your answer.

Journal

1. Have you ever lost (through death, distance, divorce, or the like) a close friend or relative, of whom you keep something (an article connected with that person or a photo) that reminds you of that person and what that person added to your life? If so, what is that symbolic item, and how does it connect you with that person?

2. Think of something you have at home (on a shelf, in a drawer, on a wall, in a scrapbook) that you keep because it reminds you and connects you with something important from earlier in your life. (Sometimes these symbolic keepsakes are called *souvenirs,* from the French word meaning "to remember.") What is this object, and what does it symbolize to you?

The Sacraments as Symbolic Actions

sacrament as defined by the Catechism: an efficacious sign of grace, instituted by Christ and entrusted to the Church, by which we receive the life of God through the work of the Holy Spirit

Activity

Look around your school for symbols. Make a list of these symbols and what they represent.

Because symbolic actions often are the best way to communicate what we want to express and reveal to others, Christians from the very beginning have felt the need to communicate their faith through symbolic actions as well as through words. This is because words alone are not enough to convey everything that the sacraments are about. The **sacraments** express things that can indeed be put into words, and yet words alone cannot say them as fully and as richly as they deserve to be said. The sacraments are the Church's way of saying what the Christian life is all about. To put it briefly, the sacraments are all about the life of God, and the Christian life is a way of participating in the mystery of God.

Just saying that, however, does not convey the full impact of the Christian life. Just saying that does not reveal its richness. And so the Church down through the centuries has tried to communicate what the Christian life is all about, not only in words but also in symbols, especially those sacred symbols called sacraments. The definition of sacrament found in the margin will be explored in more detail in this chapter and the next.

Discussion

In a small group, discuss the following questions:

1. Brainstorm at least ten symbolic gestures (for example, shaking hands with someone, turning your back on someone). List these on a sheet of paper, along with what they mean.

2. How does each of these gestures say something more or better than words alone do?

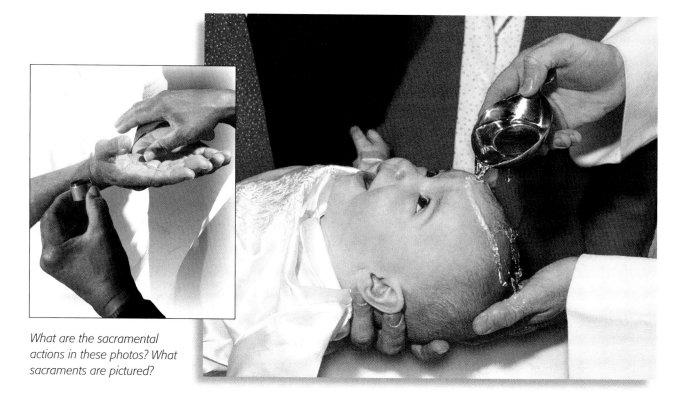

What are the sacramental actions in these photos? What sacraments are pictured?

Sacramentals

Sacramentals have been part of the Church's life for many centuries. Some of them are simple rituals, such as making the sign of the cross when giving a blessing or when blessing oneself—"In the name of the Father and of the Son and of the Holy Spirit." You may have heard someone say, "When I was a child, my grandmother used to kiss me good night on the forehead and make a sign of the cross with her thumb. I always felt peaceful and ready for bed when she gave me her blessing." The sign of the cross is one of the most ancient Christian sacramentals. Genuflecting before the Blessed Sacrament is a sacramental action that became popular in the Middle Ages when it was customary to kneel before someone of high rank.

Some sacramentals are ceremonies. Men and women who join religious communities profess their vows in such ceremonies by which they are consecrated for service to God. There are very elaborate, ancient ceremonies for the dedication of churches, for the coronation of kings and queens, and for the installation of bishops and the pope. Other sacramentals are blessings. For example, there are simple rituals for the blessing of animals and fields, fishing boats and new houses.

Other sacramentals include individual or communal prayer services: the Rosary, the Stations of the Cross, and Benediction of the Blessed Sacrament. These and similar devotions focus our attention on some aspect of our faith and deepen our awareness of the mystery that they present to our attention.

Some sacramentals, finally, are symbolic objects: crucifixes, icons, rosaries, statues, mosaics and paintings of holy persons and important events in salvation history. What makes them sacramental is not the quality of art but their ability to raise our hearts and minds to God. Relics and holy cards, scapulars and medals are also reminders of our Christian call to holiness. Holy water and blessed oil, ashes and palms, candles and incense are sacramentals that are used at special times in the Church's liturgical life.

A wide variety of art forms and sacramental objects are apparent in this view of S. Marco in Venice, Italy.

sacramental a sacred sign that is similar to the sacraments in some ways, by which spiritual meanings and realities are signified or by which spiritual blessings are able to be obtained by God's grace through the prayers of the Church

Discussion

In the large group, discuss the following questions:

1. With what sacramentals are you familiar?

2. When do you make use of sacramentals? Why do you do so?

3. What sacramentals are used during the liturgies you attend? Why are they used?

Symbols as Revelations

Symbols speak to us. They tell us what they are about. Thus, the water of Baptism suggests that Baptism on a natural level has something to do with what water means to people: In some circumstances water signifies cleansing; in others it means life. The symbol has meaning in ordinary life; it says something to those who perceive or experience it. All symbols are like this. They reveal in signs things that literally we cannot see. They speak to us about things that literally we cannot hear. They help us feel things that literally we cannot touch. Symbols enable us to experience realities that are beyond the reach of the senses. They make it possible for us to know what is real, even though the reality is something of a mystery to us.

In dramatic symbol, spring follows winter by gently overcoming it.

Take thoughts, for example. How do we know the thoughts of others? We cannot get inside their heads. But we can get to know their thoughts through that marvelous symbolic invention called language. By speaking to us, people give us audible signals that tell us what they are thinking. Language is a symbol system that makes the communication of thoughts possible.

Feelings are very similar. We cannot literally get inside other people to experience what they are feeling, but they can show us verbally and nonverbally what is going on inside them. A sigh, a scowl, a relaxed or tense body, a smile, tears—these are all signs that help bridge the gap between other people's inner lives and our own. Body language, gestures, and facial expressions are other sets of signs that make the communication of feelings possible.

How do we get to know another person's character or personality? Again, both the problem and the solution are the same. Character and personality are not tangible, visible realities. Still, they are real. They are intangible, invisible realities. We could even call them spiritual realities, since they make up a person's moral and emotional nature. We can get to know what people are like inside by observing what they do and listening to what they say. Their outward behavior reveals their inner nature to us. Once again, external signs play the role of symbols that communicate invisible or spiritual mysterious realities to us.

 ## Activities

1. In many ways, intangible or spiritual realities are more important than tangible or material ones. Even money is less important than the pleasure, satisfaction, or prestige it can buy for us. After coming up with a personal list of ten such realities, explain in an essay why they are important and what life would be like if they were absent (for example, if there were no such thing as love, courage, family, or similar intangibles).

2. Make a symbolic work of art (painting, drawing, sculpture) and explain the symbolism to others in the class.

In the large group, discuss the following questions:

1. What does "revelation" mean to you?

2. What are some revelations that you have experienced in your life or discovered on your own?

3. What are some nonreligious revelations that you have heard about?

4. What does revelation mean in a religious sense (for example, the Bible contains God's revelation)?

Take yet another example: spring. How do we know that spring has arrived? We cannot see it or hear it or touch it or smell it. Spring (like the other seasons, for that matter) is an unseen reality that is knowable only through concrete signs: We have experienced spring through these signs: the budding of trees, the singing of birds, the warming of the air, the sweet smell of new grass. So much of what we think we know directly, upon reflection, turns out to be known only indirectly, through symbols.

Symbols, then, reveal much of reality to us. Without our spiritual ability to "see through" symbols, as it were, all we would know are sensations: colors, sounds, touches, tastes, and smells. We would never know those intelligible, invisible realities that are most meaningful to us: friendship and love, nature and society, justice and beauty.

WHAT THE CATECHISM SAYS

The signs and symbols of the sacraments are rooted in natural signs of God found in creation and culture. People need and use natural signs such as light and dark, wind and fire, water and earth, tree and fruit, to communicate their thoughts, emotions, and spiritual yearnings. People also use signs based on their social nature: language, gestures, actions; washing and anointing, eating and drinking in family and community. Jesus used signs such as these in his teaching and in his miracles. Many of the symbols we use in our sacraments were first used by the Jewish people as signs of their covenant with God: anointing, laying on of hands, sacrifices, and especially the Passover. Christ gives new meaning to our signs and symbols; in him they are signs of grace. Today the Holy Spirit continues to work in the Church through its sacramental signs. The sacraments in turn point to and make present the salvation gained through Christ and anticipate the joy and wonder of eternal life with God in heaven.

See the *Catechism of the Catholic Church,* #s 1145–1152.

THE CASTLE

Once upon a time there was a wonderful prince. He lived in a valley where he was loved by all the people. He and his people worked together, ate together, and celebrated together. There was great peace and harmony in the land because of the love they all had for one another.

One day the people decided to show their great admiration for the kindly prince.

"Let us build him a castle," they said, "a fine home for him to live in, even better than those of other princes."

"Together we will build the most wonderful castle the world has ever seen," they explained, "for with our prince we are beyond doubt the happiest people on earth."

It did, indeed, turn out to be the most marvelous castle imaginable. The walls were hewn from rare marble, so fine as to be almost transparent. The towers were made from precious stones—one of ruby, one of sapphire, one of emerald, and one of onyx. The floor was inlaid ivory and the roof gold. People everywhere agreed that it rivaled the sun in brilliance and beauty.

Word of the castle began to spread beyond the valley. At first the curious came from nearby. Then travelers began arriving from far and wide. It became necessary for the villagers to set up inns and restaurants to provide for the needs of these tourists. The greater the influx of travelers, the greater became the commerce in the village.

The villagers knew that their good fortune was due to the wonderful castle. In order to assure their continued prosperity, they would regularly polish its stones and clean its towers. The castle continued to sparkle like a jewel, drawing visitors from the world around.

Then village grew into a city. There was commerce and industry. But with the trade came rivalry, with rivalry jealousy, with jealousy hate, and with hate contention. There was no longer peace in the valley.

Finally, one day the wonderful prince emerged from the castle. The people had all but forgotten that he lived there. Without saying a word, the prince walked around the castle seven times. When he was done, the castle collapsed.

"Why have you done this?" the angry people shouted.

"I have done nothing," the prince replied. "Seven times I walked its circumference searching for your image in its walls and on its towers. I found none. The castle no longer reflected the hearts of the people. It could stand no longer."

Fables for God's People by John R. Aurelio.

Discussion

In the large group, discuss the following questions:

1. In what sense was the castle a symbol?
2. Why did the castle, as a symbol, collapse?
3. What did the castle, at first, reveal? In the end?

Review Questions

1. What is a symbol? A symbolic action? A sacramental? A sacrament?
2. What does it mean to say that a sacrament is a symbolic action?
3. What do symbols reveal?
4. What does it mean to say that the sacraments are rooted in natural signs of God?

The cathedral in Cologne, Germany.

Revelation as Symbolic

People who do not believe in God sometimes find it a little strange that religious people believe in things they cannot see. It should be obvious by now, however, that everybody, whether religious or atheist, believes in things they cannot see. Anyone who believes in thoughts and feelings, character and personality, nature and society, love and justice, believes in realities that are not, strictly speaking, visible.

Through symbols, we all come in contact with invisible and spiritual realities that we take for granted. But religious people also do one more thing that nonbelievers do not, and this is the basic difference between them. Religious people look at the world around them, and they perceive something that the unbelieving are not aware of. They stand before a majestic vista, and besides seeing the awesome wonder of nature, they perceive the majesty of God. They look up into the starry heavens, and besides sensing the vastness of the universe, they feel the infinity of God. They walk into a beautiful cathedral, and besides admiring the architecture, they lift their hearts to God. They read the Bible, and besides hearing voices from the past, they listen to the ever-present word of God.

In brief, Christians and other religious people see many things as symbolic of God. Through the world around them they come in contact with a spiritual reality beyond all others, and they allow it to communicate itself to them. They allow nature and art to be symbols of God for them, bridging the gap between the human and the divine. When they have what are called "religious experiences," they are opening themselves up to the **revelation** of God through tangible and visible signs.

When we think about it, therefore, what we call revelation is not really strange at all. It's simply an extension of our natural human power to perceive spiritual realities that our senses cannot see and touch. Our religious experiences are times when we pay attention to a reality beyond the natural world. Religious experiencing is our way of moving through symbols to come in contact with a **"supernatural"** reality. Revelation is what we experience when God is revealed to us through symbols.

revelation anything that is revealed or disclosed; also, the act of revealing or disclosing; for Christians, God's self-communication, realized by words and actions over time, and fully in Jesus

supernatural above and beyond what is natural, usual, ordinary

Jews and Christians often speak about the Bible as revelation, as God's revealed word. In fact, however, the Bible began to be written long after the Judeo-Christian revelation had begun. Abraham lived around 1800 B.C., the Israelites entered the promised land around 1200 B.C., and the prophets spoke their message of divine judgment around 800 B.C., but much of the Old Testament as we have it today was not put together until around 400 B.C. The stories that we find in the Scriptures are the written record of a revelation that was already taking place for centuries.

Since God is a spiritual reality, we cannot see him directly. In this sense, the ancient Israelites were probably no different from ourselves. Yet they perceived God acting in their lives, and so they recounted and saved marvelously vivid stories from generation to generation about what God had done and said to them. Most likely, though, God appeared and spoke to them the same way that God is revealed to us—through symbols and through events that they perceived as symbolizing God's presence, power, and will.

When Abraham felt the need to break from his past, renounce human sacrifices, and move to a new land where he could live a new life, he heard and experienced the yearning as the call of God. When Abraham's descendants miraculously escaped from slavery in Egypt, they knew the hand of God was involved. When they received the Law that gave them a way to live in harmony and peace, they perceived the commandments as coming from God. When they conquered the land that Abraham had once settled in, they acknowledged it as a gift from God and a promised land. When their tiny kingdom was later conquered and destroyed, they saw it as the righteous punishment of God.

Unlike other ancient peoples who perceived God only in nature, the Israelites perceived God acting and speaking in their own history. The events that they experienced together were symbolic in a way that was unique. The Judeo-Christian revelation began among a people for whom history was sacred because it revealed God to them. It began among a people for whom historical persons such as the prophets were living symbols, for they communicated God's message to them. It began among a people for whom events and persons could therefore be sacramental, in the sense that they were signs of a sacred and mysterious reality, the reality of God.

Research

Artists have depicted God in many ways, even though God as a spiritual reality cannot be seen. Find some artists' depictions of God. What do these images symbolize about him? Share your impressions with the class.

Activity

Look back at a time in your life and see how God may have been guiding or protecting you, even though you did not realize it at the time. In an essay, explain what happened and how you see the presence of God in the experience. Connect this to the idea that the Israelites found God in their history *after* they had lived through it, and then when they wrote about it later, they portrayed God as a visible character in the story.

Jesus—The Sacrament of God

messiah Hebrew term for the anointed one; *Christ* is the Greek term (It is related to chrism, a type of oil used for anointing.)

incarnation literally, enfleshment; used to describe how the Son of God, the Second Person of the Blessed Trinity, became human in order to bring about the salvation of all people

The Jewish people were prepared by their own religious tradition for another unique revelation of God. At the time that Jesus was born, many of them were expecting a **messiah,** an anointed one, a Christ. And when Jesus began his public ministry, at least some Jews believed that he was the one for whom they had been waiting.

Outwardly Jesus looked like any other man, but when he spoke, it was as if God was speaking to his listeners' hearts. Those who followed him saw those who were sick healed of physical and spiritual ills, and they sensed the power of God at work. They saw Jesus' compassion for those who were poor and lowly, and they beheld the mercy of God for all people. They saw Jesus chase the money changers from the temple, and they realized that the justice of God was in their midst. When Jesus told his hearers about his Father's love, they knew that he was talking about the same love that he was showing to them. When Jesus forgave people for their sins, they felt it as God's forgiveness. When Jesus gathered a community of disciples around himself, they felt joined together in the Spirit of God.

Jesus made God visible for people who believed in him. He acted the way that God would act, if God could be seen. He spoke the way that God would speak, if God could be heard. He embodied everything that they believed about the God whom they knew does not have a body. He was filled with the Holy Spirit; he was the **incarnation** of the God who is pure spirit.

In this sense, then, Jesus was a living symbol of God in the world. In his presence, people felt the presence of something more than a man. In his words, people heard more than just a man's ideas and feelings. In his deeds, people saw more than just human power at work. Through who Jesus was, they saw who God is. Through what Jesus said, they heard God speaking to them. Through what Jesus did, they felt God acting in their lives.

Thus Jesus was and is the unique sacrament of God, the living symbol of invisible divinity. He fully reveals the mystery of God and shows us that reality in flesh and blood, words and deeds. He reveals the life of God, a life of self-giving and compassion, a life of forgiveness and love, a life of service and concern.

✝ Activity

Read the ninth chapter of the Gospel according to John, the story of a man cured of blindness who recognizes God's power in Jesus. How does the Scripture passage illustrate the importance of symbolic action in the ministry of Jesus? Respond in an essay, an oral report, or a skit.

Discussion

In the large group, discuss the following questions:

1. What does it mean to say that Jesus is a sacrament of God?

2. Explain in your own words, perhaps using stories from the Gospels, connections you perceive between what Jesus said and did and what you imagine God to be.

3. If you have any questions about this concept, what are those questions?

SCRIPTURE

The following Scripture passages illustrate the importance of symbolic action in the ministry of Jesus and in the early Church:

Jesus says that people can tell who he is by what he does.

When John heard in prison what the Messiah was doing, he sent word by his disciples and said to him, "Are you the one who is to come, or are we to wait for another?" Jesus answered them, "Go and tell John what you hear and see: the blind receive their sight, the lame walk, the lepers are cleansed, the deaf hear, the dead are raised, and the poor have good news brought to them. And blessed is anyone who takes no offense at me."

Matthew 11:2–6

Discussion

In the large group, discuss the following questions:

1. What are the symbolic actions done or referred to in each of these readings?

2. Of what are the actions symbolic?

3. What do these readings tell us about Jesus as sacrament of God?

4. Why is faith necessary for those who follow Jesus?

5. Why are words not enough to prove one's love?

It takes faith to perceive what is revealed symbolically.

When Jesus had finished these parables, he left that place.

He came to his hometown and began to teach the people in their synagogue, so that they were astounded and said, "Where did this man get this wisdom and these deeds of power? Is not this the carpenter's son? Is not his mother called Mary? And are not his brothers James and Joseph and Simon and Judas? And are not all his sisters with us? Where then did this man get all this?" And they took offense at him. But Jesus said to them, "Prophets are not without honor except in their own country and in their own house." And he did not do many deeds of power there, because of their unbelief.

Matthew 13:53–58

The disciples recognize who Jesus is through what he does.

Once when Jesus was praying alone, with only the disciples near him, he asked them, "Who do the crowds say that I am?" They answered, "John the Baptist; but others, Elijah; and still others, that one of the ancient prophets has arisen." He said to them, "But who do you say that I am?" Peter answered, "The Messiah of God."

Luke 9:18–20

Love shows itself in action.

We know love by this, that he laid down his life for us—and we ought to lay down our lives for one another. How does God's love abide in anyone who has the world's goods and sees a brother or sister in need and yet refuses help?

Little children, let us love, not in word or speech, but in truth and action.

1 John 3:16–18

The Church—A Sacrament of Jesus

Jesus lived the life of God to the fullest, but he did not keep that life to himself. He shared his spirit, the Spirit of God, with those who believed in him as the Messiah and who acknowledged him as their Lord and Savior. He communicated the life of God to his followers, the first disciples, and they in turn communicated it to others. Still, there is a difference. Jesus was a singular incarnation of the life of God. Moreover, his followers found that, in order to live God's life, they could not do it alone. They had to do it together, as a community united with Christ.

By living together and supporting one another, the first Christians found that they could live the life of Jesus. By sharing what they had and by forgiving one another, they could share what Jesus had communicated to them as a body of disciples. By praying for one another, they could experience the healing power that Jesus had manifested to them. By loving one another as he had loved them, they could know the love of God. We could say that the early Christians were sacraments to one another, the way that Jesus in their midst had been a sacrament to them. In this sense, then, the **Church** was a sacramental Church from the very beginning.

But the first Christians also discovered that they were not to be sacraments to themselves alone. Just as they had been attracted to the life of God by the life and ministry of Jesus, soon others began to admire that life in the Christian community and wanted to have a share in it. In fact, the apostles and evangelists declared that the good news of Jesus (the word *gospel* means "good news") was that the life of God was now available to everybody! It was not just for the Israelites who had the Law and the prophets, but for everyone who would accept Jesus as the Word (another way of saying "symbol") of God and enter into the life of the Church. For the life of the Church was that new life which Jesus had promised them, a life that made them less and less the way they used to be, and more and more like Jesus.

Church the community of the people of God that draws its life from Christ

gospel the good news of God's mercy and forgiveness revealed by Jesus in his life, death, and resurrection, and proclaimed by the Church to the whole world

"Alleluia" (stitching and applique) by Sister Helena Steffens-meier SSSF, twentieth century.

Jesus had talked about that new life, but primarily he lived it. It was by living the life of God that he symbolized and communicated that life to others. In the same way, then, the early Church symbolized and communicated the life of God by proclaiming it and by living it. Christians got together regularly to pray and share what they remembered about Jesus. They ate together at least once a week at "the Lord's Supper," and they made sure that everyone in the community had enough food to get them through the other days. They opened their houses to those who were homeless and gave clothing to those who were poor. They prayed over those who were sick and laid hands on them for healing. When they were asked why they cared so much for one another, they explained that this was the way that Jesus taught them how to love. They invited those who wanted to enter their community to be symbolically immersed in water and to rise into a whole new way of life.

The early Church was thus a sacramental Church because together it was the "Body of Christ" (to use Paul's term), revealing that same life of God which Jesus, the unique incarnated sacrament of God, had revealed as a singular person. The Church was, we could say, a sacrament of Jesus just as Jesus was the sacrament of God, for it symbolized to the world the unique spirit of Jesus, the Spirit of God. As the *Documents of Vatican II* tell us:

> By her relationship with Christ, the Church is a kind of sacrament of intimate union with God, and of the unity of all mankind, that is, she is a sign and an instrument of such union and unity. . . .
>
> In that body [of the Church], the life of Christ is poured into the believers who, through the sacraments, are united in a hidden and real way to Christ who suffered and was glorified. . . . Giving the body unity through Himself and through His power and through the internal cohesion of its members, [the Holy] Spirit produces and urges love among the believers.

"Dogmatic Constitution on the Church," #s 1, 7.

To say "I love you" to the world in a way that said it better than words, God gave us Jesus, the sacrament of God. To stay with the world and to be with us until the end of time, Jesus gave us the Church, the people of God, the sacrament of Jesus and the sacrament of salvation.

THE BODY OF CHRIST

During the Second World War, some soldiers were patrolling a European town that had been bombed the day before. Checking for civilians who might be trapped in the rubble, one of them looked in a church whose roof had caved in. As a Catholic, he recognized a statue of the Sacred Heart lying on its side. Calling for help, he and his buddies righted the statue, which was pretty much intact, except that the hands of the Christ figure were broken off. After searching in vain for the missing hands, the soldier wrote some words on the statue's pedestal before he left. The words read, "I have no hands but yours."

This sentiment echoes a prayer of Saint Teresa of Ávila:

Christ has no body now but yours,
no hands, no feet on earth but yours.
Yours are the eyes through which he looks
with compassion on this world;
Yours are the feet with which he walks to do good;
Yours are the hands with which he blesses all the world.
Christ has no body now on earth but yours.
Amen.

Journal

What image would you use to explain the Church as the Body of Christ? Why would you use that image?

DiSCUSSioN

In the large group, discuss the following questions:

1. When does the Church behave in ways that you imagine Jesus would behave?

2. Are there times when people in the Church (as a whole or as individual religious institutions) behave in ways that Jesus would not? What are some of those cases?

3. In such cases, what ought to be done so that it is more evident that the Church is a sacrament of Jesus? Explain.

Review Questions

1. How has God been revealed to people in the past?

2. What does it mean to say that Jesus is the sacrament of God?

3. In what sense is the Church a sacrament of Jesus?

4. Why is the Church called the Body of Christ?

Summary

Symbols are more common than we realize. When we think about symbols, we usually think about visual images that represent sports teams, business corporations, schools, countries, and so on. Actually, though, all communication takes place through symbols—written and spoken words, gestures, and body language are all symbolic. Actions and gestures are particularly symbolic. As the saying goes, "Actions speak louder than words." We reveal who we are by how we behave. In this sense, sacraments are symbolic actions of the Church. When Christians participate in sacraments, they are saying, "This is what we are." Sacraments are also symbolic actions that point to, reveal, and mediate God. They enable Catholic Christians to find God, the same way that the ancient Israelites found God revealed in their history, and the same way that the first followers of Jesus saw God in what he did and said.

Scripture

For just as the body is one and has many members, and all the members of the body, though many, are one body, so it is with Christ. For in the one Spirit we were all baptized into one body—Jews or Greeks, slaves or free—and we were all made to drink of one Spirit. . . . Now you are the body of Christ and individually members of it.

1 CORINTHIANS 12:12–13, 27

Prayer

*May God be gracious to us and bless us
    and make his face to shine upon us,
that your way may be known upon earth,
    your saving power among all nations.
Let the peoples praise you, O God;
    let all the peoples praise you.
Let the nations be glad and sing for joy,
    for you judge the peoples with equity
    and guide the nations upon earth.
Let the peoples praise you, O God;
    let all the peoples praise you.
The earth has yielded its increase;
    God, our God, has blessed us.
May God continue to bless us;
    let all the ends of the earth revere him.*

PSALM 67

Scripture

Now the whole group of those who believed were of one heart and soul, and no one claimed private ownership of any possessions, but everything they owned was held in common. With great power the apostles gave their testimony to the resurrection of the Lord Jesus, and great grace was upon them all.

ACTS 4:32–33

Prayer

You who live in the shelter of the Most High,
who abide in the shadow of the Almighty,
will say to the LORD, "My refuge and my fortress;
my God, in whom I trust." . . .
Because you have made the LORD your refuge,
the Most High your dwelling place,
no evil shall befall you,
no scourge come near your tent. . . .
Those who love me, I will deliver;
I will protect those who know my name.
When they call to me, I will answer them;
I will be with them in trouble,
I will rescue them and honor them.
With long life I will satisfy them,
and show them my salvation.

PSALM 91:1–2, 9–10, 14–16

Sacraments and Divine Life

The Followers of Jesus

The door slammed shut behind Jonah and his two new friends. It seemed strange to have been so excited just an hour before and now to be so confused. What had they done? Why were the men who grabbed them so angry? The cell was unlit, dirty, and dank. Jonah looked at his companions, his eyes trying to focus in the dark. At least the quiet and the isolation gave him a chance to talk to these two men he hardly knew.

There were so many questions to ask. Just this morning he had been Jonah, the crippled beggar. It had been his identity for the forty years of his life. He knew no other role. What exactly had happened? He began a mental review of the day. Sarah had taken him to the Beautiful Gate at the temple to beg for alms from the faithful entering to pray. It was just past three o'clock when these two men entered the area. He called to them for an offering. They stopped and looked at him intently. They seemed ordinary enough, but why were they so intent? He focused on them, and then the taller one spoke. What was it he said? Something about not having any money, but giving me something else in the name of, what was that name . . . ah, yes, Jesus, the Nazarene.

Jonah continued his reflection, "Then he took my hand. He was so strong and sure, and suddenly, suddenly everything was different. I felt a strength I had never known. I could walk! . . . I could jump! . . . I could dance! People came running from all directions. And then the taller one, Peter, began to talk to them. It was strange talk. On the one hand he scolded them, and then he forgave them for their ignorance that had caused this Jesus person to be put to death. He talked about the prophets and a Messiah and the forgiveness of sins and times of refreshment.

Chapter Three

"And then the priests and the guards came and took us away. But my mind was so jumbled and confused. Now I can listen and hear more clearly. Why do I feel such a peace when I am near these two, Peter and John? What is their secret?"

Jonah spent the night talking with Peter and John about this man, Jesus. They gladly shared their good news about the Messiah and about the community Jesus inspired. (Based on Acts 3:1 to 4:3.)

The Catholic Church designates seven of its rituals as sacraments. Many Protestant Churches call only two ceremonies (Baptism and Communion) sacraments. Some other denominations do not use the word at all, even though they may have similar ceremonies.

They devoted themselves to the apostles' teaching and fellowship, to the breaking of the bread and the prayers.

Awe came upon everyone, because many wonders and signs were being done by the apostles. All who believed were together and had all things in common. . . . Day by day, as they spent much time together in the temple, they broke bread at home and ate their food with glad and generous hearts, praising God and having the good will of all the people. And day by day the Lord added to their number those who were being saved.

Acts 2:42–44, 46–47

Jesus had said and done things that were sacramental in themselves, revealing and bestowing the love and power of God to people, and inviting them to share in his divine life. In the same way, the first Christians soon found themselves saying and doing things which were sacramental, even though (as we saw in the first chapter) it was quite some time before they grouped these activities together under the Latin word *sacramentum*.

Research

Read John 14:9–14; Matthew 12:46–3:2; John 15:13–15; Matthew 19:16–21. From these readings, list the qualities Jesus may have wanted to see his followers develop.

Discussion

In the large group, discuss the following questions:

1. Imagine that you are the young man Jonah in the chapter's opening story. What would be your feelings at that moment? What would you be thinking?

2. Jesus was a sacramental person who said and did things that manifested God to the people around him. Is Jesus a sacrament of God today? Explain your answer.

Journal

Is there someone who is a sacramental person to you? That is, have you met someone or do you know someone whose attitude and behavior give you hints or clues about what God might be like? Describe that person and explain how he or she was sacramental for you.

The Sacramental Actions of the Church

What were these symbolic and sacramental actions of the Church? To some extent we have already discussed them in Chapters 1 and 2, especially in terms of how they relate to the need for humans to celebrate key events and stages of life—both the natural life and the spiritual life. But here we should talk about them again in order to show how they are extensions of the sacramental ministry of Jesus.

WHAT THE CATECHISM SAYS

Throughout his life, Jesus' words and actions were saving, because they anticipated his suffering, death, and resurrection. The mysteries of Christ's life are the foundations of the sacraments. Through the Church and its ministers, Jesus continues his saving work.

See the *Catechism of the Catholic Church*, #1115.

THE SACRAMENTS OF THE CATHOLIC CHURCH

The Sacraments of Initiation	The Sacraments of Healing	The Sacraments at the Service of Communion
Baptism	Reconciliation (Penance)	Matrimony
Confirmation	Anointing of the Sick	Holy Orders
Eucharist		

Activities

Choose one of the following:

1. Use your imagination to design a celebration of something that you think is worth celebrating. What symbols or other indicators would you use (for example, words that could be said) to let people know what the celebration is about? Who are the people that would be doing the celebrating? How would they participate in the celebration? Write out what you have imagined, or, even better, act out the celebration you have designed, or, better still, really have such a celebration. Share and discuss your celebration with the class.

2. In your imagination, design a ceremony in which one or more people receive something that is real but not tangible (for example, recognition, honor, forgiveness, assurance, acceptance). What symbols or other indicators would you use (including words that are spoken) to let people know what is happening at this ceremony? What role or roles would they play in the ceremony? Write out what you have imagined, or, even better, act out the ceremony you have designed, or, better still, hold a real ceremony. Share and discuss your celebration with the class.

3. In your imagination, design a ceremony in which one or more people are changed in some real but intangible way (for example, induction into a club, a change in job or rank or social position, expulsion from a group). What symbols or other indicators would you use (including words that are spoken) to let people know what is happening at this ceremony? What role or roles would they play in the ceremony? Write out what you have imagined, or, even better, act out the ceremony you have designed, or, better still, hold a real ceremony. Share and discuss your celebration with the class.

Activity

Read Luke 24:13–35, the story of Emmaus. In small groups, create modern-day skits based on the story and present them to the class. Discuss the emotions you experienced as an actor and as a spectator.

Journal

The chapter suggests that we can learn about God and about God's life by meditating on the world around us and by reflecting on the Gospel stories about Jesus. Try doing this for yourself: Look at nature or read a Gospel story, and then ask yourself what the scene or story reveals about God. Journal on what you learned through doing this exercise.

Eucharist: Celebration of God's Life

Jesus was undoubtedly a person who celebrated life and shared it with his friends. One of the ways he did this most often was by eating with them. The Gospels are filled with accounts of Jesus visiting people and having meals with them. On at least two occasions, he blessed bread and fish. When he did so, those who had come out from the town to hear him preach found that miraculously there was enough food for everyone to have their fill. Another time Jesus and his friends attended a wedding feast at Cana, and, at his mother's suggestion, he provided the best wine for the occasion. Many times Jesus used the image of a banquet to symbolize what it was like to share the new life of God, in order to help his listeners understand something of the reign of God. Jesus must have eaten often with his disciples, and all four Gospels record his last memorable supper with his closest friends. During this meal, Jesus blessed bread and wine and shared it with them, saying, "This is my body" and "This is my blood."

The early Christians continued Jesus' practice of sharing food and celebrating their new life together. They called it simply the *Breaking of Bread* or the *Lord's Supper*, because, when they shared it in memory of him, they experienced the reality of their Lord's presence in a special way. Another way to say this is that they experienced a sacred reality made possible by a sacrament.

The story of the two disciples on the road to Emmaus recognizing Jesus in the shared meal vividly recalls the importance of this sacrament (Luke 24:13–35). As Jesus had so often done, they gave thanks to God for the new life he had given them, and so another name for this special Christian meal with bread and wine was **Eucharist,** from the Greek word meaning "to give thanks" or "thanksgiving" to God. Some Christians in the first century even came to call their weekly dinner together an *agape supper* or "love feast." It was out of this meal, during which stories about Jesus were shared, letters from apostles were read, instructions on the Christian life were given, and prayers for the community were said, that our Christian liturgy evolved.

 **Activity**

The Greek word for love in the New Testament (which was written in Greek) is *agape,* which can be translated as "love" or "care." In an essay, explain what you understand about the attitudes and behaviors that are characteristic of *agape,* giving examples that illustrate what you are saying.

 Journal

Look up 1 Corinthians 13:1–7, Paul's famous passage on love that is often used as a Scripture reading at weddings. Replace the word *love* with phrases that use the words *care* and *caring.* Journal on examples of the kind of people who might fit the description of what you have rewritten for verses 4–7.

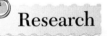 **Research**

Using a biblical concordance (a reference book that lists every place in the Bible that key words appear), find five New Testament passages that use the word *love* and retranslate them using *care, care about, take care of,* and so on. How does your retranslation sharpen or modify the meaning of these passages?

AGAPE

If you read the New Testament, you see that the word *love* appears often. Jesus says, "You shall love your neighbor as yourself" (Matthew 22:39), ". . . love one another as I have loved you" (John 15:12), and even, "Love your enemies . . ." (Luke 6:27). Equally famous are the words from the First Letter of John: "God is love, and those who abide in love abide in God, and God in them" (1 John 4:16).

If you were able to read the New Testament in the original Greek, you would see that the words translated as "love" are the noun and verb forms of *agape.* The trouble with this translation, however, is that the English word *love* is primarily a feeling word; it is most often used to express a feeling of affection for someone ("Harry loves Sally.") or liking something ("I love rock 'n' roll"). So translating *agape* as "love" makes it sound as though Jesus is telling us to like our neighbors and even our enemies, and it makes John sound as though he were saying that God is a good feeling.

The Greek word *agape* is much more an action word than a feeling word. In order to convey this idea, theologians have spoken of it as self-giving love, unconditional love, selfless love, and even self-sacrificing love. But there is also a simple word in English that conveys much of what *agape* conveys in Greek. The word is "care," in the sense of "care for," "care about," or "take care of."

Probably the best image of *agape* in the sense of care or caring is the way a loving and responsible parent cares about and takes care of a child. Babies need to be fed, diapers need to be changed, crying needs to be attended to—regardless of what time of day or night it is, and regardless of how the parent feels. Caring and considerate moms and dads will do what needs to be done because they have made the well-being of their children a top priority. They put their children's needs ahead of their own feelings and wants. They go the extra mile day in and day out.

So when Jesus says to his followers, ". . . love one another as I have loved you," he is really saying, "Take care of one another the way I have." When he talks about loving our neighbor as ourselves, he means that we should care about other people the way we care about ourselves. And when he talks about loving our enemies, he means treating them with care and respect in order to overcome hatred with kindness and in order to replace suspicion with trust.

Likewise, when John says, "God is love," or elsewhere, "God so loved the world that he gave his only son" (John 3:16), he is talking about a God who cares. The spirit of God therefore is a caring spirit, and the spirit of Jesus is a spirit of caring. Living in the Spirit means caring about the world we live in, and especially caring about others. It means taking care, it means being responsible and considerate, it means putting the needs of others ahead of less significant wants and desires on our part. That's the Jesus way to live. That's what the sacraments, in seven different ways, communicate and celebrate.

Baptism: Immersion in God's Life

disciple someone who is willing to learn from a specific teacher; more generally, a follower; derived from a Latin word that refers to a student. For Christians, a disciple is one who accepts Jesus' message, follows him, and lives according to his teachings.

Baptism from the Greek word for immersion, the name of the first of the three Sacraments of Initiation; the sacrament of new life in God and of incorporation into the Church

initiation the process of becoming a member of a group; the process by which an unbaptized person prepares for entrance into the Christian community and membership in the Church

Jesus was an inviting person. He welcomed others to share the life of God with him and to learn to live it more fully. Those who accepted his invitation became his **disciples** (from the Latin word meaning "students"). They sometimes even left their homes and businesses to become immersed in the life of the little community that formed around Jesus.

While the Gospels tell us of Jesus' baptism in the River Jordan by his cousin John, we do not know if Jesus himself ever baptized people in water. However, since the Greek word for *baptism* means simply "to immerse," the early Christians adopted water baptism as a symbolic way of initiating converts into the community into which they were being immersed. For them, going down into the water and coming up again symbolized their disappearance from their old life and their emergence into the life of Christ shared by the community.

The rapid growth of the early Church communities around the Roman Empire certainly suggests that the early Christians were eager to spread the good news of Jesus, just as he had spread the good news of God's reign throughout Galilee and Judea. Christian **Baptism** and **initiation** into the community was therefore a logical extension of Jesus' own way of going out to people and inviting them to share the life of God with him.

Journal

To better understand the concept of immersion in God's life, compare two times in your own life:

1. One time when you were in a new situation but felt somewhat awkward and didn't know what to do

2. One time when you were in a new situation and got really into it so that you felt at ease and knew what to do

   What did you learn from getting "immersed" in the second situation?

Baptism by immersion at the Easter Vigil once again has become a common practice in the Catholic Church.

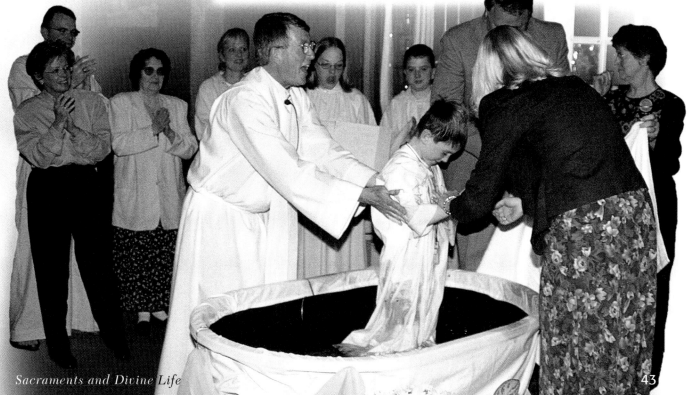

Confirmation: Affirmation of God's Life

But Jesus did more than just invite people to share in his life. He also supported and strengthened his followers by communicating his own Spirit to them. He confirmed their faith in him and their trust in God by telling them that they now shared in his spiritual power. Sometimes he even sent his disciples out to do the same kinds of things that they had seen him do—teach and heal—and they came back amazed that they could do those things!

Jesus was probably very comfortable showing his feelings by touching people and hugging his friends, as people of the Mediterranean are even today. These are natural ways of affirming one another and communicating confidence to one another. We can easily imagine Jesus playfully slapping Peter on the back or walking with his arms over the shoulders of his friends as they traveled from town to town.

The early Christians naturally picked up on this very human way of expressing their love for one another and confirming newcomers into their community life. The New Testament speaks of a "laying on of hands" through which the apostles communicated the Spirit of God to those who had already accepted the good news of Jesus. And when converts were initiated into their new community, their Baptism was not complete until they had in this way been embraced by the leader of the local church.

In time, the Church added anointing to the embracing or the laying on of hands as symbolic of the pouring of the Holy Spirit into the lives of new Christians. Eventually in the West, as the number of Christians grew too large for bishops to preside over all Baptisms, the bishop's **Confirmation** of the initiates was separated from the ritual of Baptism in water. Baptisms were then performed by the parish priest. But Confirmation as we have it today still goes back to Jesus using touch to affirm and confirm those who believed in him and to communicate his Spirit to them.

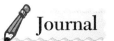

Journal

If you have been confirmed, what do you recall about the event? What does it mean to you now?

Confirmation the Sacrament of Initiation that completes Baptism and celebrates the gifts of the Holy Spirit

Chapter Three

Christian Initiation and the Sacraments of Initiation

Rite of Christian Initiation of Adults the process of gradual initiation into the Christian community and the rites that celebrate the various stages of that process, culminating in the Sacraments of Initiation

Sacraments of Initiation Baptism, Confirmation, and Eucharist; the sacraments that are at the foundation of the Christian life

catechumenate the first formal stage of formation and education in the Rite of Christian Initiation of Adults

catechumen an unbaptized person who has celebrated the rite of entrance into the catechumenate and who is preparing for full membership in the Christian community

scrutinies rites of repentance celebrated with the elect during Lent

The Rite of Election is often held at a central location in a diocese.

The ***Rite of Christian Initiation of Adults*** (RCIA for short) is a series of liturgical ceremonies designed to lead new Christians along the journey of faith to full membership in the Church through the **Sacraments of Initiation.** In the United States, where many of those entering the Catholic faith have already been baptized in other denominations, the RCIA is adapted to meet their special needs, and somewhat parallel rites are celebrated with them. It is better to think of the RCIA as a process of gradual initiation into the life of the Christian community rather than as a single rite. The liturgical rituals celebrate the important stages in the initiation process.

The first ceremony for unbaptized inquirers is the rite of acceptance into the **catechumenate,** or time for learning. They receive a sponsor to be their special friend and mentor in the Catholic Church, and they spend at least a few months meeting regularly with other **catechumens** and sponsors to receive instructions and discuss what they are learning about the Catholic faith. Baptized inquirers participate in the rite of welcoming the candidates.

If at the beginning of Lent catechumens feel ready to request Baptism and join the Church (and if their sponsor or godparent and catechists agree with their decision), they celebrate the rite of election or enrollment of names. This rite signifies their choosing and being chosen to proceed on to full membership in the Church. Already-baptized candidates celebrate the rite of calling the candidates to continuing conversion. Frequently these ceremonies take place in the cathedral, where the catechumens and candidates from all the parishes in the diocese are welcomed by the bishop, the chief pastor of the diocese. From this time until Easter, the catechumens are referred to as the *elect*.

During Lent itself, another series of ceremonies helps the elect to spiritually prepare for their Baptism. **Scrutinies** are special rites in which the parish community prays for the unbaptized that they may experience spiritual healing and strengthening. The elect and the candidates continue to meet on a regular basis with the parish RCIA team. They are reminded of the importance of the Lord's Prayer and the Creed in the life of a Catholic Christian.

These newly baptized men
hold their baptismal candles
during the Easter Vigil.

As Holy Week approaches, the elect and candidates are encouraged to pray and fast with the other members of the community who are similarly preparing for Easter. On Holy Saturday those about to be baptized are signed for the last time with the oil of catechumens. Later that night, at the Easter Vigil, the elect and their sponsors and godparents meet with the assembled community for their solemn reception into the Church. Their Baptism symbolizes their identification with the death and resurrection of Jesus in the paschal mystery. Their Confirmation strengthens them and the Eucharist nourishes them as they become disciples of Christ.

The RCIA does not end with Baptism, however, for Baptism marks only the beginning of the life of faith within the Church community. A further period of instruction called *mystagogy* makes them more aware that the mystery of Christ means dying to self and serving others. The neophytes (newly baptized) and those others who have joined the Catholic Church are encouraged and helped to find the way that they can best contribute to the life of the community into which they have been welcomed.

Activity

Interview a person in your parish who has been initiated into the Catholic Church through the RCIA. Before the interview, write down five or six questions that you want answered. After the interview, organize a summary to present to the class; then respond to any questions the class may have.

Review Questions

1. What are the seven sacraments of the Catholic Church?

2. What are the Sacraments of Initiation?

3. In the teaching of Jesus, what did the image of a banquet symbolize?

4. What does the term *agape* mean? To what sacrament does it particularly relate?

5. Through what process are unbaptized adults initiated into the Catholic Church?

Reconciliation: Reconversion to God's Life

Jesus was concerned with people's entire welfare. He cared about their suffering from diseases over which they had no control, but he also cared about the suffering they brought upon themselves through their own selfishness and sinfulness. The healing needed to remedy guilt and alienation was forgiveness and love, so time and again Jesus manifested God's willingness to forgive sinners and help them lead more moral lives.

Jesus was also concerned that those who claimed to follow him should show forgiveness toward one another, regardless of how many times the other person sinned against them. And he admonished his disciples to forgive even their enemies, just as he had done, assuring them that as they forgave others God also forgave them.

From the number of parables about forgiveness in the Gospels, we can see that the early Christian community saw the importance of living a life of forgiveness. The first Christians remembered and retold these stories before they were written down, not only as reminders to themselves, but also as a means of instructing newcomers about what the Christian life entailed. The early Christian community also developed more formal procedures for warning sinners and helping them to see the error of their ways, and these practices eventually led to a ritual of public repentance as the first expression of the Sacrament of **Reconciliation.**

Reconciliation the Sacrament of Penance in which, through the words and actions of a priest, God forgives the sins of a repentant person who confesses and resolves not to sin again

✝ Activity

Create an artistic representation—drawing, painting, collage, computer graphic, poem, story, song, instrumental music—of forgiveness and reconciliation. Present your work to the class.

The forgiveness of sins so important in the ministry of Jesus is carried on in the Church today through the Sacrament of Reconciliation.

Anointing of the Sick: Healing by God's Life

Jesus often touched people in order to heal them. Whatever else our image of Jesus might contain, we always think of him as ministering to people who were physically ill and spiritually distressed. The Gospel according to Matthew sums up this picture of Christ in just a few verses:

Jesus went throughout Galilee, teaching in their synagogues and proclaiming the good news of the kingdom and curing every disease and every sickness among the people. So his fame spread throughout all Syria, and they brought to him all the sick, those who were afflicted with various diseases and pains, demoniacs, epileptics, and paralytics, and he cured them.

Matthew 4:23–24

Using his sacramental touch and healing words, Jesus showed God's desire and power to help the helpless. He manifested divine authority over physical and spiritual evils, and he assured his followers that they too could exercise that authority in his name. The New Testament contains a number of accounts in which the apostles acted as Jesus did, healing the sick and curing the ill who appealed to them for help. The Acts of the Apostles and the various letters reveal that the church in Jerusalem also organized ministerial programs to attend to the needs of those who were widowed and orphaned, sick and elderly. And it celebrated a sacramental ritual for anointing the sick for their recovery. Local churches in other parts of the Roman Empire had their own ways of continuing Christ's healing ministry, and out of these practices the liturgical Sacrament of **Anointing of the Sick** as we know it today developed.

When possible, the Anointing of the Sick is celebrated in the community.

Anointing of the Sick
the Sacrament of Healing for those who are in danger of death due to illness or old age, consisting of anointing with oil, imposition of hands, and prayers for physical and spiritual healing and the forgiveness of sins

✏️ Journal

Write about a time when you were ill.

1. How did you feel physically? Emotionally? Spiritually?

2. What feelings and attitudes changed when you recovered?

3. What decision(s) did you make following the illness? Why did you make that decision or those decisions?

Matrimony: Union in God's Life

The wedding day celebrates a covenant relationship that is meant to be one of lifelong, faithful love.

Of all the sacraments, **Matrimony** (from the Latin word for marriage) looks like it might be the hardest to trace back to the life and ministry of Jesus. Although we know from the New Testament that Peter was married, Jesus himself was not married. While he approved of marital fidelity and attended a wedding feast, Jesus, as portrayed in the Gospels, did not give as much attention to marriage as he did to other aspects of the Christian life. And it is obvious that marriage existed long before Jesus and Christianity came on the scene.

Yet the New Testament clearly shows that Jesus and Christianity did introduce something new to marriage. Jesus' teaching that "what God has joined together, let no one separate" (Matthew 19:6) indicates that when a man and woman are united in marriage, people should not try to separate them. And the author of the Letter to the Ephesians likened the love between Christian spouses to the love between Christ and the Church, indicating that both husbands and wives should give themselves completely to the service of the other. (See Ephesians 5:25–32.)

Certainly this was a change from the traditional custom, according to which the woman was the servant and the man was the master of the household. Jesus had said, "Just as I have loved you, you should love one another" (John 13:34), and that meant even going so far as to lay down one's life for the other, including in marriage.

What Christianity introduced to marriage, therefore, was the ideal that husbands and wives should always put their spouse's needs and welfare above their own.

Christian families are the domestic Church, sharing the agape *love that Jesus shared with his followers.*

To say it simply, the love that bonds Christian marriages together is the love of Christ, which is divine love, a love of complete self-giving. Jesus gave himself completely to the people to whom he ministered, and he gave his life for the community of those who gathered around him, those who became the Church. In return, Jesus' disciples gave themselves completely to the service of their Lord, even sometimes to the point of martyrdom. In other words, the love with which they loved Jesus was the same *agape* love with which he loved them, divine love, given and received.

Even before a specifically Christian wedding ceremony developed, therefore, there was something specifically Christ-like about marriages between Christians. Although marriage as a social institution existed before Jesus, marriage as a Christian institution begins and finds its meaning in the Christ-like love that is at the heart of it. Christian marriage lasts until the death of one of the partners, then, because the mutual love of the spouses reflects the everlasting love between Christ and the Church. The Sacrament of Matrimony is the Church's way of symbolizing in marriage the generous self-giving love of Christ, inviting Christian men and women to enter more fully into an unbreakable union of divine *agape.*

DisCuSSioN

In a small group, discuss the following questions:

1. What are the qualities of a truly Christian marriage?

2. What can adolescents do now to develop some of the qualities necessary for a good Christian marriage?

Chapter Three

Holy Orders: Service to God's Life

the Twelve   the disciples closest to Jesus, also called *apostles* in the Gospel according to Luke

Although Jesus invited everyone to follow him, he also called a few to be special ministers in continuing his work. The most obvious of these were Peter, James, John, and the rest of **the Twelve** who accompanied him throughout much of his ministry and with whom he shared his Last Supper. Jesus entrusted the Twelve with the mission of being his witnesses to others and of telling them about the new life that Jesus had shown them.

But, as the community of believers grew, the Twelve could not do everything that had to be done. They began to appoint some others to serve the special needs of the community. In addition, there were people such as Paul, Mark, and Barnabas who answered God's call by spreading the good news of Jesus to the non-Jews who lived around the Roman Empire. They founded new communities wherever they went and placed others in charge of those communities when they left to continue their own missionary work. The letters of Paul list some of the local churches founded by the early followers of Jesus in Rome, Corinth, Galatia, Ephesus, Philippi, Colossae, and Thessalonica.

The New Testament letters also give us a picture of the wide variety of ministers in the early churches, some of whom were appointed and some of whom performed their service simply because their gifts were needed in the Church: bishops or supervisors, presbyters or elders, deacons and deaconesses, prophets, teachers, administrators, healers, and those who performed works of charity. The letters to Timothy and Titus also show that church leaders were selected with special care, and that many of them were prayed over with the laying on of hands so that God would bless their ministry.

The ordained minister is called to service in the Church.

From the variety of ministries in the Church, we can see that from the very beginning Christians were concerned about continuing the ministry of Jesus and extending it far and wide and into every important area of life. Jesus lived a life of service to others, and so using one's gifts in the service of others was a hallmark of the Christian life. As the Church grew by leaps and bounds, most Christians did not have a special ministry in the Church. But for a long time what we consider "social services" (education, care of those who were sick and elderly and hospitality for strangers) were carried on by Church members who devoted their lives to the service of others.

Christians attached great importance to the unity of the Church and continuity with the ministry of Jesus. Not everyone who aspired to positions of leadership had the interests of the community at heart, however, and not everyone who claimed to preach the gospel taught the authentic message of Jesus passed on by the Twelve. The concern for unity and continuity in the Church led to a system of training and ordaining pastors in the Church. There were the bishops and priests (originally called **presbyters**) who were given responsibility for dioceses and parishes. To them were given the important functions of preaching and teaching, presiding at the Eucharist and the other sacraments. Men were ordained with the laying on of hands, the symbolic ritual of commissioning mentioned in the New Testament. Eventually, those serving in official capacities progressed through a series of ordinations that admitted them to the various ranks or orders in Church administration. The Sacrament of **Holy Orders** thus became a means of maintaining proper order and correct teaching in the Church, as well as a means of insuring that the sacramental ministry of Jesus would always have a central place in the life of the Christian community.

presbyter the term used in the early Church for an elder or community leader; still used today in reference to the second of the Holy Orders; the word *priest* is derived from this word

Holy Orders the sacrament of apostolic ministry exercised in the Church, bestowed through the laying on of hands; the three degrees or orders of the sacrament are deacon, priest, and bishop

Journal

Describe a priest or deacon whom you admire. How has that person helped you? How does he inspire you?

Review Questions

1. What are the Sacraments of Healing? The Sacraments at the Service of Communion?

2. In the Sacraments of Healing, what kinds of healing are requested? Explain briefly.

3. What is the love on which Christian marriages are based?

4. What are the three orders? What is the sign used in this sacrament?

Jesus' practice of forgiving sinners, as shown in Titian's "Christ and the Woman Taken in Adultery," is the scriptural basis for the Church's Sacrament of Reconciliation.

Institution by Christ

Research

The seven sacraments of the Catholic Church are Baptism, Confirmation, Eucharist, Reconciliation (or Penance), Anointing of the Sick, Matrimony, and Holy Orders. Indicate the sacrament to which each of the following Scriptures connects.

1 John 4:7–21
Acts 3:1–10
John 2:1–10
Luke 9:10–17
Mark 3:13–19
Matthew 10:5–7
John 20:22
John 20:23
John 8:1–11
John 3:1–5
Matthew 18:21–22
Matthew 15:29–31
Luke 9:6
Matthew 19:3–6
Acts 2:1–4
John 21:15–17
John 6:32–35

The Catholic Church teaches that the seven sacraments were instituted by Christ (see the Catechism #s 1114, 1210), but there is no Church document that specifies or spells out in detail how this instituting was done. The manner of the institution of the sacraments has therefore been a topic of theological discussion over the centuries.

In the distant past, some theologians believed that during his public ministry, Jesus himself took the Twelve aside and showed them how to perform all seven of the Church's rituals. As a matter of fact, there is clear scriptural evidence for such institution of two of the sacraments by Jesus—Baptism and Eucharist. It is for this reason that many Protestants recognize these two rites as sacraments instituted by Christ.

There is not the same clear scriptural evidence for the other five, which is why Protestants do not celebrate them as sacraments, even though they may retain them (especially marriage and ordination, and sometimes confirmation) as religious rituals. Other theologians in the past proposed that Jesus might have told his followers about the essential meanings of the other five sacraments (for example, forgiveness and healing), but he left it to the Twelve to come up with rituals that would embody and express those meanings. We know today from historical evidence, however, that this is not how the Church's sacraments evolved.

A third and more recent theory suggests that since the Church is the Body of Christ, whenever the Church developed any aspect of a sacramental ceremony for Christians, Christ was in fact doing it. This theory has the merit of explaining how Catholics can say that Christ instituted all seven sacraments while admitting that some of these ceremonies as we understand them first appeared some centuries after Jesus. A shortcoming of this theory is that it does not connect each of the seven sacraments to the life and ministry of Jesus, to which the expression "institution by Christ" points.

There are non-religious ceremonies that communicate spiritual realities, even though we do not ordinarily think about them in such terms. For example, when a person is inaugurated as president of the United States, that person is really different in some knowable but non-physical ways.

1. What does being sworn in as president give to a person?

2. What other examples do you have in which people go through non-religious ceremonies and come out somehow different from the way they were before the ceremony? Name some examples and explain them.

A fourth explanation overcomes this shortcoming by tracing the sacred realities symbolized by the sacraments to the life and ministry of Jesus. During his life, Jesus said and did things to immerse people in God's life (Baptism), to communicate his spirit to others (Confirmation), to celebrate community and God's presence among people (Eucharist), to forgive people's sins (Reconciliation), to make people well (Anointing of the Sick), to be faithful and self-sacrificing (Matrimony), and to serve others (Holy Orders). Moreover, Jesus did these things using words and actions that were sacramental, that is, he used speech and gesture to communicate spiritual realities.

The spiritual core of each of the seven sacraments can thus be traced back to the ministry of Jesus as it is presented in the New Testament. These are the spiritual realities or Christian mysteries that are celebrated in the seven sacraments—life, belonging, acceptance, growth, forgiveness, conversion, sharing, healing, strengthening, self-giving, fidelity, serving, community, renewal, transformation, and so on. In essence, sacraments come to us from the historical Jesus and from the Church, the Body of Christ.

WHAT THE CATECHISM SAYS

The sacraments were instituted by Christ. Jesus' life and ministry were salvific, that is, they anticipated Jesus' suffering, death, and resurrection—the Paschal mystery. In Christ's actions, then we see the foundations for the sacraments as they came to be celebrated in the Church. The seven sacraments touch on the stages and significant moments of life. The sacraments are "of the Church" in two ways. They are "by the Church" because they are the work of the Church which is a sacrament of Christ at work in the people of God. Second, the sacraments are "for the Church" because they make the Church by showing us the mystery of our communion with God, the Trinity. Through our initiation into the Church, we are all part of the Body of Christ, a priestly people with Christ as our head.

See the *Catechism of the Catholic Church*, #s 1114–1115, 1117–1119, 1210.

 Journal

The chapter suggests that sacraments celebrate spiritual realities that are felt and known even though they cannot be seen. To understand this concept better:

1. Think about some non-religious celebrations and figure out the spiritual realities they celebrate (for example, a birthday or anniversary party, Fourth of July parade, Thanksgiving dinner, victory party after an important game). In doing this, it is sometimes better to analyze a real experience that you have had rather than just thinking about celebrations in general.

2. Think about some time when someone gave you reassurance, courage, forgiveness, peace of mind, or something of this nature (These are all spiritual realities in the sense that we have been talking about.) through something that they said or did. What did they do, and what did this communicate to you?

Sacraments as Symbols of Divine Life

God is a mystery, in the original sense of that Greek word *mysterion*, meaning something hidden from our eyes. This does not mean, however, that it is something hidden from our minds and hearts. Twenty centuries ago, Jesus, the incarnation of God, revealed that mystery to those who encountered him. To all those who encounter him today, Jesus, in the same way, continues to reveal what the mystery of God means and feels like. And through the symbolism of ritual, the sacraments in a similar way reveal what the life of Jesus and the mystery of God are all about.

What then can we say about the mystery of God, which is revealed in Jesus and which is symbolized in the sacraments? The mystery of God is, first of all, life itself. God is the creator of the universe, the source of all life: the life of stars and planets, plants and animals, humans and purely spiritual beings. But for Christians, God is especially the source of a new kind of life, a life that goes beyond the ordinarily human. We call it an elevated human life, the supernatural life, the spiritual life, life in the Spirit.

grace the free and undeserved gift of God's life and help that enables us to respond to God's call to be his children and to act by his love

WHAT THE CATECHISM SAYS

The sacraments are observable signs with words and actions through which Christ acts to communicate **grace**. Through the action of Christ and the power of the Holy Spirit, the Church celebrates the sacraments. Independent of the worthiness of the minister, the sacraments bring about the grace they signify; they are efficacious. The sacraments bear fruit in the spiritual lives of individual Christians, whose faith is strengthened, and in the Church itself, which grows in love of God and others and witnesses to that love in the whole world.

See the *Catechism of the Catholic Church,*
#s 1084, 1127–1128, 1131P, 1133–1134.

How to Read Church Documents

The *Catechism of the Catholic Church* and other official documents from the Church sometimes make statements that are hard to understand when we compare the statement to our experience.

For example, the Catechism states (quoting Vatican II): "The Eucharist is 'the source and summit of the Christian life.'" Many times, however, we attend Sunday Mass and come away feeling that it was boring and irrelevant. Does this mean there is a contradiction between the Catechism and life as we experience it?

In a way, yes. On the surface, it seems that what the Catechism states is not accurate, not factually true—at least not all the time, and at least not for everybody. One reason why some people reject Catholic teaching is that it seems to be inaccurate and unrealistic. It certainly doesn't help the situation when priests and other Church leaders, eager to promote Church teaching, present it as something that is true all the time and in all cases.

People who read Church documents in this way, however, overlook the fact that they are often written in what can be called *normative language*. That is, they set a norm or standard against which what happens at various times and in various places can be measured.

For example, the Catholic Church teaches that marriage is indissoluble and that priestly ordination is for life. Yet we all know Catholics who have gotten divorced, and at least some of us know about priests who have left the ordained ministry. These facts do not really contradict the Church's teaching because the teaching is expressed in normative language that is abstract and general, whereas descriptive language (for example, Mr. and Mrs. Jones got divorced, or Mr. Smith is a former priest) is concrete and specific.

Normative language states what "ought to be" or "what should be," but it expresses this in abstract language using the present tense. Thus "The Eucharist is the source and summit of the Christian life" refers to the Eucharist in its essence and does *not* mean that each and every Eucharistic liturgy is concretely and factually the high point of each member of the

Discussion

Mysteries are realities that are hidden from our eyes although not from our heart and mind, that is, they are intangible, but they can still be experienced.

1. Besides life and love, which are mentioned in the chapter, what are some other things that fit this definition? (Hint: Look at personal qualities such as individual strengths and weaknesses, or at social characteristics such as group strengths and weaknesses.)

2. What did you learn about the meaning of mystery from doing this exercise?

3. What is the relationship between mystery and sacrament?

In traditional Catholic theology, the life of God is symbolized by the doctrine of the Trinity. In the Trinity, the Father and the Son give and receive divine life so perfectly that the Holy Spirit surrounds and radiates from them. The triune God is so utterly creative that all creation symbolizes and reveals the divine life that brings it into being and sustains it. This is why, for example, the wondrous works of nature often speak of God to those of us who behold them with reverence and awe.

Another name for life given and received with such perfect generosity is the mystery of love. Saint John says, "God is love, and those who abide in love abide in God, and God abides in them" (1 John 4:16b). Again, in traditional Trinitarian doctrine, theologians speak of the life that passes between the Father and the Son as divine love, and the Holy Spirit is that Spirit of love. Living in the Spirit, therefore, means living in love. It means being in love with God and all creation, the way that Jesus was. It means loving ourselves and loving other people the way that Jesus did.

So if the sacraments are about the mystery of God made known to us in Jesus, then we must say that the sacraments are all about life, and they are all about love. They are about the fulfillment of human life, our life, with divine life, and about the enrichment of human love, our love, with divine love.

Chapter Three

assembly's day as a Christian. It does mean that celebrating the Eucharist *is* essentially and *ought to be experienced as* a high point for the whole assembly and as a source of spiritual nourishment for them and other Christians.

Another way to think about this is that normative language states what happens when everything is going right. In this way of looking at a situation, the statement about the Eucharist means that when everything comes together the way it should—people really caring for one another, ministers really serving the community, liturgy that is well planned and well performed, and so on—then it is a high point for everyone involved. But, whatever their attitude and preparedness, the liturgy does nourish them for continuing their Christian walk; how well they are nourished depends on their openness to God's grace.

If going to Mass is boring or irrelevant, we know that there is something wrong, but we do not necessarily know what is wrong. Maybe the fault lies with ourselves; perhaps we are not really trying to worship as we ought. But some of the fault may be the responsibility of the presider or the liturgy committee who planned this Mass. Maybe the fault is that we live in a parish that is in a do-nothing mode and doesn't care about people's real needs. In this case, the Catechism's statement about the Eucharist may be a clue that something is not happening that ought to be happening.

Official Church documents and other resource books help Catholics understand and apply Church teachings to their lives.

Activities

1. Find statements in the *Catechism of the Catholic Church* or in other official documents that seem contrary to your experience. In class discuss what the statements mean if they are taken as normative, rather than as descriptive, statements.

2. One reason the Church uses normative language in many of its teachings is that in ancient times scientific knowledge was limited to understanding what is normal or essential to things. For example, humans were understood to be essentially rational, even if they sometimes acted irrationally, and even though they were not able to be consistently rational until they were about seven years old. This certainly did not mean that insane people or babies were considered to be inhuman. What kind of language might the Church adopt besides normative language?

3. Normative statements (sometimes called statements of principle) are also found in secular documents such as the Declaration of Independence and the Charter of the United Nations. Find examples of normative statements in documents not related to Church or religion.

Sacraments and Divine Life

The Meaning of the Sacraments

What do words mean? What do symbols mean? What do sacraments mean? The simplicity of those questions makes it appear that they are easy to answer. In fact, the question of meaning is one of the central questions in contemporary linguistics, semantics, philosophy, theology, and other human sciences. The more we learn about meaning, the more we understand that meaning—what things mean, how they mean it, to whom they mean it, and so on—is really a very complicated matter.

It is important to understand at least a few things about the meaning of meaning, however, in order to put in proper perspective what the Church (most recently in the Catechism) says about the sacraments. The most crucial thing for our purposes is that meaning occurs on different levels, as it were.

First, there is the personal level: what something means to me as an individual. Second, there is the communal level: what something means to those of us who are here. Third, there is the societal level: what something means to society in general or to a large social institution. (We might just as easily call these three dimensions or aspects of meaning rather than levels of meaning.)

We often surround ourselves with objects that hold special meaning. Which objects hold special meaning for you?

One example of personal meaning is a child's scribbling. She shows it to her mommy, who asks, "What does it mean?" and she explains what she has written or drawn. It has meaning for her but for no one else. Another example of personal meaning is a souvenir. On a desk or shelf at home you may have a rock or shell that speaks to you of where you went on vacation, what you did, and who you met, but it does not have that meaning for anyone else who looks at it.

One example of communal meaning is a family tradition, such as an annual Fourth of July barbecue or Thanksgiving dinner. It is something a family has done every year, and it means "family" to them. Going to someone else's celebration would be nice, but it would not be the same. Another example might be a car accident. To those who hear about it on the news, it may be just another story. But to the people who know those who were injured or killed, it has a deeper meaning.

Examples of societal meaning are practically endless. Words have conventional meanings that are found in dictionaries, regardless of what we might think they mean when we read them. Manners have public meanings in the sense that some behaviors are considered polite and others impolite. We are regarded as ill-mannered when we do something impolite, perhaps without realizing it. National symbols like the flag or bald eagle, religious symbols like the Christian cross, the Jewish star, or the Muslim crescent, and even corporate symbols like the Nike swoosh or the Mercedes hood ornament have their meaning publicly defined at the societal level—by society at large, by a large segment of society, or by a powerful institution in society.

Therefore, when someone asks what a sacrament means, we have to figure out which level of meaning the person is thinking about. Any sacramental celebration will always have three levels of meaning at the same time: what it means to individuals who are attending the celebration, what it means to the groups in attendance (or maybe to the whole group that is there), and what it means to the Catholic Church as an institution.

Take, for example, a Mass that is celebrated at the end of a student retreat. For someone who goofed around during the retreat and resisted taking it seriously, the Mass may mean nothing; it may be boring, or it may be a form of free entertainment. For someone who deeply participated in the retreat and was touched to the core, the Mass may be a reminder of what the person discovered and a reinforcement of decisions that he or she made.

At the same time that many individual meanings are playing in the thoughts and feelings of individual retreatants, there are also some common meanings that are occurring to everyone (or almost everyone) in the group. The retreat probably has a theme, and this theme gets recognized in the readings that were selected and prayers that were composed for this Mass. At some point during the retreat, many of the participants may have begun to feel very close, and this feeling of closeness is intensified during the closing liturgy because the feeling is meaningful to everyone there. It may also happen that something was said or done during the retreat, and this memorable event is recalled by the homilist for everyone to think about.

At the same time that all this is going on, the religious ritual at the center of this celebration is the intellectual property of the Catholic Church. The Church created it, holds something like a copyright on it, and even has official rules regulating its performance. The Mass as a Mass (not necessarily this particular celebration, but the Mass in general) has a meaning (actually, a whole set of meanings) defined by the institution whose ritual it is. This is "the meaning of the Mass" as prescribed by the Catholic Church. It is, if you will, the institutional meanings of the Eucharistic liturgy in the Catholic Church.

If you look in an official document such as the Catechism for the meaning of the Eucharist, therefore, you will not find what a particular Mass means to you personally, and you will not find what it might mean to the group of people who are with you that day. The Catechism—indeed, any public Church document—is not written at the personal or communal levels. It is always written only at the societal level—in this case, at the institutional level.

This is why when you are told, "This is what the Eucharist means," you may sometimes say to yourself, "Well, it doesn't mean that to me." The speaker is talking about the meaning of the Mass at the societal level, and you are thinking about its meaning (or lack of it) at the personal level. Part of "learning about one's faith," therefore, is coming to understand and appreciate what the Catholic Church means by its rituals, even if a particular ritual doesn't yet make much sense to you at the personal level. Even if you end up never personally appreciating a ritual or what the Church teaches about it, you still need to learn the institutional meaning of the sacraments.

Sometimes there is a conflict between the meaning that a sacramental celebration has on different levels for different people. A good example of this is the Church's rule about who may and who may not receive Communion. The rule is that Communion may be received only by Catholics in good standing with the Church and with God. You may have gone to church one Sunday with a Protestant friend and were invited to receive communion at his or her Sunday worship. Now, when that friend is visiting your parish, you would naturally like him or her to receive Communion with you.

A simple gesture can carry several levels of meaning for an individual and for a community.

Chapter Three

Journal

Take an event you have experienced, and explore the three levels of meaning for that event.

In such a personal situation, the Church's rule about receiving Communion may seem wrong. And at the level of personal meaning, it may actually be wrong, if telling your friend not to go to Communion hurts your relationship. What about the communal level? What will people who are there at Mass with you think if they know that your friend is not Catholic? At that level it depends on the values and judgments of the community with whom you are celebrating. One thing you do know is that at the institutional level, only Catholics are allowed to receive Communion.

The point here is not that the Church is right and you are wrong in wanting to invite your Protestant friend to receive Communion, or that you are right and the Church is wrong to forbid it. The point is that meaning occurs on at least three different levels, and the meanings on those levels do not always agree. Resolving conflicts such as this one is part of what it means to be an adult Catholic. Ideally, the three levels coincide, but when they don't, Church members recognize that the institutional meaning is normative, and they aspire to appropriate that meaning into their values.

WHAT THE CATECHISM SAYS

In exploring the meaning of the sacraments, the Catechism tells us that the sacraments are "of Christ" and "of the Church"—by and for the Church, the Body of Christ. These concepts have been explored in this chapter. The sacraments are also "of faith," that is, they "not only presuppose faith, but by words and objects they also nourish, strengthen, and express" faith (Catechism, #1123). Because of the saving work of Christ (the Paschal mystery), the sacraments are "of salvation." In its sacramental celebrations, the Church affirms the understanding that for believers, the sacraments are necessary for salvation, since Christ and the Spirit work in the Church through the sacraments to transform its members (Catechism, #1129). Finally, the sacraments are "of eternal life," celebrating the mystery of Christ until he comes again in glory in the fullness of the kingdom (Catechism, #1130).

Review Questions

1. What significant moments of life are celebrated in the sacraments?

2. What do we mean when we say that Christ instituted the sacraments?

3. In what ways are sacraments said to be effective (to have spiritual effects)?

4. To what does the word *grace* refer?

5. Why does the Church use normative language in its documents?

6. What are the three levels of meaning, and how do they differ?

Summary

Earlier generations of Catholics learned that "sacraments give grace," but this manner of speaking leads to some serious misinterpretations, not the least of which is the notion that sacraments are something like faucets through which grace is poured into the soul. Another way to say the same thing in more contemporary language is to say that sacraments celebrate and in various ways communicate God's life. Still, the question can be asked: What is God's life? In one sense, we don't know for sure, because even the Bible admits that "No one has ever seen God" (1 John 4:12). In another sense, however, our faith tells us that we can learn about God through the world around us and especially through the Son of God, Jesus Christ. By meditating on creation and on the Gospel stories about Jesus, therefore, we can gain some insight into the divine vitality that was expressed first in the majesty and complexity of the universe and then in the incarnation of the Second Person of the Trinity.

Our understanding that Jesus was a sacramental person who said and did things that manifested God to people can now be extended to the seven liturgical sacraments. What each of the sacraments celebrates and communicates can be traced back to the life and ministry of Jesus. The spiritual realities symbolized by the sacraments come to us through the power of the Holy Spirit at work in the Church, the Body of Christ.

Chapter Three

Scripture

Blessed be the God and Father of our Lord Jesus Christ! By his great mercy he has given us a new birth into a living hope through the resurrection of Jesus Christ from the dead, and into an inheritance that is imperishable, undefiled, and unfading, kept in heaven for you, who are being protected by the power of God through faith for a salvation ready to be revealed in the last time. In this you rejoice, even if now for a little while you have had to suffer various trials, so that the genuineness of your faith—being more precious than gold that, though perishable, is tested by fire—may be found to result in praise and glory and honor when Jesus Christ is revealed. Although you have not seen him, you love him; and even though you do not see him now, you believe in him and rejoice with an indescribable and glorious joy, for you are receiving the outcome of your faith, the salvation of your souls.

1 PETER 1:3–9

Prayer

Happy is everyone who fears the LORD,
who walks in his ways.
You shall eat the fruit of the labor of your hands;
You shall be happy, and it shall go well with you.

PSALM 128:1–2

Scripture

Do you not know that all of us who have been baptized into Christ Jesus were baptized into his death? Therefore we have been buried with him by baptism into death, so that, just as Christ was raised from the dead by the glory of the Father, so we too might walk in newness of life.

ROMANS 6:3–4

Prayer

By God's gift, through water and the Holy Spirit, we are reborn to everlasting life. In his goodness, may he continue to pour out his blessings upon all present, who are his sons and daughters. May he make them always, wherever they may be, faithful members of his holy people. May he send his peace upon all who are gathered here, in Christ Jesus our Lord. Amen.

RITE OF BAPTISM FOR CHILDREN, #70.

Baptism: Immersion in God's Life

CHAPTER OVERVIEW

Welcomed into the Life of God

Baptism from the Greek word for immersion, the name of the first of the three Sacraments of Initiation; performed by full or partial immersion in water, or by pouring water over the head of the candidate, while the presider proclaims, "I baptize you in the name of the Father, and of the Son, and of the Holy Spirit."

*At the very dawn of creation
your Spirit breathed on the waters,
making them the wellspring of all holiness. . . .*

*May all who are buried with Christ in the death of baptism
rise also with him to newness of life. . . .*

*The God of power and Father of our Lord Jesus Christ
has freed you from sin
and brought you to new life
through water and the Holy Spirit.*

Rite of Baptism for Children, #s 54 and 62.

These poetic phrases from the baptismal ritual highlight the essence of **Baptism** as we explored it earlier. Through Baptism we are welcomed into the life of God in the Church. Through Baptism we are initiated into a community that loves and accepts us. In Baptism we are reminded that the life of God must be passed on to each new generation, and that it must reach out to those who have not yet been touched by it. Baptism says that divine love means being immersed in the joys and sufferings of others, welcoming and accepting others as children of God and sharing life with them as fully as possible.

How then does the rite of Baptism reflect these truths? To discover the essence of the rite we need to look back again to our roots and see the transitions that have brought us to this point.

Journal

1. What have you been told about your Baptism, or, if you were older, what do you remember about it?

2. Why were you baptized?

Early Christian Baptism

At the beginning of Christian history, the vast majority of converts were adults, and so they were baptized as adults. Some Christian denominations today refuse to baptize infants because they think that Baptism should always be done the way they think it was done in the early Church. Like most Christian Churches, the Catholic Church recognizes and practices infant Baptism, but it views adult Baptism as clearly expressing the full meaning of the sacrament.

In the Gospel according to John, Jesus has a conversation with a religious leader of the Jews and says, ". . . no one can enter the kingdom of God without being born of water and Spirit" (John 3:5). And at the end of Matthew's Gospel, he commands his followers, "Go therefore and make disciples of all nations, baptizing them in the name of the Father and of the Son and of the Holy Spirit" (Matthew 28:19). In both instances Jesus is speaking to adults about adult conversion.

This is certainly the way the early Christians understood it. The apostles preached the good news about Jesus and God's kingdom to grown men and women, and they baptized all those who accepted their message. These Baptisms were initially done "on the spot" and quite informally; as soon as people believed the good news, they were baptized and joined the community of those living Jesus' way of life. Take, for example, the story of the Ethiopian official, some of which was quoted in chapter 1:

The Lord's angel said to Philip, "Go south along the desert road that leads from Jerusalem to Gaza." So Philip left.

An important Ethiopian official happened to be going along the road in his chariot. He was the chief treasurer for Candace, the Queen of Ethiopia. The official had gone to Jerusalem to worship and was now on his way home. He was sitting in his chariot, reading the book of the prophet Isaiah.

The Spirit told Philip to catch up with the chariot. Philip ran up close and heard the man reading aloud from the book of Isaiah. Philip asked him, "Do you understand what you are reading?"

The official answered, "How can I understand unless someone helps me?" He then invited Philip to come up and sit beside him.

The man was reading the passage that said,

"He was led like a sheep on its way to be killed.
He was silent as a lamb,
whose wool is being cut off,
and he didn't say a word.
He was treated like a nobody
and did not receive a fair trial.
How can he have children
if his life is snatched away?"

The official said to Philip, "Tell me, was the prophet talking about himself or about someone else?" So Philip began at this place in the Scriptures and explained the good news about Jesus.

As they were going along the road, they came to a place where there was some water. The official said, "Look! Here is some water. Why can't I be baptized?" He ordered the chariot to stop. Then they both went down into the water, and Philip baptized him.

After they had come out of the water, the Lord's Spirit took Philip away. The official never saw him again, but he was very happy as he went on his way.

Acts 8:26–39 (CEV)

✏️ **Journal**

1. How would you have responded to Philip?

2. If you think you would have asked to be baptized, why do you think you would have done so?

✝️ **Activity**

Work with your parish priest and the Protestant minister to arrange to attend a baptismal service at a Protestant Church that practices adult Baptism or believer's Baptism. (Some Protestant Churches, like the Catholic Church, practice infant Baptism. Ask your teacher for a suggestion of a denomination to observe. It would be good to discuss your plans ahead of time with your parents. Get as close as possible to where the Baptism takes place. Write up a report or give an oral report on what you saw and your reactions.

Baptism: A New Way of Life

In his letters to communities of Christian converts, Paul reflected on the experience of Baptism and wrote about what it meant to him and other adult converts. He said it was like dying with Jesus and being raised with him to new life; it is an experience of the **Paschal mystery.** In their old life, they may have been sinners or even criminals, but Baptism washed all of that away and dedicated them to the life of God. When they came out of the baptismal water, they were clothed in Christ and became God's daughters and sons:

. . . in Christ Jesus you are all children of God through faith. As many of you as were baptized into Christ have clothed yourselves with Christ. There is no longer Jew or Greek, there is no longer slave or free, there is no longer male and female; for all of you are one in Christ Jesus.

Galatians 3:26–28

A fifth-century baptistry in Ravenna, Italy.

Paschal mystery Christ's work of salvation accomplished through his passion and death, leading to his resurrection and ascension; the mysterious way that goodness comes out of self-sacrifice or dying to self

grace from the Greek word for gift, used in Christian theology to mean any gift from God, including the spiritual gifts symbolized and received through the sacraments; the free and undeserved gift of spiritual power that enables us to live the life of God and be God's daughters and sons

In their new community they all had one Father, they were motivated by one Spirit, and they were joined together as one body—the Body of Christ. Paul was explaining the experience of conversion to people who had changed in midstream from one way of life to another.

How then did Baptism get turned around from adults to children? Undoubtedly, some of those who believed the good news that a brand new way of life was possible were parents, and when they joined the Church, they brought the whole family. Sometimes, too, entire households—adults, children, and those who worked for the family as servants or slaves—came into the Christian community all at once. When children were baptized, it was understood that they were baptized in the faith of the Church and that the **grace** of Baptism was a gift from God unmerited by anyone. Baptism brought true freedom to everyone over whom the blessed waters flowed.

Chapter Four

Christianity spread rapidly because many people were attracted to the way of life that Jesus announced and that God's Spirit made possible. At times, the Roman government regarded the followers of Jesus with suspicion because they were "too different." After three centuries, however, the Emperor Constantine recognized that the Christian way of life was truly good for his subjects, and he put an end to the official persecutions and signed an edict of tolerance.

Within a few generations after that, nearly everyone in the Roman Empire had been converted to Christianity, and as a result there were few adults to baptize. There were still, however, children being born into Christian families. Sometimes parents postponed the Baptism of their children until they were old enough to make their own decision to follow Jesus. Eventually, though, Christian parents asked to have their children baptized the Easter after they were born. (At this time all Baptisms in the Church were performed only once a year, at the Easter Vigil.)

By the Middle Ages, infant Baptism had become the statistical norm, and, since no one enjoyed a church full of crying babies on Holy Saturday night, Baptism took place shortly after birth. All that was left of the original service at the Easter Vigil was the blessing of the baptismal water. Until fairly recently, even adult converts were initiated into the Church with the very short Rite of Baptism designed for infants. Also, until the reworking of the sacramental liturgies mandated by Vatican II, Baptisms were held with only a few family members present.

This engraving portrays an eighteenth-century Catholic Baptism.

What the Catechism Says

From the time of the early Church, Baptism into the Christian community has included a journey with stages in the initiation process. While the length of the process has varied, initiation has included conversion, proclamation and acceptance of the gospel, a profession of faith, Baptism, anointing, and Eucharist. In the early centuries of the Church, a lengthy catechumenate developed, with liturgical rites of preparation for the Sacraments of Initiation.

The preparatory rites were greatly abridged when infant Baptism became common. This practice required and requires post-baptismal catechesis, that is, teaching about the faith after rather than before Baptism. Since the Second Vatican Council, the catechumenate has been widely used for adults, along with its stages and rites, as detailed in the *Rite of Christian Initiation of Adults*. In line with the rite, the Sacraments of Initiation are celebrated at the Easter Vigil.

In the Eastern Rites of the Catholic Church, infants are initiated with Baptism, Confirmation, and Eucharist at the same time. In the Latin or Roman Rite, Baptism of infants is followed by catechesis, with Confirmation and Eucharist celebrated at or after the age of reason, thus completing the initiation process.

See the *Catechism of the Catholic Church*, #s 1229–1233.

Discussion

In the large group, discuss the following questions:

1. In the beginning, Christians were expected to begin a new life and behave differently from the non-Christians around them. Is this still true today? Explain your answer.

2. Describe how the practice of Baptism changed in the early centuries from Baptism primarily of adults to Baptism primarily of children. What advantages and disadvantages did this have? Explain.

Discussion

In a small group, discuss the following questions:

1. To which Christian communities (home, parish, school, clubs, and so on) do you belong?

2. In which ones would you say that you are immersed?

3. What beliefs, attitudes, and habits have you acquired because of your immersion in those communities?

Review Questions

1. What type of Baptism was more common in the early Church?

2. How does Baptism signify and celebrate the Paschal mystery?

3. How are the Sacraments of Initiation celebrated in the Eastern Rites of the Catholic Church? How is this similar to and different from the practice of the Latin or Roman Rite?

Vatican II Reinstatement of the Catechumenate

Rite of Christian Initiation of Adults
the process of gradual initiation into the Christian community and the rites that celebrate the various stages of that process, culminating in the Sacraments of Initiation

catechumenate the period of time when people are preparing for Baptism through a process of learning and faith sharing, and solemnized in the rituals of the RCIA

Sacraments of Initiation
the three liturgical rites through which a person is received into full membership in the Catholic Church: Baptism, Confirmation, and Eucharist

Since the Second Vatican Council, adults seeking Baptism experience a far different preparation and celebration from that used for many centuries. Returning to its early roots, the Church has reinstated the ***Rite of Christian Initiation of Adults.*** The purpose of the RCIA (as it is usually referred to, with emphasis on the rites) or the adult **catechumenate** or the order of Christian initiation of adults (names that emphasize the process and stages), is gradually to immerse people in the Christian life during the year (more or less) before their liturgical initiation into the Church at Easter. To highlight the symbolism of immersion in the Christian life, some parishes have replaced the customary baptismal font with an immersion baptismal pool.

Adults are welcomed into the Church during the Easter Vigil by participating in all three **Sacraments of Initiation.** They are baptized and confirmed in their new faith by the pastor of their parish, and they receive Eucharist for the first time at the Mass in which they are participating. In the early centuries, those who were learning about the Christian life, the catechumens, would never have been present at a full Eucharistic liturgy until their initiation. For them, it was truly a night of "firsts." The Sacraments of Initiation today, as then, are celebrated among the community that has walked the journey with the newly initiated. These sacraments lay the foundations of Christian life, which the new Christians now live in grace and charity.

Infants and young children, however, are received into the Church through the simple Rite of Baptism, which can be performed separately or in conjunction with a Eucharistic liturgy. Some parishes schedule Baptisms to take place during Sunday Mass, to emphasize the fact that Baptism into the Church is not a private matter but something to be celebrated by the entire community. It is a wonderful opportunity for the community to welcome the newest members of its family, signed as members of God's holy people. Celebrations are shared, and the sacraments are celebrations!

Activities

1. Attend a meeting for adults who are preparing for Baptism and membership in the Catholic Church. If possible, explain your reason for attending and learn from the leaders and participants what they think about the process. Report to the class what you have learned.

2. Attend an Easter Vigil service at which one or more people are baptized. (You can find out whether or not the service will include a Baptism by calling the parish during Lent.) Sit as close as possible to where the Baptism takes place. Write up a report or give an oral report on what you saw and on your reactions.

Research

1. Talk with the person in your parish who is in charge of the Rite of Christian Initiation of Adults. Find out everything you can about the process, including how it works and how successful it is. Present your report to the class.

2. Talk with a person who has been recently baptized into the Catholic Church. Ask them about the RCIA and what they think about it. Ask them about their experience of the Sacraments of Initiation, especially Baptism (what did it feel like, how did it/they affect them, and so on). Present your report to the class.

What Is Original Sin?

original sin the sin of the first man and woman and the fallen state of human nature into which every person is born, with the exception of Mary and Jesus

You may remember learning that Baptism washes away **original sin.** The Rite of Baptism refers to being "set free from sin," but does not refer specifically to original sin, and even the *Catechism of the Catholic Church* in its section on Baptism mentions it only briefly. Why is this?

Perhaps the simplest way to answer that question is to remember that the Church's understanding of original sin developed early in its history as it explored the meaning and importance of Baptism. Over the centuries, however, ordinary people's understanding of the concept of original sin lost much of its depth. Many people had a very shallow idea of it, some even imagining that original sin was like a stubborn stain to be washed out by the miracle detergent of Baptism. It wasn't and isn't always easy to fight such a misconception. The Church of the present shares a clearer understanding of original sin, but it also emphasizes concepts that are more meaningful to people today when it explains the significance of Baptism.

The Bible does not use the term *original sin*, but it does talk about "the sin of Adam." The word *adam* in Hebrew means "a human," and the Book of Genesis presents a vivid story of the first human sin. The first creation story in chapter 1 tells us that man and woman were created in the image and likeness of God, and the second creation story in chapter 2 describes the separate creation of man and woman, personified as Adam and Eve. Initially, their relationship to one another and to God their creator is harmonious, but in chapter 3 the harmonious relationship is destroyed. In the familiar biblical story of the Fall, Eve and then Adam eat of the forbidden fruit, they are inwardly transformed, and because of their transgression they are cast out of paradise, thus affecting the fate of all humans who come after them. The story teaches, among other things, that God wants people to live in harmony (with each other, with all creation, and with him) and that the fact that life is full of difficulties is not God's fault but ours.

The Catholic doctrine of original sin is based on this story. Before the Fall, the Catechism says, Adam and Eve lived in "original holiness and justice." When the first couple chose to disrupt the original harmony of paradise by disobeying God, however, they were deprived of that condition, and their descendents ever since have had to live in this condition of sinfulness or deprivation. Both their action and the resulting condition (which we might think of as the human nature that all people are born with) are referred to in Catholic theology as *original sin*. (You will learn more about the Hebrew understanding of sin in the chapter on Reconciliation.)

"The Crucifixion" by Maurice Denis (1870–1943).

Discussion

In the large group, discuss the following questions:

1. What were you taught, when you were younger, about original sin?

2. What do you think about the explanation presented here?

Journal

In general, how have you experienced the effects of original sin in the world around you?

Art: "Resurrection of Christ" by Peter Paul Rubens (1577–1640).

The Catechism does not use the expression, "washing away original sin" to talk about the effects of Baptism, as was done in the past, because its view of original sin and Baptism is both biblical and nuanced. If we think of sin as disrupting or breaking a relationship with God or other people, we can think of original sin not as a stain on the soul but as a lack of harmony in our relationships—something that we can all relate to. Baptism does not automatically restore harmony in our lives, but it provides the possibility of harmonious relationships. In other words, immersion in the new life of an active Christian community makes it possible to take that life into ourselves, with the assurance that all our past sins are forgiven, no matter how serious they might have been.

Jesus lived the life of God on earth, unaffected by the deprivations associated with original sin. He lived in harmony with God the Father, gathering a community of disciples around him, immersing them in his way of life, and communicating his Spirit to them. Through his life and teaching, his unjust execution, and his resurrection to new life, Jesus restored the possibility of living the way God originally intended humans to live. His disciples in turn invited others to enter into the life of God by joining the Christian community. Baptism by immersion in water was the sign through

which people became immersed in the life of Christ being lived by the Christian community. In traditional theological language, Baptism brings the grace of justification that enables people to relate to God with faith, hope, and love, to experience and respond to the work of the Holy Spirit, and to grow in holiness and virtue.

WHAT THE CATECHISM SAYS

The grace of Baptism is experienced in a twofold way. Just as immersion in water represents death and resurrection, purification and renewal, Baptism purifies us from our sins, both original sin and personal sin, and brings about our rebirth in the Holy Spirit.

See the *Catechism of the Catholic Church*, #1262.

Baptism and Salvation

The Catholic Church teaches that Baptism is necessary for salvation. This teaching is based on the response of Jesus to Nicodemus: "Very truly, I tell you, no one can enter the kingdom of God without being born of water and Spirit" (John 3:5). And so the Church is called to proclaim the good news of Jesus to all the world and to baptize in Jesus' name. But we know that, on one hand, not everyone has the opportunity to be baptized and that, on the other hand, God is loving and merciful. So the Catechism tells us: "God has bound salvation to the sacrament of Baptism, but he himself is not bound by his sacraments" (#1257).

The Church has long understood that physical Baptism is not the only way to experience this sacrament and salvation. An unbaptized person who dies a martyr for the faith is saved. Likewise, catechumens who die before being baptized and, indeed, all who desire Baptism and have repented of their sins are assured that salvation is theirs. And those people to whom the gospel is not preached, but who live good lives, are doing all that God asks of them and can be saved. Even those who have heard the gospel, but do not understand its necessity, can be saved—first among these are the Jews, whose covenant with God stands forever. "God our Savior . . . desires everyone to be saved and to come to the knowledge of the truth" (1 Timothy 2:3–4).

Sometimes children die without being baptized, and some children die even before being born. The Church teaches that these children are in the hands of a merciful and loving God and that we are to pray for their salvation. We are reminded that Jesus said, "Let the little children come to me: do not stop them . . ." (Mark 10:14). In the funeral liturgy for a child who died before Baptism, the presider prays:

> *God of all consolation,*
> *searcher of mind and heart,*
> *the faith of these parents [N. and N.] is known to you.*
> *Comfort them with the knowledge*
> *That the child for whom they grieve*
> *Is entrusted now to your loving care.*
> *We ask this through Christ our Lord.*
> *Amen.*
>
> ORDER OF CHRISTIAN FUNERALS, #254.

WHAT THE CATECHISM SAYS

The usual ministers of Baptism are bishops and priests. In the Latin Rite, deacons also are ordinary ministers of the sacrament. However, because of the Church's belief in the necessity of Baptism for salvation, in an emergency, anyone, even an unbaptized person, can baptize, as long as he or she has the right intention and uses the words of Baptism. To have the right intention means to intend to do what the Church does in Baptism. The words of Baptism are: "I baptize you in the name of the Father, and of the Son, and of the Holy Spirit."

See the *Catechism of the Catholic Church*, #1284.

SAINTS PERPETUA AND FELICITY

The story of Perpetua and Felicity is one of the earliest records of Christian martyrdom. They and several other catechumens were arrested in Carthage, North Africa, in 203. Perpetua was the twenty-two-year-old wife of a man of high rank and the mother of an infant son. Felicity was a slave who was eight-months pregnant at the time of her arrest. While under house arrest, they were instructed in the faith and baptized.

Shortly after being transferred to prison, the small group of Christians was sentenced to death. While they were in prison, one of their jailers became a believer because of their witness. Felicity gave birth to a girl while awaiting her death. The group became part of the games in the amphitheatre, where they were gored by wild animals before their throats were cut.

In all the early stories of martyrs and Church calendars, Perpetua and Felicity were honored as martyrs and saints. Their feast day is March 7. In 1907, an ancient inscription concerning them was discovered in the church in Carthage where they were buried.

 ## Activities

1. Read more about Saints Perpetua and Felicity, and share your findings with the class.

2. Find out about other martyrs of the Church who were catechumens or newly baptized at the time of their deaths. Report to the class.

Review Questions

1. What is the purpose of the Rite of Christian Initiation of Adults?

2. What is the meaning of original sin?

3. Who may baptize? Why?

The Role of the Godparents

Journal

1. What is your relationship to your godparents?

2. Is your relationship with your godparents what you would want it to be, or would you want it to be different in some way? Explain your answer.

---

godparent Baptism sponsor who takes on the responsibility to help the newly baptized person to live a Christian life

---

sponsor an active Catholic who accompanies a catechumen during his or her journey toward Baptism, offering spiritual support and participating in the Rite of Christian Initiation of Adults

---

Rite of Baptism for Children the ritual of Baptism specifically for infants and children; Christian formation follows Baptism as the children grow

---

Satan the devil; a biblical figure, originally an argumentative member of God's heavenly court (see Job 1:6–12), later identified with the snake or serpent in the story of the Fall (see Genesis 3:1–15), and eventually believed to be the head of all the evil spirits in the world. Satan therefore symbolically stands for any and all forms of immorality.

---

baptismal vows promises made at Baptism by the person baptized, or by the parents, godparents, and assembly, to reject sin and confess the Christian faith

---

What is the reason for having **godparents?** The tradition of godparenting goes back to when adult candidates for Baptism had to ask a Christian friend to act as a teacher and role model, and to be their **sponsor** when they asked to be received into the Church. After the rise of infant Baptism, godparents were often expected to raise their godchildren in the faith if the parents died.

This is why, until fairly recently, godparents had an important role in the Baptism of infants. And this is still why godparents are expected to be active Catholics and good role models in general and models of faith for their godchildren, not just relatives or friends of the family. The role of the godparent is not to be taken lightly. Today both the parents and the godparents have an important part in the Baptism of children. However, the parish community is also asked to assume some responsibility for anyone who is baptized in the parish.

If we look at what is said and done in the rite, we can see how the ***Rite of Baptism for Children*** is an adaptation from the *Rite of Christian Initiation of Adults.* After the initial prayers in the ceremony, the celebrant (a priest or deacon) turns to the parents and godparents and asks three questions:

> *Do you reject **Satan?***
> *And all his works?*
> *And all his empty promises?*

The rite provides alternate questions for the presider:

> *Do you reject sin so as to live in the freedom of God's children?*
> *Do you reject the glamour of evil, and refuse to be mastered by sin?*
> *Do you reject Satan, father of sin and prince of darkness?*

> RITE OF BAPTISM, #57.

To these questions, the adults answer: "I do." Then the celebrant puts three more questions to the adults, asking if they believe in God the Father, Son, and Holy Spirit. Once again the adults answer: "I do."

The adults are giving witness to their own Christian faith and the faith in which they pledge to raise the child. When they are confirmed later in life, the children will be asked to repeat on their own the **baptismal vows** that were spoken at their infant Baptism by their parents and the faith community.

Discussion

In the large group, discuss the following questions:

1. In the early days, candidates for Baptism had sponsors or godparents who vouched for them in front of the community and who helped them live a Christian life after Baptism. Do you think this was a good idea? Why or why not?

2. The Church has a rule that only active Catholics can be godparents. What do you think are some of the Church's reasons for this rule?

The Words and Actions of Baptism

The central and essential act of Baptism is the same for both adults and children—either a triple pouring of water over the head or an immersion in water and the words that the celebrant speaks while performing the ritual: "I baptize you in the name of the Father, and of the Son, and of the Holy Spirit."

When adults are baptized, they are confirmed immediately afterward, with a special oil called **chrism.** Something similar to this is done in the *Rite of Baptism for Children*, when the child is anointed with chrism. This is not, however, the Sacrament of Confirmation, for this anointing does not signify the "seal of the Holy Spirit"; rather, it is referred to as the "chrism of salvation." This anointing marks the newly baptized as one saved by and incorporated into Christ.

Next comes a part of the ceremony that is rather nice, but the full symbolism of it is not as powerful in infant Baptism as it is in adult Baptism. The child receives a white garment, signifying that he or she has become a "new creation" and has been "clothed . . . in Christ." Technically the white baptismal gown ought to be put on *after* the Baptism, but very often infants are brought to Baptism already dressed in white. Then, after they are baptized, they are covered with a white cloth instead of being reclothed.

When adults are baptized, they receive a white garment that covers their old clothes entirely. And when adults are baptized by immersion, they literally take off their old clothes and put on a new white robe—not in front of everybody (to be sure!), but everybody at the Baptism sees them leave completely wet and then reappear in a fresh white garment. This is a powerful symbol of putting off the old creation and putting on Christ.

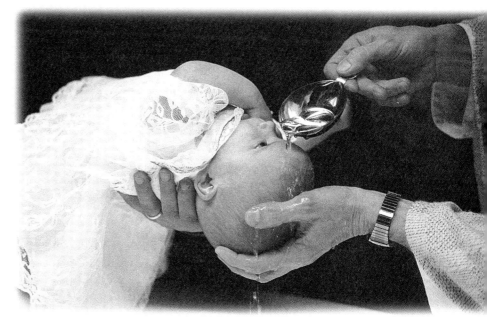

chrism blessed oil used in the Sacraments of Baptism, Confirmation, and Holy Orders

The last ceremonial act in the *Rite of Baptism for Children* that is adapted from the RCIA is the receiving of a candle, lit from the Easter candle. During the Easter Vigil, each of the newly baptized adults is presented with this symbol of the "light of Christ" with which they have been enlightened, and the "flame of faith" which now burns brightly in their hearts. During an infant Baptism this symbol is entrusted to the parents and godparents with the understanding that they will do all that is needed to help the child appreciate what the candle represents. (Some families adopt the custom of lighting the baptismal candle on the anniversary of the Baptism to reflect, renew, and celebrate this special day.)

Expectations of Baptism

It is clear that the meaning of infant Baptism is connected to the meaning of adult Baptism. A child is received into the Church in the same way that an adult is received, and with the same expectation that he or she will be an active member of the Church. Any person, whether infant or adult, is helped to grow in his or her faith and commitment to Christ by participating in the life of the Christian community.

SYMBOLS IN THE RITE OF BAPTISM

- **Water**—life, refreshment, renewal, cleansing
- **Immersion**—dying and rising, being renewed, refreshed, cleansed
- **Sign of the cross**—referring to the crucifixion of Jesus, it signifies that the one who receives it is a follower of Christ
- **Anointing with oil (chrism)**—life, strengthening, salvation
- **White robe**—new life, new beginning
- **Candle**—Christ, the light of the world; the spiritual illumination received from Christ through the Christian community (from parents and other Christian adults) and from taking the words of Jesus to heart; it also refers to how Christians are to be "the light of the world" (Matthew 5:14)

Activity

Attend a baptismal service at which an infant or child is baptized. (You can find out when Baptisms are scheduled by calling your parish office.) Sit as close as possible to where the Baptism takes place. Write up a report or give an oral report on what you saw and what you think about it.

Discussion

In a small group, discuss the following questions:

1. What are some different meanings that water can have?
2. What are the circumstances in which those different meanings are more obvious?

Review Questions

1. What is the role of a godparent?
2. What are the essential words and actions of Baptism?
3. What are the baptismal vows?
4. What concrete signs are used in Baptism? What is the meaning of each sign?

"The Baptism of Jesus,"
St. Cecilia's Church,
Hastings, Nebraska.

The word *Baptism* comes from a Greek word that literally means "immersion." John the Baptist got his name from the fact that he immersed people in the Jordan River when they said they would renounce their sinful way of life and be converted to a life of honesty and justice.

In those days John the Baptist appeared in the wilderness of Judea, proclaiming, "Repent, for the kingdom of heaven has come near." . . . Then the people of Jerusalem and all Judea were going out to him, and all the region along the Jordan, and they were baptized by him in the river Jordan, confessing their sins.

Matthew 3:1, 5–6

It is because of the nature of this baptism that John resisted baptizing Jesus:

Then Jesus came from Galilee to John at the Jordan, to be baptized by him. John would have prevented him, saying, "I need to be baptized by you, and do you come to me?" But Jesus answered him, "Let it be so now; for it is proper for us in this way to fulfill all righteousness." Then he consented. And when Jesus had been baptized, just as he came up from the water, suddenly the heavens were opened to him and he saw the Spirit of God descending like a dove and alighting on him. And a voice from heaven said, "This is my Son, the Beloved, with whom I am well pleased."

Matthew 3:13–17

Other Jews at the time of Jesus also practiced a form of baptism, asking converts to symbolize their unity with the Israelites who had crossed the Jordan River into the promised land by being immersed in water when they embraced Judaism.

Baptism: Immersion in God's Life

The primary meaning of the Sacrament of Baptism is immersion into Christ's death and resurrection to new life in Christ, which is why some Protestant churches and some Catholic parishes prefer the symbolism of full immersion to the pouring of water. A secondary meaning of Baptism is the washing away of original sin and, for adults, the personal sin and guilt of their lives up to this moment when they begin to live in a community that reflects the forgiveness and compassion of God.

For children, in particular, the primary meaning of Baptism is the most important. Through Baptism, new Christians are symbolically immersed in the community of faith and the life of God. Through Baptism, children are welcomed into the faith community of their own family (the domestic Church), their local parish, and the universal Church. Baptism is the beginning of their learning how to live the way that Jesus lived and wants his followers to live.

WHAT THE CATECHISM SAYS

The word *baptism* comes from the Greek word *baptizein,* which means to plunge or immerse. In Baptism the person being baptized is buried in Christ's death and reborn in his resurrection.

> *… when you were buried with him in baptism, you were also raised with him through faith in the power of God, who raised him from the dead.*
>
> **Colossians 2:12**

Thus the newly baptized person is a new creation:

> *So if anyone is in Christ, there is a new creation: everything old has passed away; see, everything has become new!*
>
> **2 Corinthians 5:17**

See the *Catechism of the Catholic Church,* #1214.

Research

Talk with an older Catholic (someone your grandparents' age) about his or her understanding of Baptism. In a class discussion, report on and compare your findings.

Activity

Read the story of Jesus' baptism in the other Gospels: Mark 1:9–11, Luke 3:21–22, and John 1:29–34. Write a brief essay on these questions:

1. What similarities and differences do you find in the accounts?

2. What is the essential message in the accounts?

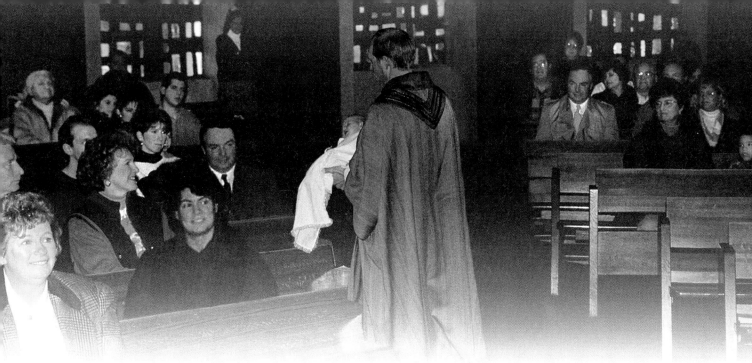

Immersion in the Christian Community

The parish community promises to share its faith and Christian life with those who are baptized and their families.

Because Baptism means immersion in the Christian community and the Christian life, the Church is concerned that the symbolism of Baptism should be actively lived out by every Catholic child. In the past, when being Catholic meant living very differently from Protestants, Jews, and nonbelievers, Catholic parents simply went to their parish priest and arranged for their children's Baptism. It was not a matter of "if," but "when."

Today, however, the world is more complex. Large parishes, interfaith marriages, and a variety of lifestyles make it impossible for pastors to be sure that every parent who comes to them will really raise their child in the Catholic Church and the Christian faith. For this reason, many pastors, before proceeding with the plans for Baptism, inquire whether parents are or intend to be active members of the Church. Sometimes it is not a matter of "when," but "if."

For similar reasons, most parishes today have a Baptism preparation program—not for the children but for the parents. Young couples need to understand what they are committing themselves and their children to when they ask for Baptism in the Catholic Church. The preparation program clarifies their role as Christian parents and supports them in that role, and it also gives them an opportunity to meet other parents of young children in the parish. Preparing for their child's Baptism helps parents become more aware of the meaning of their own Baptism and of personal immersion in the faith community.

The faith community is first of all the Christian family into which the child is born and in which the baptized child will be nurtured as a child of God. Second, the faith community is the Catholic parish where people can meet and support one another, worship together, and grow in their faith together. And third, the faith community is the Catholic Church of the diocese, the nation, and the world, sharing a common faith and commitment to the Christian way of life.

For just as the body is one and has many members, and all the members of the body, though many, are one body, so it is with Christ. For in the one Spirit we were all baptized into one body—Jews or Greeks, slaves or free—and we were all made to drink of one Spirit.

1 Corinthians 12:12–13

Discussion

In the large group, discuss the following questions:

1. Sometimes a pastor may refuse to baptize a child whose parents are not practicing their faith. What do you think of this policy? Why?

2. What are the strengths of your parish community?

3. How can these strengths benefit newly baptized members and their families?

The life of God in one sense is a mystery, but in another sense there is nothing mysterious about it at all. The life of God is the life that Jesus lived and still lives in the Church. It is the way of life that Jesus revealed by trusting in his Father, by caring and reaching out to others, by healing their hurts and forgiving their sins. It is a life that is animated by God's Spirit of love and sharing, self-giving and fairness, openness and honesty, fidelity and unity. It is our life as adopted children of God, members of Christ, and temples of the Holy Spirit, incorporated into the Body of Christ, the Church.

In the end, the life of God is the life of Jesus living in us. It means, to put it starkly, a life of death and resurrection. It means dying to ourselves and living for others, as Jesus did. It means dying to sin and selfishness and being raised to a new level of loving and caring. It means new birth, new growth, and new life. Baptism marks the beginning of that new life of discipleship.

WHAT THE CATECHISM SAYS

Christ is our high priest and mediator. Our Baptism in Christ "gives a share in the common priesthood of all believers." Through Baptism, we are consecrated by the anointing of the Holy Spirit to be a new people and to take part in Christ's priestly vocation. According to our own vocations, we are called to participate in Christ's mission to bring the good news of salvation to all the world.

See the *Catechism of the Catholic Church*, #s 784, 1268, 1546.

Journal

- What is a life of discipleship?
- What does such a life mean for you?

Research

Look in the *Catechism of the Catholic Church* and see what it says about the Sacrament of Baptism in the full article (1213–1274) or in the summary at the end (1275–1284).

1. Which statements do you find easy to understand? Which statements do you find hard to understand? Give reasons for your evaluations of the statements you chose.

2. Which statements might some people misinterpret as implying that Baptism has magical or automatic mystical effects? How would you respond to this misinterpretation?

Chapter Four

The baptized are marked with the Spirit.

The Indelible Seal of Baptism

One aspect of the traditional Catholic theology of Baptism that is found in the Catechism has to do with something that is called "an indelible spiritual mark," "the baptismal seal," "the sacramental character," and "the sign of faith." How are these terms to be understood? Some of the letters in the New Testament speak about Christians being sealed or stamped with the Holy Spirit:

> But it is God who establishes us with you in Christ and has anointed us, by putting his seal on us and giving us his Spirit in our hearts as a first installment.

2 Corinthians 1:21–22

> In [Christ] you also, when you had heard the word of truth, the gospel of your salvation, and had believed in him, were marked with the seal of the promised Holy Spirit; this is the pledge of our inheritance toward redemption as God's own people, to the praise of his glory.

Ephesians 1:13–14

The Book of Revelation (7:3–4) presents a vision of 144,000 whose foreheads are stamped with a seal that marks them as servants of God. The meaning of the seal in the letters of the New Testament is not always clear; in Revelation the reference is to something that happens just before the second coming of Christ.

During the first centuries of Christianity, theologians asked whether people needed to be rebaptized if they left the Church and later wanted to become Christians again. A few places actually practiced rebaptism, but the majority did not. The more common practice was a sacramental Reconciliation with God and the Church.

Around the year 400, Saint Augustine put forth a theological justification for the majority practice, and in doing so he appealed to Scripture texts such as the ones cited above. His interpretation was that Baptism imparted something like a spiritual tattoo that permanently marked the baptized as belonging to Christ. In fact, the Greek word for "seal" also meant a scorched brand on cattle and sheep that was used to prevent rustling. Augustine assumed that a seal of this sort would have to be permanent, and so he argued that, if the baptized are indelibly marked with the seal of the Spirit, then there is no reason to rebaptize anyone. It would do nothing more than print a new tattoo on top of the old one. In time, Augustine's explanation for the practice of baptizing people only once became accepted as a matter of Church doctrine.

The above phrases, cited in the Catechism, are therefore understood at first glance as older theological explanations for the practice of not allowing people to be admitted to Baptism if they have already been baptized in a different Christian Church. Otherwise there is a danger that the terms will be taken in a fundamentalistic way that supports magical beliefs about Baptism, a kind of being "zapped" by God.

A more contemporary explanation for the Catholic practice of not rebaptizing people can be found in our understanding of family. When a person is born into a family, he or she immediately becomes a member of that family forever. Afterward, a person may get separated from his or her family (parents may die, the person may run away from home, or so on). But nothing can erase the fact that from the moment of birth a person had a biological relationship to his or her parents, siblings, and all other blood relatives. Even an adoptive family presents a similar situation because once a child is legally adopted, he or she has a permanent relationship to the adopting parents and their family. In the same way, when we are born into the family of God through Baptism, we enter into a spiritual relationship with God and with all other Christians. We become spiritually a child of God and brothers and sisters of Christ. We may later get separated from this family by not practicing our faith, but even sin cannot undo these spiritual connections to God and the Church.

Baptism brings with it a permanent relationship with God and the Christian community.

Chapter Four

Or we may grow up in a branch of the Christian family that is not Catholic. The Church's practice of not rebaptizing people can therefore be understood as a way of symbolically recognizing that everyone who is baptized is a member of the Christian family called to worship in the community of faith. And so if they want to join the Catholic community of faith, they need only to reaffirm their baptismal faith by a profession of Catholic faith and possibly the Sacrament of Confirmation.

Discussion

In the large group, discuss the following questions:

1. What were you taught, when you were younger, about the baptismal seal or character?

2. What do you understand about this traditional Catholic belief?

3. What is your reaction to the explanation presented here?

Journal

What does the baptismal seal mean to you personally?

Review Questions

1. What is the relationship between Jesus' baptism and the Sacrament of Baptism?

2. What are the three levels of the Christian community into which we are immersed at Baptism?

3. What do we mean by *the priesthood of all believers?*

4. To what does the indelible seal of Baptism refer?

Summary

Baptism is the first of the three Sacraments of Initiation through which people are received into the Christian community. Persons of any age can participate in this liturgical rite which celebrates God's life within the person and spiritual regeneration.

As in the early days of the Church, adult Baptism by immersion in water is considered the norm for understanding the meaning of Baptism. For centuries, however, it has been a common practice for Christian parents to have their children baptized when they are still infants.

The Sacrament of Baptism is rich in symbolism and significance for family and parish as well as for those who have already been baptized, for during the ceremony all are invited to reaffirm their baptismal promises.

Scripture

There is one body and one Spirit, just as you were called to the one hope of your calling, one Lord, one faith, one baptism, one God and Father of all, who is above all and through all and in all.

EPHESIANS 4:4–6

Prayer

God, the all-powerful Father of our Lord Jesus Christ, has given us a new birth by water and the Holy Spirit and forgiven all our sins.
May he also keep us faithful to our Lord Jesus Christ for ever and ever. Amen.

CHRISTIAN INITIATION OF ADULTS, #583.

Scripture

When [the followers of Jesus] had prayed, the place in which they were gathered together was shaken; and they were all filled with the Holy Spirit and spoke the word of God with boldness.

ACTS 4:31

Prayer

God our Father,
you have given us new birth.
Strengthen us with your Holy Spirit
and fill us with your light.
Grant this through our Lord Jesus Christ, your Son,
who lives and reigns with you and the Holy Spirit,
one God, for ever and ever.
Amen.

OPENING PRAYER,
VIGIL MASS OF PENTECOST.

Confirmation: Affirmation of God's Life

CHAPTER OVERVIEW

Having Spirit
The Holy Spirit in the Old Testament
Jesus and the Spirit of God
Empowered by the Spirit
The Sacrament of Confirmation in History
Alternate Ways to Celebrate Confirmation
Gifts of the Spirit
Charisms
The Life of the Spirit
The Seal
Our Personal "Yes"
The Rite of Confirmation
Sponsors and Names
Confirmation and Christian Service
Summary

Having Spirit

The sportscaster yelled into the microphone, "Listen to that crowd roar! What spirit! The team is back on the field. Ten seconds to go. . . . Can the team spirit carry the game? They're on the nine yard line, . . . eight, seven, six, . . . a touchdown! It's over! The home team wins 13 to 12. What a game! . . . Listen to those fans! What spirit! . . . You can't be in this stadium and not feel it!

spirit an ancient word with many meanings, including breath, life, vitality, inner qualities, personality, invisible reality

We all experience spirit in one way or another. Yet in our modern way of talking, we seldom refer to it as spirit. One of the exceptions is the way people still talk about school spirit and team spirit, as in the selection above. Not paying attention to the experience of spirit cripples our understanding of spirit. It also interferes with our ability to understand what people were talking about in ancient times when they talked about spirit.

What is this mysterious reality we call **spirit?** We often find ourselves using words that make spirit sound like a thing. This was true even in ancient times, when people explained good and bad (and sometimes crazy) behavior by attributing it to being "possessed by a spirit," that is, by a spiritual entity other than the person himself or herself. At the same time, an understanding of God's Spirit, the Holy Spirit, as a personal presence, a capacity for love is at the core of an appreciation of the Sacrament of Confirmation.

In ordinary English, we sometimes use the word *spirit* to refer to a certain quality of life. When we're happy, we say that we're in good spirits. When we're depressed, we say our spirits are low. In talking about someone who doesn't worry very much, we say that she or he is a carefree spirit. In talking about someone who does a lot of volunteer work, we applaud a generous spirit. In the same vein, we talk about the spirit of patriotism, the spirit of wonder, the spirit of adventure, and so on.

Most people tend to recognize spirit when they "see" it.

Not only individuals but also groups can have an identifying spirit. We speak about team spirit, community spirit, even the spirit of our nation. Families have different spirits: it's that certain something that emanates when they are all together, a certain quality of their life that's different from the spirit of other families. Parishes, too, have different spirits. Some may be energetic while others are rather listless, some may be very liturgically oriented while others are more active in social justice issues. And each of the religious orders in the Church (Benedictines, Franciscans, Dominicans, Jesuits, and so on) in some way carries on the spirit of its founder.

The nature of spirit is hard to define. Spirit is very real, but it is also very elusive. The same is true of the Holy Spirit. First and foremost, we have to realize that the Holy Spirit is not a thing, not even a spiritual thing. Imagining the Holy Spirit as a thing is a mental trap that is easy to fall into, especially when we hear about "giving" and "receiving" the Holy Spirit. Even some theologians in the past fell into this trap, so we needn't feel bad if we have fallen into it, too. We have plenty of company.

Discussion

To get a better feel for the way the word *spirit* was used in the past, translate the following adjectives into phrases that use the word *spirit*. For example, instead of saying that a person was generous, people in the past might have said that the person had a generous or benevolent spirit. Also, for each phrase reach a consensus on the name of a person (either a real individual or a fictional character) whom you think has that quality or spirit. Share your examples in the large group.

| courageous | immoral | crazy or insane |
| fearful | unusual or weird | caring for others |

Discussion

Think of a movie or television program in which someone's spirit is transformed by undergoing a change of heart, mind, or behavior, or in which someone "receives" a new spirit (for example, self-confidence, courage, kindness) from someone else (for example, a mentor, a teacher, a coach). In the small group, share your examples, and then discuss the following.

1. Even though you might not have originally thought about this change in the character's attitude or behavior in terms of spirit, use this term now to describe and analyze what you perceive in that character.

2. How did doing this exercise help you understand and appreciate how the word *spirit* is used in the Scriptures and in theology?

 Journal

Think of a time when someone communicated his or her spirit to you or a time when an experience "gave you a spirit" that you did not have before. Describe what happened, first in ordinary language and then using the more ancient way of talking about it—using the word *spirit*.

The Holy Spirit in the Old Testament

Who then is this **Holy Spirit** we say we believe in? We could look into the Scriptures and Church's doctrines for an answer, but remember that both the Bible and the doctrines come from people reflecting on their own experience.

Turning now to the Old Testament, we can get a sense of what the biblical writers were referring to when they used the word *spirit*. In describing the emotions behind people's behavior, they often used phrases such as *the spirit of anger, the spirit of jealousy,* and *the spirit of courage.* But sometimes the authors also said that certain individuals and groups had the spirit of God. How is this different?

Moses is said to have had the spirit of God when he courageously faced the pharaoh and led the Israelites out of Egypt. King Saul is said to have lost the spirit when he was unfaithful to God's law, and as a result David was anointed as a sign that the presence of God was enabling him to act with courage and honesty, justice and mercy, and all the qualities of a good king. Solomon was renowned for the spirit of wisdom that God had given him. The prophets were moved by the spirit of God to denounce injustice and call the people back to righteousness.

From these instances and others in the Old Testament, we see that whenever God's spirit enters in, life gets better, and whenever God's spirit is not present, things get worse. The Spirit of God brings goodness into the world. When we see people doing good, we catch a glimpse of God's creative and sustaining spirit.

*"The Anointing of David,"
Sacred Heart Church in
Freeport, Minnesota.*

Holy Spirit, God's spirit, Spirit of God, Spirit of the Lord, Holy Ghost

different ways that Scripture and Christian tradition name the invisible spiritual reality that is God; the third Person of the Holy Trinity; the personal love of the Father and the Son for each other

Research

A concordance is a reference book to the Bible that notes the texts in which various words are found. Use a concordance to find two of the Old Testament references to people mentioned in this section. Give the references and summarize each of them. Explain how the concept of spirit or Spirit comes across to you in each reference.

Discussion

Until the mid-twentieth century, the Holy Spirit was referred to as the Holy Ghost. In the large group, discuss the following questions:

1. What do you think were some of the disadvantages of using the old name?

2. What do you think are some of the advantages of using *Holy Spirit*?

Jesus and the Spirit of God

Because their Jewish heritage taught them to look at goodness and see God's spirit at work, people looked at what Jesus did and saw more. The simplest summary of Jesus' ministry is that "he went about doing good" (Acts 10:38). Jesus did not look different from other people, but he acted very differently.

"Baptism of Christ," by Andrea del Verrocehio. The head of the kneeling angel on the left was painted by Leonardo de Vinci when he was an apprentice.

He treated alike those who were rich and those who were poor, he invited women as well as men to his table, he didn't hate the Romans. To the accused he was merciful, to the outcast he was understanding, to the lonely he was friendly. With the weak he was unassuming, but with the powerful he was daring. When he touched those who were sick, they were healed. When he told people that their sins were forgiven, they knew that it was so. When he taught them, they felt the word of God speaking to their hearts.

In their Jewish way of naming what they saw in Jesus, people said that he was *meshiach*, anointed with the spirit of God the way that Moses and King David and the prophets were. God's spirit was upon him and within him, giving him the power to do good. (The word *messiah* comes from the Hebrew *mashiakh* [mĕ-shee-ACH].)

Turning to the New Testament, we read that Jesus was filled with the Holy Spirit.

Now when all the people were baptized, and when Jesus also had been baptized and was praying, the heaven was opened, and the Holy Spirit descended upon him in bodily form like a dove. And a voice came from heaven, "You are my Son, the Beloved; with you I am well pleased." . . .

Jesus, full of the Holy Spirit, returned from the Jordan and was led by the Spirit in the wilderness . . . .

Luke 3:21–22, 4:1a

"Christ in the House of Martha and Mary"
by Jan Vermeer (1632–1675).

The author of the Gospel according to Matthew quotes the prophet Isaiah to explain that Jesus is empowered by the Holy Spirit:

"Here is my servant, whom I have chosen,
my beloved, with whom my soul is well pleased.
I will put my Spirit upon him,
and he will proclaim justice to the Gentiles."

Matthew 12:18

Those who knew him closely, though, also knew that that was just the way that Jesus was. It was *his* spirit that they felt when they were near him. It was *his* spirit that energized them and gave them confidence and hope. To them, the **spirit of Jesus** and the spirit of the messiah and the spirit of God all seemed to be the same spirit, a wholesome spirit, a healthy spirit and a healing spirit: a holy spirit.

Reflecting on this experience of spirit and on what Jesus had said, the early Christians came to understand Jesus' spirit, or God's spirit, as a reality in itself, a separate reality, a personal divine reality. They called it the Holy Spirit, or referred to it simply as the Spirit.

spirit of Jesus, spirit of Christ, spirit of the Lord, Holy Spirit, Holy Ghost different ways that Scripture and Christian tradition name the invisible spiritual reality that motivated and empowered Jesus, and that motivates and empowers those who commit themselves to following him

Research

1. Pick up a New Testament and read about Jesus in the four Gospels. Based on what you read, in an essay describe Jesus' personality or character using the word *spirit* as would have been done in ancient times.

2. Jesus gathered a group of followers (disciples or students) around him, and he communicated his spirit—God's spirit—to them. Look for places in the Gospels that can be understood in this way, and in an essay or other medium, describe the qualities of spirit that Jesus was communicating to those around him.

DiSCUSSioN

Many times people have fallen into the trap of thinking about the Holy Spirit merely as a thing that can be given in sacraments and received by people. The term *grace* has also often been thought about in this way, since God's life within us—another way to talk about God's spirit—is likewise a gift from God. In a small group, discuss the following questions:

1. When have you heard someone talking about the Spirit or grace as a thing to be received?

2. When have you found yourself thinking about these spiritual realities in this way? Explain what you were thinking at that time.

Empowered by the Spirit

empowered strengthened, energized, given the ability to do something

Jesus' followers didn't completely understand exactly how it happened, but somehow after his resurrection Jesus was able to assure them that this same Spirit entered their lives. Looking back, one disciple said it happened shortly after the resurrection.

When it was evening on that day, the first day of the week, and the doors of the house where the disciples had met were locked for fear of the Jews, Jesus came and stood among them and said, "Peace be with you." After he said this, he showed them his hands and his side. Then the disciples rejoiced when they saw the Lord. Jesus said to them again, "Peace be with you. As the Father has sent me, so I send you." When he had said this, he breathed on them and said to them, "Receive the Holy Spirit. If you forgive the sins of any, they are forgiven them; if you retain the sins of any, they are retained."

John 20:19–23

Another follower recounted a later experience on the feast of Pentecost.

When the day of Pentecost had come, they were all together in one place. And suddenly from heaven there came a sound like the rush of a violent wind, and it filled the entire house where they were sitting. Divided tongues, as of fire, appeared among them, and a tongue rested on each of them. All of them were filled with the Holy Spirit and began to speak in other languages, as the Spirit gave them ability.

Acts 2:1–4

This Pentecost painting is from the church of St. Maron in Minneapolis.

From the way the Holy Spirit energized them and enabled them to do the same sorts of things that Jesus had done, they knew it was that same divine Spirit that had **empowered** Jesus—the Holy Spirit of God.

Becoming a Christian in those early days meant being willing to receive that same Spirit. Sometimes people received the Spirit suddenly and dramatically, when they were prayed over and had hands laid on them, asking for the Spirit (Acts 8:17; 19:6). The apostles sometimes communicated the Spirit through the laying on of hands.

> *Now when the apostles at Jerusalem heard that Samaria had accepted the word of God, they sent Peter and John to them. The two went down and prayed for them that they might receive the Holy Spirit (for as yet the Spirit had not come upon any of them; they had only been baptized in the name of the Lord Jesus). Then Peter and John laid their hands on them, and they received the Holy Spirit.*
>
> Acts 8:14–17

More commonly, however, the Spirit's influence was gradual. People were attracted by the spirit that they saw in Christians, and they asked to be initiated into the life of the community. Through living with Christians and praying with them, they slowly absorbed the Spirit of Jesus into their own lives. The initiation process may have taken months or even years, but when it was over, the candidates were immersed in water and anointed with oil as a sign that they were now fully immersed in God's life and anointed with God's Spirit. In the words of Jesus in his conversation with Nicodemus, they were "reborn of water and the Spirit."

> *Jesus answered, "Very truly, I tell you, no one can enter the kingdom of God without being born of water and Spirit. What is born of the flesh is flesh, and what is born of the Spirit is spirit. Do not be astonished that I said to you, 'You must be born from above.' The wind blows where it chooses, and you hear the sound of it, but you do not know where it comes from or where it goes. So it is with everyone who is born of the Spirit."*
>
> John 3:5–8

"Jesus and Nicodemus" by James J. Tissot (1836–1902).

Chapter Five

The Spirit of God works in us and through us.

From this reflection on the Scriptures we can say that the Spirit of God is a presence within us impelling us to be all that God wants us to be as persons and to do good in the world, especially good for other people. We also see that ordinarily the presence of the Spirit is realized gradually and over time. We should also see that the way we know we have the Spirit within us, other than by faith, is by the way we act. That's also the main way that other people know we have the Spirit—by looking at the way we behave and seeing the Spirit of God at work in us and through us.

There is one peculiar thing about the Holy Spirit. This is the fact that the only way to realize the presence of God's Spirit is to go out and act as Jesus would want us to act. We have to live that Spirit and reflect the Spirit—the essence of the Christian life.

How do we do this? The answer is simple—not easy, but simple. We do it by doing it! We receive the Holy Spirit by doing the works of the Spirit. We accept the Holy Spirit into our lives by living according to the Spirit of Jesus, so that his Spirit becomes more and more our spirit. We allow God's Spirit to grow in us every time we do good for ourselves and others, and bring goodness into the world.

WHAT THE CATECHISM SAYS

The Spirit of the Lord rested on Jesus, the longed-for Messiah and the Son of God. Conceived by the Spirit, Jesus lived his life and carried out his mission with the fullness of the Spirit. Jesus promised that the Holy Spirit would be poured out on his followers. Following the experiences of the Spirit on Easter and Pentecost, the followers of Jesus went forth to proclaim God's mighty works and to baptize those who believed. Through the laying on of hands, all who were baptized received the Spirit. This laying on of hands is seen as the beginning of the Sacrament of Confirmation, which extends the grace of Pentecost in the Church.

See the *Catechism of the Catholic Church*, #s 1286–1288.

DiSCUSSioN

In a small group, discuss the following questions:

1. How can someone be said to empower others? Give some examples of empowerment as you understand it.

2. The New Testament presents different imaginative stories depicting Jesus imparting his Spirit to the disciples (for example, in the Gospel according to John, Jesus breathes on them) or depicting the disciples receiving the Holy Spirit (for example, in Acts of the Apostles, the Spirit rushes in as wind and fire).

   • What aspects of those stories are hard to believe if you take them literally?
   • What do you think the authors of those stories were trying to communicate to their readers?

Divided tongues, as of fire, appeard among them. —*Acts 2:3*

Research

Using a concordance, look up the word *spirit* and see what you can learn about the human spirit, the Spirit of God, the spirit of Christ, and the Holy Spirit. Are these different spirits or the same spirit? How can you tell?

Activity

New Testament authors used various types of imagery (Jesus breathing on his disciples, the Holy Spirit coming down as of a rushing wind and tongues of fire) to communicate the elusive notion of receiving the Spirit of God. If you were a Gospel writer, how would you have represented that idea? Using other arts (for example, drawing, music, sculpture, drama, pantomime), how would you do it? If time permits, do so and present your results to the class.

interview

Sometimes people don't pay any attention to the power of the Holy Spirit that is available within them until they are so down and out that they will try anything to climb out of the hole that they are in. Twelve Step programs such as Alcoholics Anonymous, Narcotics Anonymous, Alanon, Alateen, and so on refer to God or the Spirit simply as a "higher power." Such programs help people get in touch with their "higher power" in order to straighten out their lives. People with religious backgrounds, of course, name that higher power *God* or *Christ* or the *Holy Spirit*.

1. Under the direction of your teacher, interview a person in a Twelve Step program who is in recovery from an addiction and ask if the person would share with you his or her experience of the higher power within and how being in contact with this higher power helps him or her maintain sobriety.

2. With other members of your class who have conducted similar interviews, present and discuss what you have learned to the entire class.

Review Questions

1. In the Old Testament, how was the Spirit of God experienced?

2. How did Jesus experience God's Spirit?

3. How did the early Church experience the Spirit?

4. How do people who see us or hear about us know that we have received the Holy Spirit?

The Sacrament of Confirmation in History

Let's turn now to the task of explaining what the Sacrament of Confirmation means. The explanation is somewhat difficult because the sacrament has been understood in various ways during the twenty centuries of the Church's history. Part of the variety arises from the two different ways that the rite has been performed (in conjunction with or separate from Baptism), but even the separated rite has been given a number of meanings down through the centuries. For example, the rite talks about receiving the Holy Spirit. But isn't the Holy Spirit received in Baptism? How can the Spirit be received twice?

Scripture tells us that the Spirit indeed is received through conversion and Baptism.

> Peter said to them, "Repent, and be baptized every one of you in the name of Jesus Christ so that your sins may be forgiven; and you will receive the gift of the Holy Spirit. For the promise is for you, for your children, and for all who are far away, everyone whom the Lord our God calls to him."
>
> Acts 2:38–39

This statue of Peter stands high over the crowd in St. Peter's Square in Vatican City.

In its early days the Church was not very large, and the bishop of each community presided over the initiation of new candidates every year at the Easter Vigil. The majority of candidates, of course, were adults, and in that single evening they were baptized and confirmed, and then they shared their first Eucharist with the whole Christian community.

By the fourth century, however, the Church had grown so large that it was impossible for one bishop in each city to be present at all the initiations that needed to take place every year at Easter. Bishops gave the pastors of local parishes the responsibility for Baptism and Eucharist, but, in the western or Latin-speaking part of the Roman Empire, they held on to the role of being the one who would confirm the new Christians in their faith. The bishops wanted to make sure that they personally welcomed every person into their community. Doing this, however, meant that the Confirmations had to be done at other times during the year. Over time Baptism and Confirmation in Western Europe came to be separated by years. The name *Confirmation* began to be given to the separated ritual in the fifth century.

DiSCuSSioN

Some Scripture passages (such as Acts 1:5) speak about being "baptized in (or with) the Holy Spirit." In a large group, answer the following questions:

1. If the Greek word for "baptized" is also the word for "immersed," what does this suggest about the meaning of that scriptural phrase?

2. To what kind of behavior might this refer?

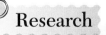

Research

Search magazines, books, or the Internet for the story of a person of the twentieth or twenty-first century who gave his or her life for the Christian faith. Share the story with the class. Prepare three to five discussion questions, and lead a discussion after the sharing of the story.

Some theologians in the Middle Ages noticed the question raised by the separation of Confirmation from Baptism. They suggested that at Baptism the Spirit gets people started in the Christian life, but that at Confirmation they are given an increase and deepening of baptismal grace and an additional strengthening by the Holy Spirit. This suggestion evolved into the idea that Confirmation turns baptized Christians into "soldiers of Christ"—an explanation that was common into the twentieth century in the western part of the Church, or the Latin Rite. The "strengthening" idea seemed to fit the words of the Confirmation ceremony, but it did not explain how people made it through life on the grace of Baptism alone, since at times in the past many people were never confirmed.

Looked at historically, then, the meaning of **Confirmation** is not very clear at all. Yes, it is a confirmation of Baptism by the bishop, a confirmation that makes stronger the confirmed person's bond with the Church. And yes, it is an affirmation of Baptism by the candidates. But the words of the sacrament say that it is more than that. How are we to make sense of those words today?

We might see the confirming, affirming, strengthening of the Spirit as a boldness in proclaiming the gospel and in doing the right thing. The Spirit of God is a spirit of boldness; recall the Scripture at the beginning of this chapter:

When [the followers of Jesus] had prayed, the place in which they were gathered together was shaken; and they were all filled with the Holy Spirit and spoke the word of God with boldness.

Acts 4:31

And so, we are tapped by the Spirit to follow in their footsteps. The Spirit of God is also a spirit of courage, even in the face of death.

But filled with the Holy Spirit, [Stephen] gazed into heaven and saw the glory of God and Jesus standing at the right hand of God. "Look," he said, "I see the heavens opened and the Son of Man standing at the right hand of God!" But they covered their ears, and with a loud shout all rushed together against him. Then they dragged him out of the city and began to stone him; and the witnesses laid their coats at the feet of a young man named Saul. While they were stoning Stephen, he prayed, "Lord Jesus, receive my spirit." Then he knelt down and cried out in a loud voice, "Lord, do not hold this sin against them." When he had said this, he died.

Acts 7:55–60

Throughout history and right down to the present day, many Christians have died for their faith. They have courageously stood before unbelievers and proclaimed the good news in word and action, even when their proclamation was dangerous. With the Spirit's strength, they faced even martyrdom for the sake of the kingdom of God. We may not be called on to give our lives for Christ, but we may sometimes have to face ridicule and prejudice for our Christian beliefs and practices. The Spirit is with us and within us as we stand up to and challenge those values in our culture that draw people away from God and goodness.

Alternate Ways to Celebrate Confirmation

Some Catholic liturgists and theologians point out that the original sequence of the Sacraments of Initiation was Baptism, Confirmation, Eucharist, but today, if Confirmation is delayed, it is Baptism, Eucharist, Confirmation. They argue for a return to the original sequence for these sacraments, and in fact there are some dioceses and countries where children prepare for Confirmation just before they make their First Communion at about the age of seven.

The Sacraments of Initiation are celebrated together in Orthodox and Eastern Rite Churches.

Eastern Rite Catholics and Orthodox Christians practice Confirmation along with infant Baptism, although their name for the sacrament is *Chrismation* (anointing with chrism). Children are baptized, chrismated, and given the Eucharist (usually in the form of a few drops of the consecrated wine) shortly after they are born.

Since this is a different liturgical practice than the one in the Latin or Roman Rite of the Catholic Church, it is bound to be understood somewhat differently. In other words, its theology is necessarily a little different. While the Eastern Churches emphasize the unity of the Sacraments of Christian Initiation, the Western Church puts more emphasis in Confirmation on the communion of the one confirmed with the larger community that is represented by the bishop.

Research

1. With advice and direction from your teacher and parish priest, interview a priest of an Eastern Rite (Catholic) or an Orthodox church about his Church's understanding of the liturgical initiation of children, which includes the ritual of Chrismation. Write down what you learn and share it with the class.

2. With a representative from your parish or diocese, discuss the order of the Sacraments of Initiation in your diocese; the following questions will help guide your discussion. Write up your findings and report them to your teacher or the class.

   - What is the practice in your diocese?
   - How does the practice in your diocese affect its theology of Confirmation? For example, how is Confirmation understood theologically if children are confirmed when they are around seven years old rather than when they are teenagers?

Activity

With advice and direction from your teacher and parish priest, attend an Eastern Rite (Catholic) or Orthodox celebration of the Sacraments of Initiation for children. Reflect on the experience and share your reflections with the class.

Gifts of the Spirit

One understanding of Confirmation is that it increases the gifts of the Holy Spirit in us. The "gifts of the Spirit" are first named in the Book of Isaiah.

> The spirit of the LORD shall rest on him,
>   the spirit of wisdom and understanding,
>   the spirit of counsel and might,
>   the spirit of knowledge and the fear of the LORD.
> His delight shall be in the fear of the LORD.
>
> Isaiah 11:2–3a

gifts of the Spirit
capabilities or dispositions (sometimes called strengths or virtues) that help us follow the promptings of the Holy Spirit and grow in our relationship with God and others

From this quote of Isaiah, Christians have traditionally identified seven aspects of God's Spirit as **gifts of the Spirit:** wisdom, understanding, knowledge, right judgment (counsel), courage (fortitude), reverence (piety), and wonder and awe (fear of the Lord). Paul listed many other gifts of the Spirit in the following passage:

> Now there are varieties of gifts, but the same Spirit; and there are varieties of services, but the same Lord; and there are varieties of activities, but it is the same God who activates all of them in everyone. To each is given the manifestation of the Spirit for the common good. To one is given through the Spirit the utterance of wisdom, and to another the utterance of knowledge according to the same Spirit, to another faith by the same Spirit, to another gifts of healing by the one Spirit, to another the working of miracles, to another prophecy, to another the discernment of spirits, to another various kinds of tongues, to another the interpretation of tongues. All these are activated by one and the same Spirit, who allots to each one individually just as the Spirit chooses.
>
> 1 Corinthians 12:4–11

The seven flames represent the gifts of the Spirit.

Chapter Five

From what we have learned about the spirit of Jesus, we should at least add some other qualities that are often referred to as the fruits of the Spirit: charity, joy, peace, patience, kindness, goodness, generosity, gentleness, faithfulness, modesty, self-control, and chastity. Still other qualities flow from the Spirit: mercy, compassion, justice, forgiveness, caring, concern, even outgoingness. In the early Christian community that lived in the Spirit, we can see even more fruits: hospitality, sharing, self-giving, friendliness, and enthusiasm. And let's not forget the all-important **theological virtues:** faith, hope, and love. There are as many ways to name and live God's Spirit as there are ways of being good, doing good to others, and bringing goodness into the world. These are some of the ways described by Paul in his letter to the Christians in Rome:

The Spirit of God is a spirit of *agape,* selfless love.

. . . hope does not disappoint us, because God's love has been poured into our hearts through the Holy Spirit that has been given to us.

Romans 5:5

Faith is represented by a cross, hope by an anchor, and love by a heart. What symbols would you use for the theological virtues?

When Christians follow the example and teachings of Jesus, they are empowered by the Spirit. They are united more firmly with Christ and are rooted more strongly in their relationship with God, whom they regard as a loving Father.

But you are not in the flesh; you are in the Spirit, since the Spirit of God dwells in you. Anyone who does not have the Spirit of Christ does not belong to him. But if Christ is in you, though the body is dead because of sin, the Spirit is life because of righteousness. If the Spirit of him who raised Jesus from the dead dwells in you, he who raised Christ from the dead will give life to your mortal bodies also through his Spirit that dwells in you. . . .

For all who are led by the Spirit of God are children of God. For you did not receive a spirit of slavery to fall back into fear, but you have received a spirit of adoption. When we cry, "Abba! Father!" it is that very Spirit bearing witness with our spirit that we are children of God, and if children, then heirs, heirs of God and joint heirs with Christ—if, in fact, we suffer with him so that we may also be glorified with him.

Romans 8:9–11, 14–17

theological virtues
faith, hope, and love; spiritual gifts that enable us to act as children of God and followers of Jesus

The Spirit of God is a spirit of peace and joy in those who are in right relationship with God.

For the kingdom of God is not food and drink but righteousness and peace and joy in the Holy Spirit.

Romans 14:17

The world is charged
    with the grandeur of God.

. . . the Holy Ghost over the bent

    World broods with warm breast
        and with ah! bright wings.

—"God's Grandeur"
by Gerard Manley Hopkins

The Spirit of God assists us as we live in community with others.

May the God of steadfastness and encouragement grant you to live in harmony with one another, in accordance with Christ Jesus, so that together you may with one voice glorify the God and Father of our Lord Jesus Christ.

Romans 15:5–6

The Spirit of God is a power for hope and inner growth and development.

May the God of hope fill you with all joy and peace in believing, so that you may abound in hope by the power of the Holy Spirit.

Romans 15:13

THE GIFTS OF THE HOLY SPIRIT

Wisdom—the ability to know with the heart and see things with the eyes of faith, to see ourselves as God wants us to be and to act as God wants us to act

Understanding—the ability to be aware of what is around us, to see the relationships and connections between things, and to discern the consequences of choices

Knowledge—the ability to benefit from education and experience in order to distinguish between truth and falsehood, and thereby do the right thing

Counsel (right judgment)—the ability to give and accept good advice flowing from prayer, Scripture, Church teaching, and the guidance of others in the faith community

Fortitude (courage)—the ability to know, stand up for, and do what is right and good, even when that is difficult

Piety (reverence)—the ability to give faithful love and honor to God, and to treat all others and creation itself with respect

Fear of the Lord (wonder and awe)—the ability to respond with adoration, praise, and thanks to God who is holy, powerful, wise, bountiful, and merciful

THE FRUITS OF THE HOLY SPIRIT

Charity—the highest form of love *(agape);* God's love in us, directed toward others

Joy—the confident happiness that comes with love

Peace—the inner harmony that comes from living in right relationship with others

Patience—the ability to cope with difficult circumstances

Kindness—sympathy and affection toward others

Goodness—the conviction to do what is right and avoid evil

Generosity—the ability to give freely

Gentleness—the ability to act tenderly

Faithfulness—loyalty to God, relationships, and beliefs

Modesty—respectful dress, speech, and conduct toward others

Self-control—self-discipline and responsible use of freedom

Chastity—living one's sexuality appropriately according to one's vocation

Many of the gifts and fruits of the Spirit are evident in the principles of Kwanza.

DiSCUSSioN

In a small group, discuss the following question:

How can the spiritual realities of faith, hope and love be regarded as gifts? Explain your answer.

 ## Activities

1. For each gift and fruit of the Spirit, name a person who embodies that quality and explain how the person does so.

2. For each of the seven principles of Kwanzaa, name the gifts of the Holy Spirit and the fruits of the Spirit that would help a person live out the principle:

   • Umoja—unity
   • Kujichagulia—self-determination
   • Ujima—collective work and responsibility
   • Ujamaa—familyhood and cooperative economics
   • Nia—purpose
   • Kuumba—creativity
   • Imani—faith

Journal

1. What are some qualities within you that you would identify as life-giving spiritual energies—in theological terms, gifts of the Holy Spirit within you?

2. What are some of your qualities that you would not want to label in this way?

Research

The "gifts of the Spirit" mentioned in Isaiah 11:2–3a are listed, but they are not defined there. Look up this passage in a Bible commentary and see what scholars have to say about these qualities. Then compare the explanations with the definitions given in this section and with your own understanding of these gifts, pointing out similarities and differences.

Charisms

There is a dimension of life in the Spirit that is not found in most Catholic parishes, even though it is recognized and approved by the Catholic Church. This dimension is mentioned in a few places in the New Testament, notably 1 Corinthians 12:4–11 and Romans 12:6–8, and it is called *charismatic* (from **charism,** and originally from the Greek word for gift) or *pentecostal* (referring to the story of what happened to the followers of Jesus on Pentecost). It is emphasized today in Catholic charismatic prayer groups and in Protestant Pentecostal churches.

Two evidences of having received the Holy Spirit are speaking in tongues and sharing the gospel with others, as this story from the Acts of the Apostles relates.

> *While Apollos was in Corinth, Paul passed through the interior regions and came to Ephesus, where he found some disciples. He said to them, "Did you receive the Holy Spirit when you became believers?" They replied, "No, we have not even heard that there is a Holy Spirit." Then he said, "Into what then were you baptized?" They answered, "Into John's baptism." Paul said, "John baptized with the baptism of repentance, telling the people to believe in the one who was to come after him, that is, in Jesus." On hearing this, they were baptized in the name of the Lord Jesus. When Paul had laid his hands on them, the Holy Spirit came upon them, and they spoke in tongues and prophesied—altogether there were about twelve of them.*
>
> *He entered the synagogue and for three months spoke out boldly, and argued persuasively about the kingdom of God.*

Acts 19:1–8

Paul cautioned his listeners about putting too much value on the lesser gifts at the expense of the spiritual gift of *agape* love.

> *If I speak in the tongues of mortals and of angels, but do not have love, I am a noisy gong or a clanging cymbal. And if I have prophetic powers, and understand all mysteries and all knowledge, and if I have all faith, so as to remove mountains, but do not have love, I am nothing. If I give away all my possessions, and if I hand over my body so that I may boast, but do not have love, I gain nothing.*

---

charism   a spiritual gift; today the term usually refers to special abilities in ministry

Research

1. Read 1 Corinthians 12:4–11 and Romans 12:6–8. What gifts are mentioned? How do you see some of these gifts at work in the Church today? Write a short essay responding to these questions.

2. Read 1 Corinthians 12:12–31. Creatively express your understanding of this passage with music, dance, poetry, story, sculpture, painting, or mixed media.

Now there are varieties of gifts, but the same Spirit.

—1 Corinthians 12:4

Love is patient; love is kind; love is not envious or boastful or arrogant or rude. It does not insist on its own way; it is not irritable or resentful; it does not rejoice in wrongdoing, but rejoices in the truth. It bears all things, believes all things, hopes all things, endures all things.

1 Corinthians 13:1–7

A true charism is a gift or grace of the Holy Spirit that benefits the Church, either directly or indirectly. It helps the person live as a Christian and serve the common good of the whole Church. An enthusiasm for God can uplift the individual and all those he or she meets. Loving kindness toward others draws people to the person exhibiting this gift and encourages them to respond, in turn, with loving kindness toward the people they meet. The Spirit works through all Christians to draw all people into relationship with God, who is love.

And now faith, hope, and love abide, these three; and the greatest of these is love.

—1 Corinthians 13:13

✝ Activities

1. Using the resources available to you (especially adults in your school or parish) and with advice and direction from your teacher and parish priest, locate a Catholic charismatic prayer group and arrange for a group of students to attend one of their meetings. Either before or after the meeting, talk with one of the group's leaders about their understanding of the Holy Spirit and the gifts of the Spirit. Describe your experience and explain what you learned to the members of your class who did not go with you.

2. With advice and direction from your teacher and parish priest, use the resources available to you (for example, look up "Churches" in the Yellow Pages to find if there are any churches in your area that call themselves "Pentecostal," "Charismatic," "Apostolic," "Assembly of God," or "Church of God in Christ"—these are some of the more common denominations that emphasize the special gifts of the Spirit such as praying in tongues), locate a Protestant congregation that calls itself Pentecostal or charismatic. Arrange for a group of students to attend one of their church services or prayer meetings. Either before or after the service, talk with one of the ministers about his or her understanding of the Holy Spirit and the gifts of the Spirit. Describe your experience and explain what you learned to the members of your class who did not go with you.

Review Questions

1. Why did the Sacrament of Confirmation develop in the West as a sacrament separated in time from Baptism?

2. What does it mean to be strengthened by the Holy Spirit?

3. How does the celebration of Confirmation differ between the East and the West? How does the theology differ?

4. What are the seven gifts of the Holy Spirit? What is their purpose?

5. What are the theological virtues? Why are they gifts from God?

6. What is a charism?

The life of the Spirit is seen in faith and action.

The Life of the Spirit

Neither Baptism nor Confirmation fills us completely with the Holy Spirit, as though we were an empty tank and the Spirit a ghostly something that is magically poured into it. Even theologically this conception is absurd. If God's Spirit in its totality filled us completely, we would be God! Who among us would claim that privilege?

We must therefore return to a more sober and more realistic interpretation of how these sacraments "give" us the Holy Spirit. They give us the Spirit by offering the Spirit to us in symbols, by saying in a symbolic way, "This is what the Spirit of God, the spirit of Jesus, is all about." And we receive the Spirit by allowing the life of God to enter our lives. In and after our Baptism as infants we receive the life of the Spirit passively for the most part, through our family and the Christian community we live in. In and after Confirmation, if we are old enough to act on our own initiative, we ourselves are expected to activate that life of the Spirit.

Young people or adults who are preparing for Confirmation must be believers—must profess the faith—and must be in right relationship with God. They must want to celebrate the sacrament and must prepare to live more as disciples of Christ and witnesses to him. Their Christian life ought to be evident in the Church community and in all the other situations in which they find themselves—school, neighborhood, social groups, work, and so on. There should be no doubt about their Christian values and way of life.

Prompted by the insight that the Spirit is active within us and that we grow in the Spirit, some parishes (and Catholic high schools) present opportunities to involve young people in doing good things for themselves (developing their growth in the Spirit), for their parish, and for the people in their neighborhood, both before and especially after their Confirmation. Catholic parishes and high schools nurture the growth of the Holy Spirit in young people by assisting them in youth clubs and sports activities, in spiritual growth retreats and Bible study groups. They facilitate the movement of the Spirit in young people who may be looking for direction in a frequently confusing world. They encourage young people to do peer ministry and to help each other out in school. They find ways to let them work in the parish (or school) in a variety of liturgical and service ministries. They set up programs so that the young people can have hands-on experience working with those who are poor and underprivileged, for social justice and world peace.

Parents who are concerned to see their children grow in God's Spirit should also try to make such opportunities available for them. In many ways, of course, they already do this by raising their children well and being role models for them, by seeing to their education, especially in the faith, and by helping them get involved in athletic, social, and cultural activities. All of this increases their children's potential for being and doing good. There is much that can be done by suggestion and by example during the teenage years.

WHAT THE CATECHISM SAYS

The purpose of preparation programs for Confirmation is to lead people to a closer relationship with Christ so that they can better live out their discipleship in the Church and in the world around them. Prayer is an important part of this process as people prepare for an increase of the gifts of the Holy Spirit.

See the *Catechism of the Catholic Church*, #s 1309–1310.

DISCUSSION

It is an established practice to prepare groups of young people who are about the same age (the ages are different in different dioceses) for the Sacrament of Confirmation. In the large group, answer the following questions:

1. What do you think about this practice?

2. If you were the bishop of a diocese, what Confirmation policy would you want to establish (age, preparation)? What would be your reason for that policy?

3. If you were the pastor of a parish, what would the Confirmation preparation program look like? What would be your reasons for recommending that type of program?

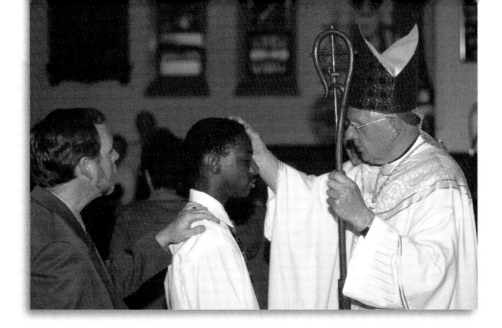

The Confirmation of teenagers is common in the United States. The minimum age for Confirmation is generally set by the bishop of the diocese.

THE SEAL

The Catechism uses traditional theological language in saying that Confirmation "imprints on the soul an indelible spiritual mark." This "spiritual mark" or "character" or "seal" is a sign that a person belongs to Christ. The seal of the Holy Spirit in Confirmation marks a person for life as a disciple of Christ. Through the action of the Holy Spirit, Christ has given the person the power to proclaim and witness to him in word and action. Because this seal, like the mark of Baptism, is for life, Confirmation is a once-in-a-lifetime sacrament. The one confirmed henceforth is called to live out a Christian life for the benefit of the Church and their world.

interview

1. Investigate the Confirmation preparation program in your home parish by talking with the person in charge of it and by attending some of the sessions. Evaluate the program in terms of whether or not it seems to be successful, in light of what you learned so far from this chapter. Is the program as good as it can be, or do you have suggestions for making it better?

2. With one or two other students in your class, locate the person in your diocese (perhaps in the catechetical, religious education, or youth ministry office) who is responsible for implementing the diocesan policy on Confirmation and its preparation. Interview that person (by phone or e-mail, if necessary), asking for an explanation of the policy and an evaluation of the strengths and shortcomings of the Confirmation programs in the diocese. Make an oral or written report of what you learned.

Discussion

In the large group, answer the following questions:

1. How might the seal of Confirmation be misinterpreted in a magical or automatic fashion?

2. How might this traditional teaching be understood as describing a permanent change in the spirit of a person who has affirmed his or her faith through the Sacrament of Confirmation?

Chapter Five

Our Personal "Yes"

In Confirmation we see and hear in words and symbols what God's Spirit is all about. We add our personal "Yes" to the "Yes" that was spoken by our parents and godparents at our Baptism. We affirm our belief in the Spirit, what the Spirit does and can mean to us in our lives. But the "Yes" that matters most, the affirmation that will make a real difference in our lives, is the one we say and do every day after our Confirmation day.

When is that day? When does Confirmation take place? Actually there are two ways that the rite is performed. One way is in conjunction with Baptism, the other is as a separate ceremony.

When adolescents or adults are received into the Church through the Rite of Christian Initiation of Adults, they are confirmed at the Easter Vigil right after they are baptized. Their Baptism and Confirmation are integrated into a single ceremony, during which they also share in their first Eucharist. They celebrate all the Sacraments of Initiation, much as was done during the earliest centuries of Christianity.

Today most Catholics in the West are baptized shortly after they are born, and some time passes before their Baptism is confirmed by their bishop, the chief pastor of the diocese and the ordinary minister of Confirmation. If, at the time of Confirmation, they are old enough to affirm what was done for them at Baptism, they stand up and say that they understand and accept what it means to be a Christian.

This is why the Rite of Confirmation, when it is performed separately, includes a repeating of the baptismal vows. When the candidates were baptized as infants, their parents and godparents made those promises to witness to the faith into which the child was being baptized. Now it's their turn to affirm that they want to live as followers of Christ, and that they want to do that in the Catholic Church.

Research

The Catechism, in paragraph 1303, talks about the effects of Confirmation. Statements such as these can improperly be taken in a magical way, that is, as implying that these effects automatically result from the performance of the Confirmation ritual. In contrast, such statements ought to be taken in a realistic way that agrees with Christian experience.

- How might the effects listed in paragraph 1303 be understood to be magical and automatic?
- How might they be understood realistically in a way that makes sense in terms of Christians' experience of Spirit?

WHAT THE CATECHISM SAYS

Throughout this chapter the effects of Confirmation have been explored. Here is how the Catechism summarizes them.

- Confirmation is a special outpouring of the Holy Spirit.
- Confirmation brings an increase of baptismal grace and deepens it.
- Confirmation roots us further in our relationship with God our loving Father.
- Confirmation unites us more firmly to Christ.
- Confirmation brings an increase in the gifts of the Holy Spirit.
- Confirmation unites us more firmly with the Church.
- Confirmation gives us the special strength of the Holy Spirit to spread and defend the faith by word and action. It calls us to be witnesses of Christ.

See the *Catechism of the Catholic Church*, #s 1302–1303, 1316.

QUINCEAÑERA—THE HISPANIC RITE OF PASSAGE INTO WOMANHOOD

Those who prefer to see Confirmation as a rite of passage into Christian adulthood often point to the lack of such a ceremony in our religious and secular culture. The *quinceañera* is an important exception.

In Mexico and among Hispanics of Mexican origin in the United States, a young woman celebrates her fifteenth birthday (*quinceañera*) with a Mass of Thanksgiving (*Misa de acción de gracias*) and an elaborate party. The celebration marks the young woman's entrance into adulthood or womanhood. In the past she was considered eligible for marriage following this celebration. Today, the celebration may mark the time when she is permitted to date.

Generally the Mass is attended only by relatives. The young woman is escorted by her parents and *padrinos* (godparents), and she is seated before the altar for the Mass. She is usually accompanied by several *damas* (maids of honor) and *chambelanes* (chamberlains), family members and friends.

The family chooses the Scripture readings for the Mass. The homily typically stresses the importance of a life lived by good moral principles. The young woman is encouraged to live with responsibility, faith, and charity toward others. At the end of Mass the young woman places a bouquet on the altar honoring Mary, usually Our Lady of Guadalupe.

Research

Research *quinceañera* or another rite of passage to adulthood and report your findings to the class.

DiSCuSSioN

In the large group, answer the following questions:

1. If you have already been confirmed in the Catholic faith, what explanations of Confirmation and the Holy Spirit were you given at that time?

2. What do you think about those explanations today?

 Activity

This chapter presents an understanding of Confirmation as a personal affirmation by ourselves and those around us—the Church—that we have received God's Spirit and that we want to continue to grow with the life of God within us. In an essay, oral presentation, or creative expression, communicate your understanding of this. What do you think about this as an explanation or theology of Confirmation? (For example, does it make sense in terms of what you remember about your own Confirmation, or in terms of how you are trying to live your life today?)

The Rite of Confirmation

laying on of hands
an ancient ritual gesture of approval, blessing, and acceptance, in which one or both hands are placed on the head of the one receiving the gesture

The Confirmation ceremony itself is filled with a pageantry that is reminiscent of the days in the Middle Ages when bishops were called the "princes of the Church." The parish church may be festively decorated with flowers and banners, the choir is singing, the candidates are wearing their Sunday best or even special robes for the occasion, and the pews are filled with relatives and friends. The bishop appears in full regalia with his pointed miter, his flowing cope, and his ceremonial shepherd's staff. Both he and the *confirmandi* (the Latin term for Confirmation candidates) are the centers of attention on this special occasion.

The Rite of Confirmation, in contrast, is rather simple. Most of the ceremony is actually the episcopal Mass, the Eucharistic liturgy presided over by the bishop, which surrounds the Confirmation itself. After the Scripture readings and the homily, the rite begins with the reaffirmation of the baptismal promises, already mentioned. These promises and the rite of Confirmation within Mass emphasize the unity of the Sacraments of Initiation. Then the bishop extends his hands over the candidates and blesses them. The blessing is a very beautiful one that recalls the gifts of the Spirit's presence and then encourages those to be confirmed with these words:

Send your Holy Spirit upon them
to be their Helper and Guide.
Give them the spirit of wisdom
and understanding,
the spirit of right judgment and courage,
the spirit of knowledge and reverence.
Fill them with the spirit of wonder
and awe in your presence.

Rite of Confirmation, #25.

Originally the sacrament included a **laying on of hands**. In the current Confirmation ritual, this is replaced by the bishop extending his hands in blessing over the candidates, but the meaning is the same: gift, approval, and acceptance.

Let us pray to our Father
that he will pour out the Holy Spirit
to strengthen his sons and daughters
    with his gifts
and anoint them to be more like
    Christ the Son of God.

—Rite of Confirmation, #24

anoint from the Latin word for oil or salve, originally a pouring of perfumed oil on the head or a smearing of scented salve over the upper body

chrism the aromatic oil used in Confirmation, from the Greek word related to ointment and anointing

Research

Using the Catechism, paragraph 1289, as a basis for your answer (but you may also use other sources of information), explain how the words *chrism, Christ, Christian, anointed,* and *messiah* are related.

Discussion

Think about the Confirmation ceremony. In the large group, answer the following questions:

1. What do you like about it? What are your reasons?

2. What do you think ought to be different? Again, what are your reasons?

After the blessing the bishop **anoints** the candidates individually on the forehead with **chrism** while saying, "Be sealed with the Gift of the Holy Spirit" (#27). These words along with the extension over or laying on of hands and the anointing with chrism are the essential words and actions of the sacrament. In the Eastern Rites, other parts of the body are also anointed. Early Christians used this ritual gesture to symbolize the "pouring of the Holy Spirit" on the baptized and the "sweet scent of new life" begun in Christ. As ancient athletes also used oil to increase their speed and to ease their discomfort as they worked to strengthen their muscles, so too chrism is associated with strength. The Holy Spirit strengthens the confirmed to live as true witnesses of Christ.

After all the candidates have been confirmed, the Mass continues with the liturgy of the Eucharist, a reminder of the community that binds us together as the Body of Christ, the sacrament of Jesus. Now the People of God have been enriched with members confirmed in God's Spirit.

WHAT THE CATECHISM SAYS

In Scripture oil signifies abundance, joy, cleansing, limberness, healing, beauty, health, and strength. Anointing in Baptism is a sign of cleansing and strengthening, while that of the Sacrament of the Anointing of the Sick expresses healing and comfort. The anointing of Confirmation and Holy Orders signifies consecration and dedication to God. The confirmed Christian shares more completely in Christ's mission and receives the fullness of the Holy Spirit.

See the *Catechism of the Catholic Church,* #s 1293–1294.

✝ Activity

If it has been some time since you were confirmed, call the bishop's office (sometimes called the chancery) in your diocese and ask if you could find out about the bishop's Confirmation schedule. (It may be as few as one per month to a couple in a single week.) Explain that you are doing this as part of a class project in your religion course. With one or more other students in your class, attend a Confirmation ceremony that is within traveling distance. Report back to the class about the experience and what you thought of it.

Discussion

In a small group, answer the following questions:

1. How might a significant event change a person's spirit? Give an example from real life or fiction.

2. How might going through a ritual or ceremony change a person's spirit? Give an example from real life or fiction.

3. How does thinking about the above "spiritual changes" help us to understand the theological language used to describe the effects associated with Confirmation?

Chapter Five

The one being confirmed is anointed with chrism in the form of the cross on the head.

Sponsors and Names

Anyone being confirmed is accompanied by a sponsor. The sponsor may be one of the person's baptismal godparents (This choice stresses the connection between the two sacraments.), but need not be. The purpose of the Confirmation sponsor is to give spiritual support during the time of preparation and after the ceremony is over. A sponsor must be a confirmed, practicing Catholic with enough maturity to take on the role.

In some Confirmation preparation programs for adolescents, the sponsor takes on a kind of mentoring role. Such a mentor is asked to be a model of commitment to personal prayer, community worship, and ministry. He or she is usually asked to attend preparation sessions with the one to be confirmed and to share his or her beliefs and faith story with the candidate. Before each session, the mentor and the candidate may be asked to respond in writing to questions related to the topic to be discussed. The mentor or sponsor is encouraged to offer support by talking with, writing to, and praying with the young person.

In some dioceses, it is the practice for Confirmation candidates to choose a Confirmation name. Rites of passage are often marked with a change of name or an addition to a person's given name. Honors and degrees are often accompanied by a new title. Often a nickname is acquired when a person accomplishes something significant or does something unusual. Especially if a person does not already bear the name of a saint, an additional name may be appropriate at the time of Confirmation. The candidate may choose the name of saint whom he or she admires and would like to imitate while striving to live the Christian life more earnestly.

Discussion

In a small group, answer the following questions:

1. Whom would you choose as a mentor for the Christian life? Why?

2. What saints or outstanding Christians do you know something about?

3. What have they done that is admirable and might be worth imitating?

CONFIRMATION AND CHRISTIAN SERVICE

When they first told me I'd have to do a service project before Confirmation, I really, well, I guess you could say that I resisted the whole idea. What right did they have to tell me what to do with my time? Between school and sports and my part-time job I already had enough to do!

I chose the project that looked the easiest to me, which was helping senior citizens with their housework. I figured it shouldn't be too strenuous, and it was only for four Saturday mornings. Boy, was I in for a surprise! One look at Mrs. Woodridge's apartment and I knew it would take longer than that, even with three of us working on it. But she was so obviously pleased, and she was always so nice to us. She'd have cookies and soft drinks on hand for us, and after we got her kitchen cleaned she even baked homemade cookies for us! For energy, she said.

But there was another kind of energy that we began to feel when we worked together—a kind of happy energy, knowing that you're doing something good for someone else. The fourth Saturday was really a bummer, though. It was supposed to be the last day of our service project, but we knew there was a lot more work to do. We felt really stupid, starting a job without finishing it.

I guess you'd have to say we prayed about it, asking God what was the right thing to do. I never prayed about anything like that before. Later that week I called up Sally and Jack. They were just as miserable as I was. It didn't take much to decide to go back and help Mrs. Woodridge until the job was done. My parents couldn't believe it, but I could tell that they were proud of me.

Even though Mrs. Woodridge isn't Catholic, she insisted on coming to our Confirmation. One of her neighbors drove her, and she never stopped talking about all the good things we had done. Well, one thing led to another, and before we knew it we had agreed to help her friend the following Saturday.

That was six months ago. I don't get to Mrs. Woodridge's apartment building every Saturday myself, but one of us is usually there, along with some of the other kids we've roped into helping us. It was awkward asking them at first, but it's gotten easier since we all get so much out of it. It's almost as though the old people give us more than we give them.

We've grown a lot, too. I mean, in being more responsible. And learning to put other people's needs ahead of our own fun. We know a lot more now about how social security works, and the welfare system. The scariest time was when we confronted the landlord about fixing up the building. I never realized before that people could be so selfish.

Slowly, I'm beginning to get a handle on the meaning of the Holy Spirit, I think. I thought I understood it before, but I'm starting to believe that God's Spirit grows on you or in you. You have to live with it for a while or let it live in you before you really begin to appreciate what it's all about.

Chapter Five

DisCussioN

If you have been confirmed, did you take part in a service project when you were preparing for Confirmation? In the large group, answer the following questions:

1. What was that project?
2. What did you get out of it?

Review Questions

1. What is required of a person preparing for Confirmation?
2. To what does the seal of Confirmation refer?
3. What are the effects of the Sacrament of Confirmation?
4. How is Confirmation celebrated? What are the essential elements?
5. What is the purpose of a Confirmation sponsor?
6. Why is service a part of many preparation programs?

Summary

Through Baptism we join the family of God and celebrate receiving God's life. We are nurtured by the Christians with whom we live and worship. The life of God is also called God's spirit, and in the Christian tradition it is referred to as the Holy Spirit.

Spirit by its very nature is elusive, hard to define and hard to identify in our experience. Yet we need to develop a sense of what is meant by the word *spirit* in order to appreciate what is celebrated in this sacrament. Once we know what *spirit* refers to, we can begin to understand how we receive the Holy Spirit as members of God's family, and why we celebrate the reception of the Spirit in the Sacrament of Confirmation.

Confirmation is celebrated with an extension over or a laying on of hands and an anointing with chrism, along with the words, "Be sealed with the Gift of the Holy Spirit." Confirmation is the second Sacrament of Initiation and is closely connected with the first—Baptism—which celebrates the beginning of life in the Spirit. Confirmation celebrates an increase in the gifts of the Holy Spirit and a strengthening by the Spirit. Confirmed members of the Church have a responsibility to be witnesses to Christ in their daily lives and to be active participants in their faith communities. The Holy Spirit helps them live as the true Christians they are called to be.

Scripture

"If you . . . know how to give good gifts to your children, how much more will the heavenly Father give the Holy Spirit to those who ask him!"

LUKE 11:13

Prayer

Lord,
fulfill the promise given by your Son
and send the Holy Spirit
to enlighten our minds
and lead us to all truth.
Grant this through our Lord Jesus Christ,
who lives and reigns with you and the Holy Spirit,
one God, for ever and ever.
Amen.

RITE OF CONFIRMATION, #35.

Scripture

The cup of blessing that we bless, is it not a sharing in the blood of Christ? The bread that we break, is it not a sharing in the body of Christ? Because there is one bread, we who are many are one body, for we all partake of the one bread.

1 CORINTHIANS 10:16–17

Prayer

Lord Jesus Christ,
we worship you living among us
in the sacrament of your body and blood.
May we offer to our Father in heaven
a solemn pledge of undivided love.
May we offer to our brothers and sisters
a life poured out in loving service of that kingdom
where you live with the Father and the Holy Spirit,
one God, for ever and ever.

Amen.

OPENING PRAYER, SOLEMNITY OF THE
BODY AND BLOOD OF CHRIST.

Eucharist: Celebration of God's Life

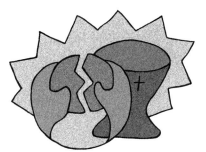

From the Beginning

The earliest account of the Last Supper in the New Testament is in Paul's First Letter to the Corinthians:

For I received from the Lord what I also handed on to you, that the Lord Jesus on the night when he was betrayed took a loaf of bread, and when he had given thanks, he broke it and said, "This is my body that is for you. Do this in remembrance of me." In the same way he took the cup also, after supper, saying, "This cup is the new covenant in my blood. Do this, as often as you drink it, in remembrance of me." For as often as you eat this bread and drink the cup, you proclaim the Lord's death until he comes.

1 Corinthians 11:23–26

The accounts of the Last Supper in Matthew, Mark, and Luke are similar in style and details. These accounts place the Last Supper within the celebration of the Passover meal, the feast of unleavened bread. This feast celebrates the Israelites' escape from slavery in Egypt and their freedom as the people of God. Our Eucharist fulfills this Passover and makes present Christ's passover from death to life; it is a memorial of his life, death, and resurrection—our most important celebration of the Paschal mystery.

The Eucharistic Prayer that we pray today contains the **consecration,** the words of institution of the Eucharist, and is based on the Scripture passages cited above.

Before he was given up to death,
a death he freely accepted,
he took bread and gave you thanks.
He broke the bread,
gave it to his disciples, and said:
Take this all of you, and eat it;
this is my body which will be given up for you.
When supper was ended he took the cup.
Again he gave you thanks and praise,
gave the cup to his disciples, and said:
Take this, all of you, and drink from it;
this is the cup of my blood,
the blood of the new and eternal covenant.
It will be shed for you and for all
so that sins may be forgiven.
Do this in memory of me.

Eucharistic Prayer II

---

consecration   Jesus' words of institution of the Eucharist at the Last Supper recited by the priest at Mass, changing the bread and wine into the Body and Blood of Christ

Communion   the consecrated Bread and Wine, perceived in faith to be the Body and Blood of Christ; also, the act of receiving the consecrated Bread or Wine

Blessed Sacrament   the consecrated Bread or Wine, especially the consecrated hosts or wafers considered apart from the Eucharistic liturgy, reserved in the tabernacle for special worship services (such as Benediction of the Blessed Sacrament) and for distribution to those who are sick

Chapter Six

Eucharist from the Greek, meaning an act of thanksgiving, an ancient name for the Christian celebration of the Paschal mystery that includes remembrance of the Last Supper and distribution of Communion

Mass from the Latin word for dismissed or sent, in this case, sent on the mission of proclaiming the good news of salvation and the kingdom of God; since the Middle Ages, a common Catholic name for the Eucharistic liturgy

liturgy from the Greek, meaning a public work or service done in the name of or on behalf of the people; in general, any formal Christian worship, especially one that follows a prescribed pattern such as a sacramental rite; sometimes used exclusively to refer to the Eucharistic liturgy

Liturgy of the Word the first major part of the Mass that includes the readings, homily, profession of faith, and general intercessions

Liturgy of the Eucharist the second major part of the Mass that includes the presentation and preparation of the gifts, the Eucharistic Prayer, and the Communion rite

These words may be so familiar to us that we can almost recite them with the priest when we hear them at Mass. We understand that they refer to Christ's institution of the Eucharist, but what exactly is the Eucharist? Is it what we call Holy **Communion,** or the entire Mass?

Catholics refer to the consecrated Bread and Wine as a sacrament in itself. We say, for example, that the **Blessed Sacrament** is reserved in the tabernacle in every Catholic church. When we say that, however, we are usually referring to just the consecrated hosts. Only enough wine is consecrated at every Mass to be distributed at that particular liturgy, and it is not reserved in the tabernacle.

Since the Second Vatican Council in the 1960s, it has become more common to speak about the **Eucharist** as a liturgical celebration. The **Mass** is more properly called a Eucharistic **liturgy,** since it is the action of the whole Body of Christ. If you look in a missalette today, you will see that the Mass has two major parts, the **Liturgy of the Word** and the **Liturgy of the Eucharist,** but together these two parts are a single act of worship, which is the liturgy that is called the Eucharist or the Eucharistic liturgy.

This liturgical approach to Eucharist is the one that we are using in this book. When we speak about the seven sacraments, we are talking about liturgical sacraments, or sacramental rituals. This broader approach to Eucharist as liturgy encourages a deeper appreciation of the Blessed Sacrament and the reception of Communion. In this chapter we will talk about the relation between Eucharist and the other liturgical sacraments, and then we will discuss the central meaning of the Eucharistic celebration.

Activity

Look up the Gospel narratives about the Last Supper and the institution of the Eucharist (Matthew 26:17–30; Mark 14:12–26; Luke 22:7–23).

1. What are some similarities?

2. What are some differences?

3. What do you think might be some reasons for the differences?

Research

The *Catechism of the Catholic Church* (#s 1328–1332) reviews many of the names by which this sacrament is called. With a group of other students, review these names and list separately the names that members of your group have heard before and the names they have never heard before. If there are other ways by which they have described Sunday worship ("going to church," "having church"), list and explain those as well. Tabulate and report your findings to the whole class.

A Sacrament of Initiation

We have already seen that Eucharist is sometimes referred to as a Sacrament of Initiation—which can be a bit puzzling since we usually think of Mass as something that happens every Sunday (or even every day), not as the start of something new. Recall that during the early centuries of Christianity, however, new members were initiated into the Church through a rather lengthy preparation process. The process culminated in their being baptized and confirmed at the Easter Vigil on Holy Saturday night, after which they participated in the Easter Eucharist in the early hours of Sunday morning. It was most fitting that this initiation took place on Easter as a sign of rebirth, and within the Eucharist, which is the sacrament that unmistakably celebrates our union with Christ and with the faith community through the sharing of sacred food.

We find an echo of this early practice in the celebration of First Communion for children. You may remember that when you were a lot younger—old enough to understand that grownups at Mass were going up to the altar and "getting something," but not old enough to "get some for yourself"—you felt left out of whatever it was that the big people around you were doing. Perhaps you didn't feel like a full member of the "parish family" that people said you belonged to. Then later, when the time for your First Communion finally arrived, you may have been as proud and happy as any new adult member of the Church. You felt like a full member of the parish family because you had been taught the meaning of Communion and you had been allowed to receive it the way everyone else does.

The separation of First Communion from Baptism and Confirmation actually developed rather late in the Church's history. In the first centuries, of course, they all came together in the long ritual of Christian initiation for adults. Even up to the Middle Ages, infants were given Communion, in the form of a small spoonful of wine, shortly after they were baptized. For a variety of liturgical and theological reasons, however, this practice was eventually abandoned in the West. It is still the normal practice in the Eastern Rites.

At the Easter Vigil the newly baptized and confirmed receive the Eucharist for the first time. Thus the Sacraments of Initiation are celebrated at the same liturgy.

Today First Communion is typically celebrated around the age of seven or eight.

The principal liturgical reason for the change in the West was that Baptism got separated from Confirmation. Any parish priest could perform the rite of Baptism, but Confirmation could be done only by a bishop. This presented a liturgical problem because, in the traditional sequence of the rites, Confirmation is supposed to occur before the reception of Communion. The solution that the Church in the West adopted was to postpone First Communion until after Confirmation.

The principal theological reason for the postponement of First Communion into later childhood had to do with questions that medieval theologians raised about the Eucharist. What should be done, they asked, if a baby spit up the wine after receiving Communion? And what spiritual benefit does an infant receive from the Eucharist when he or she is not old enough to understand what is happening? Out of reverence for the sacrament, various theologians in the West preferred to see First Communion at a later age than infancy.

As time went on, other theologians asked further questions about First Communion. What if a person was not confirmed until adolescence and had committed a mortal sin? After all, Paul had written:

> *Whoever, therefore, eats the bread or drinks the cup of the Lord in an unworthy manner will be answerable for the body and blood of the Lord. Examine yourselves, and only then eat of the bread and drink of the cup.*

1 Corinthians 11:27–29

And even if there were no mortal sins, wouldn't it be better if a person went to confession before receiving Christ in Communion? Questions such as these, again out of reverence for the Eucharist, led to the introduction of First Confession before First Communion. By the nineteenth century, the normal sequence for the sacraments had become Baptism, Confirmation, Penance (as it was then called), and Eucharist (in the form of First Communion). It was not unusual for people to go to Mass every Sunday well into their teen years without ever receiving Communion!

Liturgical Reforms

Activity

Do you have any photographs, a certificate, or other momentos of your First Communion? If so, bring them in for a class "show and tell" about your First Communion experience.

At the beginning of the twentieth century, Pope Pius X decided that a reform regarding First Communion was needed. He believed that people should not be denied Communion until that late in life, especially since Jesus himself had said, "Let the little children come to me, and do not stop them" (Luke 18:16). In 1910 the pope decreed that the normal age for First Communion should be seven. He also agreed with the theologians who insisted that everyone should go to confession before Communion. This is why the official policy in the Church is still to place First Reconciliation before First Communion.

The centuries-old concern about First Communion stemmed from a narrow focus on the Eucharistic Bread and Wine. In the Middle Ages, ordinary people were not able to understand and participate fully in the Mass because it was said in Latin. As a result, they concentrated on the one aspect of the Mass that they were able to come in contact with—Communion. The relationship to the Eucharist (understood as Holy Communion) was felt as a personal or vertical "God and me" relationship rather than a communal or horizontal "God with us" relationship. With the renewal of the liturgy since the Second Vatican Council, however, full participation is restored and the celebration emphasizes the community nature of the Eucharistic liturgy.

This emphasis also explains why Catholics' attitude toward the Blessed Sacrament has been modified. When Catholics thought about the Eucharist primarily as Holy Communion, their reverence for the Body and Blood of Christ held them back from Communion unless they first went to confession, even when they had committed no serious sins. Now that they can more fully participate in the liturgy, however, Catholics realize that preparation for Communion can take place during the Mass itself. And since the Eucharist is a sacred meal for the entire people of God, they feel that it is appropriate to go up to the altar unless they are definitely not in communion with Christ or the Catholic Church.

Discussion

The age for First Communion has varied throughout the ages. Sometimes infants received Communion when they were baptized. Sometimes people did not receive Communion until after they were confirmed during adolescence. The current practice in the West allows children who have reached the "age of reason" (about seven years old) to receive Communion. In a small group, discuss what you think the age for First Communion should be. Give reasons to support your answer.

Review Questions

1. What is the consecration?
2. To what does the word *Eucharist* refer?
3. Why is the Eucharist a Sacrament of Initiation?
4. What reform concerning Communion did Pope Pius X institute?

What Does It Mean?

The Catholic Church teaches that the Eucharist is the heart, source, and summit of the Christian life. Through the ministry of the priest, Christ gathers his Church in his sacrifice of praise and thanksgiving. Through this sacrifice, he shares with us, the Church, the grace of salvation. The Eucharist strengthens the bonds of charity between us and Christ. It reinforces the unity of the Church.

Despite this beautiful teaching, however, we can find ourselves in church asking: What does it mean? What is its purpose? Why do we go to Mass, anyway?

This is in fact a difficult question to answer. It's difficult in one sense because, as we saw in an earlier chapter, every sacramental celebration has three levels of meaning—societal (or institutional) meaning, communal (or group) meaning, and personal (or individual) meaning. The Catechism explains what the Eucharist means for the Catholic Church as an institution, but it does not say what any particular Mass means for a group or an individual.

The question is also difficult to answer because in another sense there are as many answers as the people who go to Mass. Some go out of a sense of obligation. Some go to pray privately. Some go to meet their friends or be seen by the pastor. Some go because it's part of their routine. But some also go to participate in the liturgy.

Even the notion of participation in the liturgy makes the question difficult to answer. The Mass is a fairly complex ritual that has evolved over centuries of Christian worship. It has a number of parts, each of which has its own meaning and some of which can have a number of meanings.

The purpose of the opening prayers, for example, is to lead us into the spirit of worship and make us mindful of God's presence. These prayers have a penitential flavor to them, but right after them comes a prayer of praise—a rather rapid switch in mood.

The Eucharist is celebrated in community.

homilist ordained minister who "breaks open the word"—explains the Scripture readings at liturgy and calls the assembly to live according to those readings

Journal

The gifts (bread, wine, and money) carried to the altar at the start of the Liturgy of the Eucharist represent the self-giving of those assembled for worship. What other objects might represent your personal self-giving, the giving of your family, the giving of your class?

The overall purpose of the Scripture readings and homily is to hear the word of God and see its relevance for our life. The specific meaning of every reading is different, and the lessons that the preacher or **homilist** can draw from them are equally varied. Once again we are faced with a variety of meanings that make it difficult to pin down what the Mass is all about.

The purpose of the petitionary prayers that follow is fairly obvious, as is the purpose of the Creed in which we express our faith in the God who answers our prayers. But why are the bread and wine carried up to the altar instead of just being there where the priest can reach them? And what are we supposed to be thinking as he prepares and prays over the gifts?

The Eucharistic Prayer is literally a prayer of thanksgiving, from the Greek work *eucharistia* meaning the giving of thanks. But wait, haven't we already praised God earlier in the Mass? Why then are we doing this again?

The Liturgy of the Eucharist actually contains a variety of prayers. There is the remembrance of what Jesus said and did at the Last Supper. There are prayers in which we remember and pray for the Church, its leaders, and its members; these sound somewhat like petitionary prayers again. And there are once again praises to the Father, Son, and Holy Spirit.

Then there's Communion. Just before it, there's the Lamb of God, which sounds somewhat like the Lord Have Mercy we said at the beginning of Mass. When we receive Communion, are we supposed to feel in communion with Christ, with the other people in church, with the universal Church, or what? How can we experience unity with all that singing going on? And is there any difference in meaning if we receive only the consecrated Bread and not the Wine as well?

Finally, almost before we've had a chance to sort out all the different possible meanings, the Mass is over. The priest turns to us and says, "Go forth, to love and serve the Lord." But isn't that why we came to church? Why, then, is he telling us to go out and do it?

All these questions give us some inkling as to why it's difficult to say what the meaning of the Mass is. Isn't there any way to tie the various meanings and the kinds of meanings together?

DisCussioN

In a small group, discuss the following questions:

1. What questions have you asked yourself about the meaning of the Mass?

2. Have you ever been taught about the Mass in a way that did not make sense to you? What were some of the things that were said? Why do you think they did not make sense?

3. What were you taught about the Mass that did make sense to you? Why do you think these ideas made sense to you?

4. Vatican II and the Catechism say that the Eucharist is the heart, source, and summit of the Christian life. What are some ways that this is true?

5. Look at sections 1348 to 1355 of the Catechism, which talk about the various parts of the liturgy. Which statements do you find especially meaningful? Which ones are more difficult for you to relate to?

ORDER OF THE MASS

Introductory Rites

- **Entrance song:** The assembly (the people gathered for worship) sings a hymn as the priest and liturgical ministers come to the altar.
- **Greeting:** The priest invites all to prayer and worship with the Sign of the Cross. The people answer, "Amen."
- **Blessing with holy water:** Sometimes, especially during the Easter Season, the assembly is blessed with holy water. This is done in place of the penitential rite.
- **Penitential rite:** The priest asks the people to recall their sinfulness and God's mercy, often by reciting a general confession of sinfulness or by praying, "Lord, have mercy, Christ, have mercy, Lord, have mercy."
- **Lord, have mercy:** If this prayer has not been used in the penitential rite, it is said after the penitential rite.
- **Glory to God:** All sing or pray this ancient prayer of praise.
- **Opening prayer:** All prepare themselves to hear God's word in Scripture. The priest says, "Let us pray. . . ." The people answer, "Amen."

Liturgy of the Word

- **First reading:** This reading is usually taken from the Old Testament. The lector ends by saying, "The word of the Lord." The people answer, "Thanks be to God."
- **Responsorial psalm:** This prayer taken from the Book of Psalms has a response which the assembly repeats after each verse or every few verses.
- **Second reading:** This reading is taken from the New Testament Letters by Paul and other early Church leaders. Again the lector ends by saying, "The word of the Lord." The people respond, "Thanks be to God."
- **Gospel acclamation (Alleluia):** The assembly stands and greets the good news with a word that means "Praise God!" During Lent the acclamation does not include the word *Alleluia*.
- **Gospel:** The deacon or priest reads from one of the Gospels. Before beginning the reading, the deacon or priest says, "The Lord be with you." The people say, "And also with you." The deacon or priest says, "A reading from the holy gospel according to [Matthew, Mark, Luke, or John]." The people respond, "Glory to you, Lord." After the reading of the gospel, the deacon or priest says, "The gospel of the Lord," and the people respond, "Praise to you, Lord Jesus Christ."
- **Homily:** The priest or deacon explains the meaning of God's word for us today.
- **Profession of faith (Creed):** We stand and proclaim what we believe.
- **General intercessions:** The assembly prays for the needs of the whole Church and all people. The deacon or lector reads the intercessions, each of which typically ends with "We pray to the Lord" and the people's response, "Lord, hear our prayer."

Liturgy of the Eucharist

- **Offertory song (presentation of gifts):** Gifts of bread and wine are presented to the presider and offered to God. Money is collected to be used for the needs of the Church. Usually a hymn is sung.

- **Preparation of the bread and wine:** The assembly thanks God for the gifts of food, especially bread and wine. The priest prays a prayer over each that begins, "Blessed are you, Lord, God of all creation. . . ." The people answer, "Blessed be God for ever." The priest asks God to bless and accept our gifts. The priest says, "Pray, my brothers and sisters, that our sacrifice may be acceptable to God, the almighty Father." The people respond, "May the Lord accept the sacrifice at your hands for the praise and glory of his name, for our good, and the good for all his Church."

- **Prayer over the gifts:** This prayer varies with each celebration.

- **Preface:** The priest begins the Eucharistic Prayer by recalling, in the presence of the assembly, an aspect of God's loving kindness that is a special focus for that particular Mass.

- **Acclamation (Holy, holy, holy Lord):** The people sing or pray this ancient hymn of praise that is based on the Scriptures.

- **Eucharistic Prayer:** The Eucharistic Prayer is the Church's great prayer of thanksgiving. The priest prays on behalf of the assembly and asks the Holy Spirit to bless the gifts. He uses the words of Jesus at the Last Supper, the institution narrative, to consecrate the bread and wine, and they become the Body and Blood of Christ.

- **Memorial acclamation:** There are several forms of this proclamation of the Paschal mystery.

- **The great Amen:** The priest brings the Eucharistic Prayer to a close by singing or saying, "Through him, with him, in him, in the unity of the Holy Spirit, all glory and honor is yours, almighty Father, for ever and ever." The people sing or say, "Amen."

Communion Rite

- **Lord's Prayer:** The assembly prays, using the words of Jesus.
- **Sign of peace:** All exchange a handshake or other sign of peace with those around.
- **Breaking of the Bread:** The priest divides the large consecrated host into parts, breaking off a small piece and placing it in the chalice.
- **Lamb of God:** The people sing or say a song of praise to Jesus, the Lamb of God.
- **Prayers before Communion:** The priest genuflects and holds up the Body and Blood of Christ and says, "This is the Lamb of God who takes away the sins of the world. Happy are those who are called to his supper." The people respond, "Lord, I am not worthy to receive you, but only say the word and I shall be healed."
- **Holy Communion:** Consecrated Bread and Wine are given to those who come forward to receive. The priest or Eucharistic minister says, "The Body of Christ" and "The Blood of Christ." The person receiving Communion says, "Amen."
- **Communion song or silent reflection:** A song or prayer of thanksgiving is offered.
- **Prayer after Communion:** The priest, speaking for the assembly, thanks God the Father for the gift of Christ.

Concluding Rite

- **Greeting:** The priest says, "The Lord be with you." The people answer, "And also with you."
- **Blessing:** All make the Sign of the Cross as the priest asks God's blessing. The people answer, "Amen."
- **Dismissal:** All are sent forth to carry on the work of Jesus. The priest says, "Go in peace to love and serve the Lord." The people respond, "Thanks be to God."
- **Closing song and recessional:** The presider generally leaves the sanctuary during the closing song. The assembly leaves to carry on the work of Jesus.

Activities

1. Using this summary of the different parts of the Mass, as well as the Catechism's description of the "movement of the celebration" (1348–1355) and a Sunday missalette, make a chart or pictorial representation of the variety of liturgical elements in every Eucharistic liturgy. Do this in a small group or as an individual project, and then make a presentation about it to the class.

2. By yourself or in a group, and using the understanding you have gained from reading this chapter thus far, design a Eucharistic liturgy for your class or school. Explain your rationale for the songs, prayers, decorations, and so on that you have chosen. If possible, use this liturgical plan as the basis for an actual Mass in a class, retreat, or school celebration.

Eucharist and Reconciliation

You may not realize it, but every time you attend Mass, you confess your sins! Every Eucharistic liturgy begins with a penitential rite in which we acknowledge our sinfulness and pray, "Lord, have mercy." This, in fact, is the oldest form of confession in the Church, a form of general confession that is older than private confession to a priest or public repentance before a bishop.

The Eucharist as a sacrament of unity is the basis for this understanding of Eucharist and reconciliation. In the Mass we celebrate our unity with God and with one another. When we receive the Body and Blood of Christ, we express our unity with the Father, we open ourselves to experience communion with the Son, and we acknowledge our togetherness in the Spirit that makes us the body of Christ, which is the Church.

We have to admit, though, that we do not always feel close to God or God's people. The selfishness of sin alienates us from God and isolates us from one another. Before we can truly celebrate unity, there has to *be* unity. If we are separated from God and others, we have to be reconciled before we can genuinely celebrate our togetherness in the Eucharist.

Re-conciliation means re-union. It means re-joining what has come apart. It means re-establishing a relationship that has been broken. This is why at Mass we acknowledge our need for reconciliation before we receive Communion.

The Penitential Rite is not the only opportunity for reconciliation at Mass. In the Lord's Prayer, we ask the Father to forgive us as we forgive one another. At the Sign of Peace, we put our differences aside and extend an accepting hand to each other. During the Lamb of God, we ask Christ once again to have mercy on us and grant us peace.

As we can see, the Eucharist is a sacrament of reconciliation because it is a sacrament of unity. During the liturgy we are invited to remember God's closeness to us and to come closer in our hearts to him and all people. We reestablish connections that might have been forgotten or broken. But the liturgy does not end there. It takes us beyond reconciliation to the celebration of our unity with Christ and with one another. This is why we say the Eucharist makes the Church.

Activity

In a small group, use a missalette to look for references to repentance, forgiveness, and reconciliation in the various parts of the Mass. Share your findings with the rest of the class and talk about your reactions to these statements in the liturgy.

The Eucharist is a sacrament of unity and a sacrament of reconciliation.

JUSTIN MARTYR

From the writings of Justin Martyr, we know about Christian worship in the second century. This early Christian theologian was born in Palestine, taught in Ephesus, and eventually moved to Rome. Around the year 165, Justin was arrested for being a Christian, imprisoned, beaten, and beheaded. Following is the explanation of Christian worship that he wrote to the Roman emperor around the year 150.

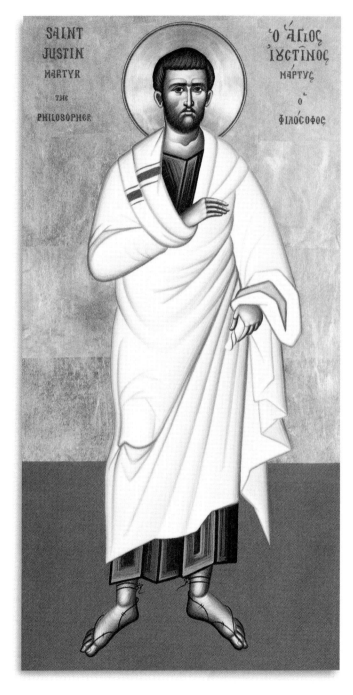

On the day we call the day of the sun, all who dwell in the city or country gather in the same place.

The memoirs of the apostles and the writings of the prophets are read, as much as time permits.

When the reader has finished, he who presides over those gathered admonishes and challenges them to imitate these beautiful things.

Then we all rise together and offer prayers for ourselves . . . and for all others, wherever they may be, so that we may be found righteous by our life and actions, and faithful to the commandments, so as to obtain eternal salvation.

When the prayers are concluded we exchange the kiss.

Then someone brings bread and a cup of water and wine mixed together to him who presides over the brethren.

He takes them and offers praise and glory to the Father of the universe, through the name of the Son and of the Holy Spirit and for a considerable time he gives thanks (in Greek: eucharistian*) that we have been judged worthy of these gifts.*

When he has concluded the prayers and thanksgivings, all present give voice to an acclamation by saying, "Amen."

When he who presides has given thanks and the people have responded, those whom we call deacons give to those present the "eucharisted" bread, wine and water and take them to those who are absent.

As quoted in the *Catechism of the Catholic Church*, #1345, from Saint Justin, *First Apology*.

DISCUSSION

In a small group, use the quote from Justin Martyr to list several similarities with the Catholic Mass today. Then list some differences.

The Breaking of the Bread in Community

One way to tie all the parts of the Mass together is to think of the entire Eucharist as a sacrament. A sacrament, as we have already discussed, is a visible sign of an invisible but experience-able reality, a mystery. It symbolically expresses and helps us get in touch with that mysterious reality. A liturgical sacrament is a communal celebration of such a mystery. Because sacraments offer spiritual effects to us, the Catechism calls them effective or efficacious signs.

In the early Church, the Christians referred to the Eucharist as the Lord's Supper or simply the breaking of bread—the community meal in remembrance of Jesus.

> *They devoted themselves to the apostles' teaching and fellowship, to the breaking of bread and the prayers. . . . Day by day, as they spent much time together in the temple, they broke bread at home and ate their food with glad and generous hearts, praising God. . . .*
>
> Acts 2:42, 46–47a

It was not a passive reception of the Bread that made the meal a Eucharistic one, however. It was the active remembering of the Last Supper and the giving thanks for the new covenant with God that Jesus had begun.

Sometimes we hear phrases like "celebrate the Mass" and "celebrate the liturgy." These phrases are not incorrect (and they're certainly a lot better than "go to Mass" and "perform the liturgy"), but they may cause us to miss a very important point. The point is that the Eucharistic liturgy *is* the celebration, and it does not make much sense to talk about "celebrating the celebration."

But if the Eucharistic liturgy is the celebration, then what's the object of the celebration? What's it all about? We are back to our earlier question, but this time we are looking for an answer outside of the Mass. It's like asking what a birthday party or an anniversary is all about. The answer is not in the celebration but outside of it, in the reality of life itself.

This folk art of the Last Supper comes from La Palma, El Salvador.

What then does the Eucharistic celebration celebrate? Now that we've straightened out the question, the place to find the answer is a little clearer. The Eucharist celebrates Christian life itself, the life that Jesus Christ has made available to us. It celebrates the life of conversion and growth that we experience in our relationship with God.

The process of dying to self and caring for others—and thereby growing in ways that we never expected—is a participation in the Paschal mystery. We participate in that mystery every time we put aside our own priorities and help someone out, every time we give time and energy to the well-being of others, every time we "die to ourselves" so that others may live, or live better because we are caring about them. Whenever we make that stretch, something new happens in us.

Jesus understood the Paschal mystery—he lived it. He cared about people; he made their lives better. And he invited them to do the same. He said, put yourself under God's reign—in other words, play by God's rules—and you'll find yourself living in what he called the kingdom of God. You'll pass over (the root meaning of the word *paschal*) from a dull life to an exciting life, from an empty life to a full life, from a life of sin to a life of grace (to say it in biblical words).

Jesus lived the Paschal mystery to the max. In doing so, he discovered what God was all about—and what he was all about. Even though he was criticized for breaking social rules and threatened for disobeying religious laws, he went on helping people and teaching his followers how to live life to the fullest. When he was arrested and given a chance to stop doing what he was doing, he didn't back off. So he was killed. But he came back, better than ever. His death and resurrection revealed the ultimate power of the Paschal mystery.

In the Eucharist, then, a Christian community celebrates the Paschal mystery as they experience it day by day and week by week. They celebrate the life of community and caring that they experience in their relationships with others both inside and outside the Church. In the Eucharist they celebrate God's life, the life that God lives in and through them, the resurrected life of Jesus that flows through the body of Christ. They celebrate the spiritual energy in their lives, the power of God revealed in the Paschal mystery. In light of what we have learned about the meaning of spirit in the chapter on Confirmation, we can say that Christians at Eucharist celebrate life in the Spirit—the Spirit of Christ, the Spirit of God, the Holy Spirit.

In the Eucharist the Christian community celebrates the Paschal mystery.

Journal

Think about a time when you participated in a Mass that was especially meaningful to you.

1. Why was that Eucharistic celebration meaningful?

2. What things contributed to the meaning of that particular celebration?

3. How did your disposition contribute to the meaningfulness of that celebration compared to celebrations at other times that were less meaningful for you?

In this respect, then, the answer is simple. Simply put, the Eucharistic liturgy is the sacramental celebration of the mysterious reality of God's life in us and in the community of faith. But life itself is anything but simple, and the same is true of the Christian life. That's where the complexity of the Eucharistic liturgy comes in. It's complex because the reality that it refers to is complex.

Discussion

In the large group, discuss the following questions:

1. Describe in your own words what you understand the Paschal mystery to be.

2. Think about movies or TV shows in which one or more characters take risks—even risking their own life—on behalf of others. What is the attraction of that kind of character, behavior, or lifestyle?

3. Fictional characters who risk or give their lives for others are called heroes. In light of this presentation of the Paschal mystery, discuss why heroes are so important in literature. Who were your personal heroes when you were growing up? What did they represent for you?

4. Think of some incidents in the life of Jesus that entailed risk-taking on behalf of others. Why might Jesus' behavior in these cases be called heroic?

Activity

1. Write down what you honestly think the Mass means to you and to other people your age.

2. Share these thoughts with other members of your class.

3. Compare what the Mass is supposed to mean (according to the Catechism and other Church documents) and what it appears to mean (according to your own experience of meaning during Masses that you attend) for young people today.

Living a Divine Life

Entering into the life of God implies conversion, turning away from being self-centered and toward caring for others. The Mass begins with a penitential rite to remind us of that and of God's mercy when we fail. Living God's life also implies reconversion whenever we discover that we have slipped back into putting ourselves first (an easy thing to do!) and that we need to turn again toward caring about others. The Mass contains reminders of this all the way through.

We learn to live God's life by listening to the word of God and putting it into practice. On the surface level we listen to the do's and don'ts of the Scriptures and change our lives accordingly (reconversion again). At a deeper level we listen to the word that God speaks to our heart through the Scriptures, revealing to us how true life is to be found, and we respond by saying "Yes, we do believe that." This is why the Creed (from the Latin word meaning "I believe") follows the readings and the homily.

Divine life has purpose and direction. When we allow ourselves to get caught up in the momentum of God's life, we feel our own life has a deeper meaning; it's coming from somewhere and it's going somewhere. The stories from the Bible tell us about our spiritual heritage. The moral messages from the Scriptures point us to our future, and the remembrance of Jesus' death and resurrection reminds us how the Christian meaning of life can be lived every day of our lives.

Service to others flows from the celebration of the Eucharist.

Living the life of God means living in dialogue with the Trinity. It implies speaking and listening in prayer, asking and receiving, thanking when our prayers are answered. But our dialogue means more than wordy conversation. It implies giving of ourselves, offering our lives to God by offering to serve others. The ritual and prayers of offering reenact and symbolize the giving of ourselves so that others may live more fully.

The Eucharist Prayer culminates with the Great Amen.

Discussion

The Catechism, in paragraphs 1391 to 1397, talks about the fruits or beneficial effects of Holy Communion. In the large group, discuss the following questions:

1. What are some ways some people might interpret those claims in a magical and unrealistic way?

2. What are some ways those claims are interpreted in a credible and realistic way?

Research

With help from your teacher or a priest, interview someone who takes Communion to people who are sick or homebound in his or her parish. Ask the person about this ministry and report back to the class or write an essay.

- How do you go about it?
- Why do you do it?
- What do you get out of it?
- What do the people you serve get out of it?

In God's life we discover that in giving we receive. We receive from God directly and from those to whom we give. In the giving and receiving, there is unity, sharing, communion. When we receive Communion, we recognize our unity with Christ both personally and communally. We encounter our Lord personally through the intimate reception of his Body and Blood, and we acknowledge his presence in the community that is also called his body—the Church. Our encounter with Christ nourishes us spiritually, increasing God's life within us.

God's life is not meant to be kept to ourselves. It is to be shared with others—the people we live with, the people we work and go to school with, even people we do not know, especially those who are poor and in need. And so at the end of Mass we are sent out on mission to live and spread the good news of God's life, to do again what we have just been celebrating.

We see, therefore, that the actual meaning of Eucharist is not confined to the Mass but involves what we do before and after Mass. If we are living with God's life in us, then Eucharist celebrates that and gives thanks for it, as its name suggests. To the extent that God's life is missing in our own life, the Eucharistic liturgy calls us back to God and points us again in the right direction. But Eucharist also does more than that, for it gives us food for our journey in communion with Christ and strength to carry on in unity with the Christian community.

WHAT THE CATECHISM SAYS

Holy Communion nourishes our spiritual life. It "preserves, increases, and renews" the grace of Baptism and helps us along our Christian journey. At the end of life, the Eucharist is our *viaticum,* "food for the way" as we journey to life everlasting.

See the *Catechism of the Catholic Church,* #1392.

Review Questions

1. Why is it difficult to say that the Eucharist has one specific meaning?

2. What meanings are found in the various parts of the Mass?

3. What is the Paschal mystery?

4. What is the connection between conversion and living God's life?

Mass as a Sacrifice

sacrifice a ritual offering made to God by a priest on behalf of the people, as a sign of adoration, thanksgiving, entreaty, and communion; originally, an act of offering, or the gift that is offered, very often accompanied by a ritual meal for the purpose of communion with the divine

In the past, Catholics commonly used the expression, "the **sacrifice** of the Mass." Even though this phrase is not used as often today, the *Catechism of the Catholic Church* speaks of the Eucharist as a sacrifice. How are we to understand this concept?

First of all, we need to remember that the meaning of the word *sacrifice* has changed over the course of two thousand years. The word itself comes from the Latin *sacrum facere*, literally to make sacred, special, or holy. Food that is blessed in a religious ceremony is made important and special through the ritual of blessing. In ancient times, when people worshiped in a temple, they brought food that then was blessed and thereby "sacrificed" or made holy because it was set apart for a special purpose.

This same food (or most of it) was later eaten by the people who had brought it for the sacrifice. The emphasis was on the eating, and this made temple worship rather enjoyable. You can also see why Christians came to call their Eucharistic meals sacrifices. Outwardly it appeared that they were doing in private homes what non-Christians did in their temples: sharing food that had been blessed or *consecrated* (a word that means, literally, made sacred together).

A second important dimension of temple sacrifice is that the blessed or consecrated food was also an offering. In a non-Israelite temple, it was offered to the god whose image was found in that temple. The sacrificed food was therefore a present to the god and, like all presents, it symbolized the devotedness of the one offering the present. The god was actually incapable of eating the food, so some of it was consumed by the temple priests on the god's behalf, and the rest was returned, as a "present from the god," to the temple worshipers.

Well aware of this ancient mode of religious worship, the early followers of Jesus brought food to their Lord's Supper celebrations, and in offering it to the rest of the community, they understood that they were also offering and showing their dedication to God. Their gift of food symbolized the way they were giving themselves to others as Jesus had taught them.

Jesus' death on the cross was also understood as a sacrifice in this way. That is to say, Jesus gave himself to the Father in death, just as he had given himself in life, ministering to people's needs. The early Christians understood that God the Father had accepted Jesus' self-offering and had shown his acceptance by returning Jesus to life on the third day.

The Eucharist is a sacrifice and a meal.

Christians at the Lord's Supper imitated Christ's self-giving in their weekly worship. Through the gifts of food—especially those of bread and wine—they offered themselves to God, only to receive those same gifts back again in the form of Communion: communion with the Father, communion with the risen Jesus, and communion with one another.

In the Middle Ages, people no longer experienced temple sacrifices and so they began to think about sacrifice primarily in terms of the slaughter of the sacrificial animal. Some Jewish sacrifices had been offered in reparation for sin, and Christians reading the Jewish Scriptures interpreted the death of Jesus as a sacrifice in this sense. This understanding lies behind the traditional theology of the "sacrifice of the Mass," which remains part of the institutional meaning of the Eucharist.

Viewed from this perspective, the Eucharist is a sacrifice offered by Christ through the ministry of a validly ordained priest. It is offered in reparation for sin, the sins of those living and those who have died, and as a means of grace, a sharing in God's life. Recalling the slaying of the Passover lamb that was eaten by the Israelites just before their liberation from slavery in Egypt, the Eucharist celebrates Jesus' sacrificial death on the cross, leading to his passover from death to new life. Jesus is the sacrificial "Lamb of God who takes away the sins of the world," and who shares his Body and Blood with his people in a new covenant for all time. The Eucharist is thus a sacrifice that enables Christians to enter into the Paschal mystery and the kingdom of God. The Eucharist makes present Christ's eternal sacrifice, through which the salvation of humankind has been accomplished.

Viewed from the earlier perspective, the Eucharist is a sacrifice because it celebrates and gives thanks for the self-giving of Jesus, and because it is a ritual in which Christians can unite themselves with his self-giving in dedicating their lives to God in service to others.

> [He] emptied himself . . .
> and became obedient to the point of death—
> even death on a cross.
> Therefore God also highly exalted him. . . .
>
> Philippians 2:7a, 8–9

Discussion

In the large group, answer these questions:

1. When you hear the word *sacrifice,* what do you think of?

2. Compare the ancient and medieval understandings of sacrifice.

3. How does calling the Mass a sacrifice help you to understand what going to Mass is supposed to be about?

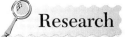

Research

With regard to the Eucharist, the word *sacrifice* can be understood as a present or offering. Refer to the *Catechism of the Catholic Church* and read paragraphs 1359 to 1361 (or 1359 to 1368, for a longer assignment), replacing the word *sacrifice* with *offering.* How does doing this affect your understanding of these paragraphs?

Mass as a Meal

The Eucharist is called a liturgical meal. How are we to understand this? Referring to the wafers that most parishes use for Communion, one Catholic remarked, "It's easier to believe it's the Body of Christ than to believe it's bread!" Some parishes don't offer the chalice to people at Mass, and if they do, all they give you is a sip of the consecrated wine—just a taste, and nothing more. Today, the physical resemblance of the Mass to a meal is more symbolic than obvious.

The Body of Christ. Amen.

But thinking of the Mass as a meal goes back to the time when it actually was more fully a meal. During the first decades of Christianity, believers got together in the evening once a week for what they called the **Lord's Supper** or the breaking of bread (see 1 Corinthians 11:17–34; Acts 2:42). During this meal, people would say what they recalled about what Jesus had said and done during his lifetime. (These stories eventually found their way into the written Gospels. This ancient practice is the reason we have a gospel reading at every Mass.)

People also had a sense of Christ's presence with them in their gathering, and especially in their sharing of food that Jesus had asked be done in memory of him (see Luke 22:19). This experience of divine presence, combined with the Christian practice of referring to the bread and wine used in Communion as "the Body and Blood of Christ," gave rise to the Catholic doctrine of the ***Real Presence***—the teaching that Christ is really present in the Eucharist.

As Christian communities grew larger, it became impossible to have a full meal at every Lord's Supper. Remember that in these early years there were no such things as church buildings; Christians met together in people's homes. Even the largest homes could not accommodate more than a few dozen dinner guests. The solution was to eat at home and then to gather elsewhere as a Christian community to celebrate a symbolic meal with bread and wine, the elements blessed by Jesus at the Last Supper, in place of the full meal with many dishes and courses.

Lord's Supper a name for Eucharistic worship that is found in the New Testament; the name often given by Protestant Churches to their communion service

Real Presence the name for Christ's presence in the Eucharistic liturgy, and especially in the Blessed Sacrament, which is believed in faith but can also be experienced by those who are open to it

Parishes that are aware of this early liturgical history sometimes try to emphasize the meal aspect of the liturgy by "setting the table" at the start of the Liturgy of the Eucharist, by using home-made unleavened bread rather than factory-produced wafers, and by offering the chalice to all those who want to receive both the Body and the Blood of Christ.

Even so, can we honestly call the Mass a meal? We can, if we remember that it is not the quantity of food that makes a meal special; it is, rather, the quality of the relationships with the people with whom we share what we have, even if it's only a little. On a long hike, we might share a candy bar and a soft drink. In a crisis when people are starving, they might share a potato or a crust of bread. When people who care about one another eat together, it's not the amount of food that's important.

WHAT THE CATECHISM SAYS

The Eucharist is called the *Paschal banquet* and the *sacred banquet* of communion with the Lord's Body and Blood. The Eucharist also commits us to the poor. When we gather around the table, we must recognize that everyone who gathers here is our brother and sister. We dishonor the table if we do not share with those in need. God is merciful and calls us to be merciful toward those in need.

See the *Catechism of the Catholic Church*, #1382, 1397.

Discussion

In a small group, discuss the following questions:

1. The Real Presence of Christ is one of the traditional Catholic teachings about the Eucharist. Can you relate this belief to your own experience? If so, describe some time when you perceived Christ's presence in the Blessed Sacrament or during Mass.

2. In some ways, the presence of Christ in the Eucharist is similar to the presence of Christ (or of God) in other situations. Is there some time, apart from the Blessed Sacrament and the Mass, when you would say that you felt the presence of Christ (or God)? If so, describe the circumstances and the experience you had.

3. What do you remember being taught about Christ's presence in the Eucharist when you were a child preparing for your First Communion? How did you understand that teaching then? How do you understand the Catholic teaching today?

The Eucharist celebration with the students of a Catholic school system took place on September 11, 2001.

 **Activities**

1. Go to Mass with a friend at a Catholic Church other than the one you normally attend. Report on your experience to the other students in the class, answering these questions:
   - How is the Mass the same as the Mass in your own parish?
   - How is it different?
   - What do you like more about that Mass?
   - What do you like less?

2. With advice and direction from your teacher and your pastor and with the permission of your parents, go with an Episcopalian, Lutheran, or Methodist friend to a Eucharistic service some Sunday (they may not have one every week). Report on your experience to the other students in the class, answering these questions:
   - How is the celebration similar to a Catholic Mass?
   - How is it different?
   - What do you like more?
   - What do you like less?

3. With advice and direction from your teacher and your pastor and with the permission of your parents, go with a Protestant friend (but not Episcopalian, Lutheran, or Methodist) to a Lord's Supper service some Sunday (they are usually not every Sunday). Report on your experience to the other students in the class.
   - How is the celebration similar to a Catholic Mass?
   - What are some differences?
   - What do you like more?
   - What do you like less?

4. With advice and direction from your teacher and your pastor and with the permission of your parents, go with an Orthodox friend to a Eucharistic liturgy some Sunday. Report on your experience to the other students in the class.
   - How is the Orthodox liturgy similar to a Catholic Mass?
   - How is it different?
   - What do you like more?
   - What do you like less?

 **Research**

Catholics understand the Bread of Life discourse in the Gospel of John (6:32–58) to refer to Christ's Real Presence in the Eucharist. Read and summarize the passage.

Review Questions

1. What does it mean to say that the Eucharist is a sacrifice?
2. In what ways is the Eucharist a meal?
3. What is the Real Presence of Christ in the Eucharist?

Summary

Eucharist is the sacrament that is most familiar to Catholics who go to Mass every week. It is also the most difficult to explain because it has many parts with many meanings, and because it carries a whole history of theological explanations whose meaning today is not always clearly understood.

Many questions have been raised about this sacrament. If Catholics participate in Eucharistic liturgies every week, why is it called a Sacrament of Initiation? If the consecrated host is called the Blessed Sacrament, then is the Eucharistic liturgy also a sacrament? Why have Eucharistic practices changed over the centuries?

Starting with the liturgy as it is currently celebrated, we can learn to understand past and present Eucharistic practices and explanations. We can also tackle the seemingly difficult question: What does it mean?

Through our study and our experience of this sacrament, we gain some understanding of these important concepts: The Eucharist is the heart, source, and summit of the Christian life. The Eucharist is a memorial of Christ's life, death, and resurrection, making it our most important celebration of the Paschal mystery. The Mass is Christ's sacrifice of praise and thanksgiving, and it is our Paschal meal. Christ is really present in the Eucharist.

Scripture

Jesus said to them, "I am the bread of life. Whoever comes to me will never be hungry, and whoever believes in me will never be thirsty. But I said to you that you have seen me and yet do not believe. Everything that the Father gives me will come to me, and anyone who comes to me I will never drive away; for I have come down from heaven, not to do my own will, but the will of him who sent me. And this is the will of him who sent me, that I should lose nothing of all that he has given me, but raise it up on the last day. This is indeed the will of my Father, that all who see the Son and believe in him may have eternal life; and I will raise them up on the last day."

JOHN 6:35–40

Prayer

Lord Jesus Christ,
you give us your body and blood in the eucharist
as a sign that even now we share your life.
May we come to possess it completely in the kingdom
Where you live for ever and ever.
Amen.

PRAYER AFTER COMMUNION,
SOLEMNITY OF THE BODY
AND BLOOD OF CHRIST.

Scripture

If a shepherd has a hundred sheep, and one of them has gone astray, does he not leave the ninety-nine on the mountains and go in search of the one that went astray? And if he finds it, truly I tell you, he rejoices over it more than over the ninety-nine that never went astray.

MATTHEW 18:12–13

Prayer

Lord our God,
you call us out of darkness into light,
out of self-deception into truth,
out of death into life.
Send us your Holy Spirit
to open our ears to your call.
Fill our hearts with courage
to be true followers of your Son.
We ask this through Christ our Lord.
Amen.

RITE OF PENANCE, #56.

Reconciliation: Reawakening God's Life

CHAPTER OVERVIEW

THE FORGIVING FATHER

The father stood at the crest of the hill in the shade of the oak tree where he prayed every afternoon. His fertile and prosperous lands belied the look of concern on his aging face. His mind wandered back in time to memories of his growing sons so different and so competitive. His mind watched them go their separate ways trying to find their identities, and his heart ached to heal their self-inflicted wounds. His younger son had been gone two years already, and the news of him was not good. His older son had stayed close by, determined to please, but lacking in joy and vision. An acorn fell, suddenly rousing the old man from his daydreams. He looked into the distance and a familiar shape and gait caught his hopeful eye.

"[H]e ran [to his son] and put his arms around him and kissed him. Then the son said to him, 'Father, I have sinned against heaven and before you; I am no longer worthy to be called your son.' But the father said to his slaves, 'Quickly, bring out a robe—the best one—and put it on him; put a ring on his finger and sandals on his feet. And get the fattened calf and kill it, and let us eat and celebrate; for this son of mine was dead and is alive again; he was lost and is found.' "

James J. Tissot

Chapter Seven

Later that evening while the father rejoiced in having his son home again, he missed his older son. He went out looking for him to bring him into the party to welcome his brother. He found his son sulking and angry. The father pleaded with his son. He loved them both.

Then the father said to him, "Son, you are always with me, and all that is mine is yours. But we had to celebrate and rejoice, because this brother of yours was dead and has come to life; he was lost and has been found."

See Luke 15:11–32, quoted: 15:20b–24a, 31–32.

We are all familiar with the story of the **prodigal** son. Jesus gave us very special messages in this simple story. If Jesus reveals God to us, then we see a God who does not focus on what we do wrong, but who cares about us no matter what we do. We also hear a call to **reconciliation** with each other, with everyone in our family and community. What do these ideas have to do with the sacrament which is now called **Reconciliation,** but which we also refer to as Penance or **confession?**

Journal

Think about the story of the forgiving father (usually called the story of the prodigal son). With which character can you more easily identify—the wasteful youth who experiences a deep conversion of heart, or the obedient youth who is a bit resentful? Why do you say this?

Discussion

Think about Jesus' parable explored here. In the large group, discuss the following questions:

1. How realistic does the story seem?

2. Do people really behave that way? Why do you say that?

3. Give examples of people who have behaved in ways similar to or different from the characters in the parable.

4. What can be learned—about God, about ourselves, about human relationships— from thinking about the parable and the way people behave?

Activity

Read John 8:1–11, the story of Jesus forgiving a woman whom others condemn. Write a poem based on this story. If you can, set the poem to music, or act it out with others in a mime or modernized skit. Share your project with the class.

prodigal wasteful, spendthrift

reconciliation overcoming emotional separation, usually through some process in which one party admits wrongdoing and another party grants forgiveness; can be between two people, between a person and God, or between a person and a community

Reconciliation the name for the Sacrament of Healing in which we seek assurance of God's love and receive forgiveness for our sins through the ministry of a priest and special words of absolution; the repentant person confesses serious sins and makes reparation

confession the act of honestly telling one's sins to another—God, another person, or in the sacrament, to a priest

Jesus said to the woman, "Go your way, and from now on do not sin again." —See John 8:1–11.

The Names of the Sacrament

Penance one of the official names for the Sacrament of Healing that is also known as the *Sacrament of Reconciliation;* the sacrament of repentance or conversion

penance originally another word for repentance or conversion; later, acts of prayer and other good works

conversion also called repentance; changing one's thoughts, feelings, and behavior; turning one's life around, at least with regard to some parts of it that are either bad or not as good as they could be

reconversion converting again, if it needs to be done, as is often the case when one is trying to change one's life for the better

People your grandparents' age were probably taught to confess their sins to a priest in a special booth called a confession box or confessional. They began by saying, "Bless me, Father, for I have sinned," and by telling the priest how long it had been since their last confession. Then they enumerated their sins (often using the Ten Commandments as a guide), telling how often they had committed each sin.

Today the Sacrament of Reconciliation is much different. Gone is the dark confessional—except in older churches, and except in movies that want to show a Catholic going to confession. It has been replaced by a well-lighted Reconciliation room that encourages open conversation and honest prayer. Gone too is the routine of enumerating sins and being questioned about them, and the words of absolution in Latin.

The usual name of the sacrament today is *Reconciliation.* The other official name—**Penance**—is used less frequently. The word **penance** originally meant something very different from what most people thought. Many thought it implied something like a penalty or punishment for sins, and they applied this concept to the acts of prayer and other works assigned by a priest to a penitent for after confession. Penance in this sense meant something done in order to make up for the harm caused by sin and to reestablish the good habits of the Christian life. But the name *Penance* in Latin, *penitentiae,* actually means **conversion,** a change of heart and mind, or even **reconversion.** The name *Reconciliation* captures this idea better.

Jesus calls his followers to conversion: "The time is fulfilled, and the kingdom of God has come near; repent, and believe in the good news" (Mark 1:15). Our Baptism celebrated our fundamental conversion toward God. But life is a journey, and we frequently fail to stay on the right track. This is why every person, as well as the Church as a whole, is called to be sincerely sorry for sinning, willing to change, and responsive to God's call to a new and better way of living. We need to be continually aware of God's love and ready to reconvert, to get back on track to caring for others and to make a firm decision to sin no more.

WHAT THE CATECHISM SAYS

In addition to the *Sacrament of Penance* and the *Sacrament of Reconciliation,* this sacrament is known by several other names. The *sacrament of conversion* points to the first step of the sinner in returning to God. The *sacrament of confession* emphasizes the essential disclosure of serious sins to a priest and our confession (in the sense of admission) of God's great mercy. The *sacrament of forgiveness* stresses God's love and willingness to forgive through the absolution of the priest.

See the *Catechism of the Catholic Church*, #s 1423–1424.

inteRView

Find an older person who is willing to talk about his or her experience as a child or teenager going to confession. Ask the person what he or she thinks was good and not so good about that older practice, and what he or she thinks about the practice of the sacrament in the Catholic Church today. Report your findings in an essay or an oral presentation.

Review Questions

1. What is reconciliation?

2. What is the message of the story of the prodigal son?

3. Explain the following names for the sacrament: Reconciliation, Penance, Confession.

4. What is meant by conversion and reconversion? Why are these important?

The Rite of Reconciliation

Looking at the Rite of Reconciliation is one way to understand what the sacrament is all about. The rite itself is a simple one. The priest welcomes us, and to set the mood he may read a short Scripture passage about God's love and forgiveness. We then talk with him about the sins and other concerns that brought us to the sacrament, while he listens and responds pretty much the way a counselor might. After we have finished, the priest asks if we are sorry for what we have done and if we are willing to repair any harm we have caused. When we have indicated that we are, he says a prayer of forgiveness and absolution. In closing, he says a few words reminding us of God's mercy and love.

The words of absolution spoken by the priest as he makes the sign of the cross over the penitent are:

> *God, the Father of mercies,*
> *through the death and resurrection of his Son*
> *has reconciled the world to himself*
> *and sent the Holy Spirit among us*
> *for the forgiveness of sins;*
> *through the ministry of the Church*
> *may God give you pardon and peace,*
> *and I absolve you from your sins*
> *in the name of the Father, and of the Son,*
> *and of the Holy Spirit.*

RITE OF PENANCE, #46.

If we go to a priest privately and ask if he would be willing to hear our confession, he is more likely to begin with an informal, "What would you like to talk about?" than with a formal ritual. And even if we go to Reconciliation in a church, we are likely to meet the priest in a small room where we can talk to one another face-to-face if we choose. In this sacrament we meet and get closer to God. Doing this through meeting and seeing another person is a better way of saying this today, and a better way of doing it, too, although some people still prefer the anonymity of the confessional or at least the screen.

Most likely, the last time you were invited to participate in the sacrament was at an Advent or Lent Reconciliation Service (or Penance Service—both names are in use). In Advent and Lent we prepare ourselves to celebrate the two great Christian feasts, Christmas and Easter, and the best spiritual preparation is reconversion.

Conversion means just what it implies: a change-over, a turn-around, an about-face. Reconversion, therefore, suggests that we need to be converted again, to change again, to turn again toward God. Because of our hectic daily lives, we may often turn every which way but God's way. The Sacrament of Reconciliation is an opportunity to turn back again toward God and Jesus' way of life. It is an opportunity not just for ourselves as individuals but for our whole faith community, since we are all part of the whole, and our actions and feelings influence the entire community for better or worse.

It is this communal aspect that we emphasize during Advent and Lent in our sacramental services in our parish or Catholic high school. We gather to be reconciled to God and to each other in the family of God. A communal Reconciliation service always begins with readings from the Bible on themes such as mercy, forgiveness, and conversion. The celebrant presiding over the service gives a homily or short instruction based on the Scripture readings. After a period of meditative silence, everyone is given an opportunity to visit a priest privately for confession and absolution.

At a Reconciliation service we listen to the word of God together as it comes to us through the Scriptures, the homily, and the silence of our meditation. When we go to confession at other times, we still need to do that listening before we speak. For this reason, the priest may begin by reading a brief selection from the Bible to allow the word of God to speak to us. Once we are in that space where we can be truly honest with ourselves and God, the dialogue can begin.

It should be a dialogue, too—not just a recitation of misbehaviors. A simple recitation may be all that children are able to give, but adult confession goes to a deeper level of communication. God does not need a mere list of the ways we've misbehaved. God already knows that. The sacrament is about what *we* need.

The word *confession* implies honesty and openness, a willingness to look candidly at our life, to admit our sinfulness, to assess our strengths and weaknesses, and a desire to improve with the help of God and others. Speaking about what is going wrong in our life (or at the very least, what is not going well) enables us to focus on it and to hear in our own words what is bothering us. When we talk about ourselves, we gather our unclear feelings and put them into words so that we can take an honest look at them. Doing this in the presence of a listening and supportive person should make it easier for us. When we unburden ourselves to a close friend, we experience this ease of communication.

The communal rite for Reconciliation reminds us that our reconciliation is with God and with the Church.

DISCUSSION

In the large group, discuss the following questions:

1. Some Catholics think that sins are never forgiven by God until they have been confessed to a priest. What do you think about when and how God forgives us?

2. When has the Sacrament of Reconciliation felt like a true celebration for you? When has it not felt like that for you?

This is one of the ways the priest can help us in the process of confession. He is there for us in the same way that a close friend is. He is giving us his time; he is making space for us to just be ourselves; he will not and cannot divulge any secret we entrust to him (this is called the sacramental seal or the seal of confession); he will listen to our inner struggle; he will offer us whatever advice he can. He is there as a representative of the Church community welcoming us back. But he is also there for us in his special role as priest, as mediator between us and God. He is standing in for the closest Friend that we can ever have. His presence helps us get in touch with God, sometimes more easily, and sometimes at a deeper level. He is acting in the name of Jesus, by the power of the Holy Spirit, and with the authority of the church, to offer us God's forgiveness.

When we come to the Sacrament of Reconciliation with the right attitude and preparation, we celebrate the forgiveness with which God responds to our contrition. Like a forgiving Father, God meets us with open arms. He has been waiting and watching for our return so that he can show us his mercy and gather us up in his loving mercy. It is this love of God, our forgiving Father, that motivates the most perfect of contrition on our part. Lesser motives can also draw us to repentance; this imperfect contrition is no less important.

DISCUSSION

In a small group, discuss the following questions:

1. Recall when you made your First Reconciliation.

   - How were you prepared for it?
   - Looking back, how good was the preparation that was given to you?
   - If you were to design a First Reconciliation preparation program, what would you retain from your own preparation, and what would you change? Give reasons to support the program you design.

2. Have you participated in a communal Penance or Reconciliation service during Advent or Lent? If so:

   - What was your experience like?
   - Did you find it helpful or not? Explain why.
   - If you were to help plan such a service for your parish, what would you keep and what would you change?

Activity

1. With other students in your class, design a Penance or Reconciliation Service for Advent or Lent.

2. In doing so, consult with books and articles which give tips for good ways to do this.

3. After the service, discuss what, if anything, could have been done better.

Research

In a Catholic encyclopedia or a book on Church history, research the practice of private confession as developed by Irish monks. Prepare a presentation for the class.

How Often Should We Go to Confession?

A generation or two ago, many Catholics felt that they needed to go to confession once a month or even more frequently, and especially before they received Communion. The official teaching of the Church was (and still is) that individual confession and absolution is the ordinary means of reconciliation for those who have turned away from God completely (those who have committed a mortal sin, to use the Catechism's language). These individuals should repent and seek reconciliation as soon as possible, and certainly within a year. Those who have committed less serious offenses (the Catechism calls them venial sins) have always been encouraged to make use of the sacrament, but there is not a strict obligation to do so.

In the earliest centuries of Christianity, only notorious public sinners were required to undergo the discipline of public repentance. In fact, ordinary Christians were expected to never need this sacrament at all! The practice of repeated confession for lesser sins did not begin until the fifth century. The Irish monks who started this practice felt that ordinary people had a need for something more than the general confession of sins found in the Mass. Their pastoral sensitivity led them to try something new: private confession combined with spiritual counseling. The intention was to encourage guided spiritual growth. By the seventh century the practice was widespread in the monasteries of Europe.

In the course of time, private confession tended to become rather legalistic. Penitents told the priest which laws of God they had broken, they received absolution, and they were given standard penances developed for each sin. Many people today are not comfortable with this legalistic attitude, however, and so the sacrament has been restored to a more pastoral practice concerned with personal counseling and spiritual healing.

These days it is not uncommon for people who have not committed a mortal sin to go to confession only when they sense a need to overcome some sinful habit or attitude that they cannot deal with by themselves. In other words, they seek the sacrament only when they feel a need for it. In reality we should go to confession as often as we really need to for our spiritual health. We should not put it off until our relationship with God has deteriorated to the point that our life is out of control.

Discussion

Recall some time in your life when you just had to tell someone about something you had done in order to get some reassurance or guidance about it. In a small group, discuss the following questions:

1. Without going into the details of your crisis, describe that experience and explain what benefit you got out of it.

2. What parallels do you see between that experience and the process of sacramental Reconciliation as it is now practiced in the Church?

Review Questions

1. Describe the process followed when making a private confession to a priest in a Reconciliation room or confessional.

2. Name some of the additional things that happen in a communal Reconciliation service.

3. How often should one go to confession?

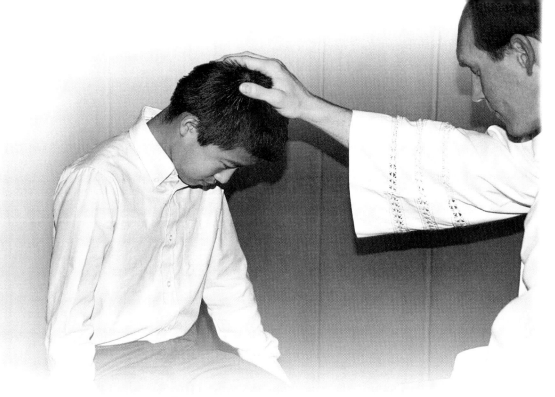

. . . may God give you
pardon and peace. . . .

—*Rite of Penance, #46.*

Spiritual Direction

The practice of private confession originated from a kind of dialogue that we have just been talking about. In the early Christian monasteries, new monks met regularly with an older monk to talk with him about their spiritual progress, to reveal the ways that they were falling short, and to receive advice and assurance of God's forgiving love. The older monk was like a father to them, encouraging them and enabling them to grow in the Christian life that they had chosen.

People living near the monasteries heard about this practice, and those who desired to improve in living the gospel sought out one of these wise "confessors" and asked him for his help and guidance. The monk gave people **spiritual direction** and became a "spiritual father" to them. The Catholic custom of referring to a priest as "Father" dates back to this early practice.

During the Middle Ages, monks carried this practice out of the monasteries and made it available to everyone. In the beginning, most of the people the monks encountered were recent converts, descendants of northern European tribes who had ransacked the Roman Empire and brought about its downfall. It seemed too much to ask these people who were perceived as uncivilized to live the gospel to its fullest. Thus the monks asked them only to live up to the minimum that God expected of them—to observe the Ten Commandments. It was a simple expedient for a seemingly simple people.

This focus on behavior also brought about another change in the practice of the sacrament. The "father confessors" had always given practical advice on how to live a more Christian life. A man who had stolen something was told to give it back and a little more besides. A woman who had gossiped was told to apologize and to set the record straight if need be. A child who had been disobedient was told to "honor your father and mother" without question. All this was geared towards *penitentiae*, or conversion in the person's moral life.

spiritual direction also called pastoral counseling; the practice of seeking and receiving spiritual and moral guidance

For good measure, the priests also prescribed prayers or other pious practices, such as fasting from food or abstaining from meat. Over the course of a few centuries, however, the penitential practices geared towards reconversion faded into mere advice with the warning "not to sin again," and the pious practices came to be regarded as penances which "made up for" the sins committed.

In the Rite of Reconciliation as it is practiced today, the original purpose of confession is again front and center. Although the priest may ask us to spend some time in prayer or in reading the Scriptures after leaving the Reconciliation room, most of what he says will often be directed more toward helping us change our life in some way. Jesus said that those who live according to his gospel will be happy and blessed. The purpose of this sacrament is to find and change whatever is preventing us from living that more abundant life.

The priest concludes by assuring us of God's forgiveness and absolving us from whatever wrong we might have done in God's sight. The last thing we need is to walk around with a load of guilt about the past! Jesus' story of the prodigal son reminds us that God is not concentrating on our sins but on merciful love. In Jesus' name the priest speaks the word of God's forgiving love for whatever we have done.

inteRView

1. Try to find someone in your parish or diocese who is a spiritual director or pastoral counselor. Learn from that person what that profession entails. What do you find attractive or unattractive about it? In your report to your teacher or your class, state what similarities and differences you see between these practices and the Sacrament of Reconciliation as it is currently practiced.

2. If there is a monastery or house of formation near where you live, arrange to visit there with one or more of your classmates. Ask your guide about the practice of spiritual direction and how it relates to the preparation and formation of members of that religious order. In your report to the class, state what parallels you see between this practice in religious orders and the current design of the Rite of Reconciliation.

3. Investigate in your diocese or community whether there are reconciliation or mediation services available to people who want to resolve their differences without resorting to physical violence or going to court. If you find one, interview someone on the staff about that organization's work. Even if this is not a Church-based service, how might it be regarded as a ministry?

 Journal

1. Is there anyone in your life who has been a spiritual guide or mentor for you? If so, who is the person?

2. What attracted you to that person?

3. What kind of help (for example, giving advice, or sometimes just listening) has that person given you?

4. If you were to be that kind of person in the future, how would you relate to the young person who comes to you for guidance?

Sins and Shortfalls

At his Bar Mitzvah, a Jewish boy reads from the Torah.

When most of us hear the word *sin*, we think of breaking a rule, a law, or a commandment. In the Scriptures, however, both the Hebrew word and the Greek word for sin mean "to fall short" or "miss the mark." The image is that of an arrow that falls short of its target. An archer who misses the target learns to hit it, not by being punished, but by aiming higher and shooting more carefully. The remedy, in other words, is to correct the error by learning how to do things better.

Hitting the bull's-eye in life starts with developing our human potential to the maximum. A lot of people, motivated by slick images in the media, believe that this means looking good and having lots of stuff. They also believe that the good life is one of pleasure and power.

Psychologists tell us, however, that these values miss the mark. Sure, we need to have a good self-image, and we need to have our physical needs met. Sure, we need a certain amount of enjoyment and relaxation, and we need a sense of self-control in order to be happy. But trying too hard to look good, to please others, to acquire more stuff, to avoid pain and experience pleasure, to run our own and other people's lives—these are sure ways to mess up our lives and wind up in the office of a counselor or therapist in order to try to get our lives back on track.

Centuries before the modern science of psychology, however, religious people understood this. The Jewish *Torah*, usually translated as "Law," is better understood as "Way"—as in *way of life*, or *the right way to live*. At the heart of the Jewish way to live is what we call the Ten Commandments (they are not numbered in the Scriptures). Actually, however, the whole Torah encompasses the first five books of the Bible and presents stories as well as instructions about the right way to live.

Blessed are the poor in spirit,
for theirs is the kingdom of heaven.

Blessed are those who mourn,
for they will be comforted.

Blessed are the meek,
for they will inherit the earth.

Blessed are those who hunger
and thirst for righteousness,
for they will be filled.

Blessed are those who are merciful,
for they will receive mercy.

Blessed are the pure in heart,
for they will see God.

Blessed are the peacemakers,
for they will be called children of God.

Blessed are those who are persecuted
for righteousness' sake,
for theirs is the kingdom of heaven.

Blessed are you when people revile you
and utter all kinds of evil against
you falsely on my account. Rejoice and be
glad, for your reward is great in heaven. . . .

Matthew 5:3–12

The Ten Commandments themselves may look like rules or laws, but when we look at them closely, we begin to see that they are basically about relationships. The first three in the traditional Catholic numbering have to do with people's relationship with God. But, if people want to have a good life, at the very least they need to avoid lying, stealing, and killing one another. So the last seven provide a minimum moral basis for people's relationships with one another.

By turning the negative *You shall nots* into positives, we can see that Judaism from its very beginning understood that the basis of the good life is honesty, generosity, and caring for one another. Falling short of these basic obligations misses the mark, and in that sense is **sin.**

In terms of living rightly, the Ten Commandments hold a prominent place, but they are not the end of the story. Jesus also taught people how to live, and he gave commandments to his followers. Jesus' most famous commandments, however, are called the **Beatitudes.** The word *Beatitudes* is from the Latin word *beatus* for "being blessed," in the sense of being happy and satisfied.

The eight Beatitudes (there are actually nine in Matthew's Gospel and four in Luke's) go beyond the basics required by the Commandments. They encourage Christians to do what God wants, to be realistic about themselves, to be generous and merciful to others, and to work for peace. Like the Commandments to the Old Testament, the Beatitudes are simply the center or heart of Jesus' way of living. In the Gospels and throughout the New Testament, Jesus' way of life is described in stories and parables, teachings and instructions.

Most of us don't think that being unrealistic, spending all our money on ourselves, or supporting military actions are sins, and yet these attitudes and actions all fall short of what Jesus asks of his followers in the Beatitudes. Jesus continually called and calls his followers to aim higher. His story of the last judgment illustrates yet another dimension of the Jesus way of life—care for those who are weak and poor in society.

sin originally understood as falling short or missing the mark; can be understood legalistically as breaking a law or commandment; can be understood relationally as weakening (venial) or breaking (mortal) a relationship

Beatitudes what Jesus taught his followers about what to do in order to be really happy and fulfilled

THE LAST JUDGMENT

"When the Son of Man comes in his glory, and all the angels with him, then he will sit on the throne of his glory. All the nations will be gathered before him, and he will separate people one from another as a shepherd separates the sheep from the goats, and he will put the sheep at his right hand and the goats at the left. Then the king will say to those at his right hand, 'Come, you that are blessed by my Father, inherit the kingdom prepared for you from the foundation of the world; for I was hungry and you gave me food, I was thirsty and you gave me something to drink, I was a stranger and you welcomed me, I was naked and you gave me clothing, I was sick and you took care of me, I was in prison and you visited me.' Then the righteous will answer him, 'Lord, when was it that we saw you hungry and gave you food, or thirsty and gave you something to drink? And when was it that we saw you a stranger and welcomed you, or naked and gave you clothing? And when was it that we saw you sick or in prison and visited you?' And the king will answer them, 'Truly I tell you, just as you did it to one of the least of these who are members of my family, you did it to me.' Then

"The Last Judgment"
by Fra Angelico (1400–1455).

he will say to those at his left hand, 'You that are accursed, depart from me into the eternal fire prepared for the devil and his angels; for I was hungry and you gave me no food, I was thirsty and you gave me nothing to drink, I was a stranger and you did not welcome me, naked and you did not give me clothing, sick and in prison and you did not visit me.' Then they also will answer, 'Lord, when was it that we saw you hungry or thirsty or a stranger or naked or sick or in prison, and did not take care of you?' Then he will answer them, 'Truly I tell you, just as you did not do it to one of the least of these, you did not do it to me.' And these will go away into eternal punishment, but the righteous into eternal life."

Matthew 25:31–46

Chapter Seven

During World Youth conferences, the Sacrament of Reconciliation is celebrated in many languages.

DiScUSSioN

The chapter suggests that Christians should not be trying to live solely according to the Ten Commandments in the Old Testament, but should also live according to the eight Beatitudes and other teachings of Jesus in the New Testament. In the large group, discuss the following questions:

1. What is your reaction to this?

2. What does Jesus' story of the last judgment tell you about what Jesus asks of his followers?

3. How can Catholics benefit from spiritual guidance in the Sacrament of Reconciliation when they find that they are not living up to the teachings of Jesus?

Research

Read the following Scripture passages. Summarize each reading in light of the text on *Sin and Shortfalls* and on what God asks of us in regard to right living.

Exodus 20:1–17
Matthew 5:3–12
Luke 6:20–26
Luke 6:27–36
John 14:15
Matthew 5:21–42
Matthew 22:34–40
John 15:12–14

Review Questions

1. What is the historical connection between private confession and the monastic practice of spiritual direction?

2. How can the Sacrament of Reconciliation be an opportunity for spiritual direction today?

3. How is "missing the mark" related to the concept of sin?

4. How is sin understood legalistically? How is it understood relationally?

5. Identify some places where the moral teachings of Jesus can be found.

6. In what ways do those teachings build upon and go beyond the Ten Commandments?

Early Development of the Sacrament

conscience the human ability to judge what is right and wrong, sometimes thought of as the voice of reason or the voice of God

repentance also called conversion or internal penance; changing one's thoughts, feelings, and behavior away from sin; turning one's life around, at least with regard to the parts of it that are sinful

As we have seen, this sacrament is an opportunity for reconciliation: reconciliation with God, and reconciliation with our own **conscience.** But it is also meant to be a chance for reconciliation with others. Another glance back at history will show why this is so.

When Christians were still being persecuted in the Roman Empire, some would inevitably give in under pressure and renounce their faith in Christ. The most intense persecutions never lasted more than a few years, however, and when the worst threat was over, some of those who had left the Church wanted to be readmitted. Remembering the example of Jesus, creative bishops devised a process known as "public **repentance.**" (*Repentance* is another word from the same root as the word *penance*, meaning conversion.) It gave people who really wanted to reconvert a chance to do so.

Later, when being a Christian was no longer illegal, the Church retained this process and used it for the moral reconversion of public sinners. People who had done things that made it impossible for them to live in the community experienced a second conversion (Baptism being the first). They were given a chance to rejoin the faith community by publicly demonstrating that they had truly undergone a change of heart and had reformed their lives.

Public repentance was a challenge in two ways. It challenged those who had not been faithful to the Christian way of life to seek and work for reconciliation with the faith community. But it also challenged the faithful in the Church community to forgive and be reconciled with people who had once turned their back on the community. This wasn't easy, especially when the faithful had lost friends and family during the persecution, or when the sinner had done something irreparable such as killing someone or destroying a marriage. It wasn't easy, but it was done. It was done because the bishops remembered the example of Jesus and his command to forgive one another as often as it takes to achieve reconciliation:

> *Then Peter came and said to him, "Lord, if another member of the church sins against me, how often should I forgive? As many as seven times?" Jesus answered, "Not seven times, but, I tell you, seventy-seven times."*

Matthew 18:21–22

DisCuSsioN

The practice of liturgical Reconciliation arose in the early Church when people who had renounced Christ and left the Church wanted to return. In a small group, discuss the following questions:

1. If this happened during a fierce persecution in which you had been tortured or had all your property confiscated because you were a Christian, how would you feel toward someone who had avoided persecution by giving up his or her faith and who now wanted to get back into the Christian community?

2. If you were the local bishop, would you make it easy or difficult for such a person to return? Why?

3. What rules would you establish for the reconciliation of such public sinners?

Stages of Moral Development

ethical, moral
pertaining to the goodness
or badness of human acts

In thinking about right and wrong, all of us pass through several phases or stages. Psychologists call this the development of **ethical** judgment, or **moral** development.

At the beginning, when we are infants and just beginning to use our mind, we judge what is right and wrong according to our feelings. If it feels good it is right, in other words, and if it feels bad it is wrong.

As our mental world expands in childhood, we develop a couple of variations of our ability to judge according to feelings.

The first can be called "reward and punishment" morality: If we do something for which we get rewarded (good feelings), we conclude that it is right, and if we do something for which we get punished (bad feelings), we conclude that it is wrong. Even before we learn to talk, we learn that what is "right" is what makes grown-ups smile, and what is "wrong" is what they yell at us or punish us for doing. Some people never move beyond this stage of moral development and grow up thinking anything is okay if they don't get caught.

Closely related to this is "approval and disapproval" morality, which leads us to do some things and avoid others according to whether we believe an action will be approved of or frowned on by others, especially the adults and children with whom we have a close relationship. Little children naturally do this, but kids in gangs and even adults in organized crime "families" seem to focus on this type of moral thinking.

We never lose our ability to base moral judgments on feelings, but in childhood our mental ability expands to include thinking and reasoning. One way we do this is by observing whether we and others are being treated equally and fairly. If everyone gets the same treatment, that's good. If someone gets more than others or less than others, that's unfair and bad. We can call this "fairness" morality. Adults appeal to this type of moral reasoning when they are negotiating over contracts.

What stage of morality is dominant in the decision making of this young woman?

Another way we learn to think morally is in terms of rules and laws. Once we become aware that there are certain standards against which individual actions can be judged (for example, the rules of a game, school regulations, and laws in society), we become able to make moral judgments not according to what we feel but according to what the law says is right. We can call this "law and order" morality. Again, we can think of people who believe that if something is not illegal, it's not immoral.

In our teen years and early twenties, we become capable of even more complex moral reasoning, looking beyond the simple application of law and order to the moral values and ethical principles on which rules and laws are based. Usually we simply accept the values that we find in the world around us, but some of us go beyond that and truly internalize them, making them our own principles of behavior. We can call this "values and principles" morality. Very often people who act according to their principles are admired and respected, even if they are not always imitated.

If moral development is a fact of human psychology, then one of the reasons why people make different moral judgments becomes very clear: they are judging people's (or their own) behavior from different perspectives—the different types of morality just described. In a sense society as a whole has also evolved through the stages of moral development, although with a great deal of backsliding. As a result, people today appeal more to values and principles than they did centuries ago, even if they do not always live up to what they say.

What also becomes clear is that the morality that we find in the Scriptures and in the Christian tradition gets interpreted in different ways by different people, depending on the type of moral judgment they are using. This is why some people look at the Ten Commandments, for example, in terms of reward (heaven) and punishment (hell), while others look at them as rules for judging people's actions, and still others regard them as expressions of moral values and principles.

Christian morality—the morality proposed by Jesus for his followers—is ultimately a matter of values and principles. We realize this today more than we did in the past, and this is one reason why our understanding and experience of the Sacrament of Reconciliation is changing.

When society generally thought of morality in terms of law and order, in terms of rules and regulations, going to confession was mostly a matter of admitting which rules we had broken and promising not to break them again. Today, as we increasingly think of morality in terms of the values and principles proposed in the Scriptures, participating in the sacrament becomes not simply an occasion to confess sins and shortcomings. It also becomes an opportunity to clarify our values and internalize the principles of Christian living.

Activity

After learning about moral development, read the story of the first humans in Genesis 3. In an essay analyze the story from the perspective of different types of moral judgment. That is, how might the story be interpreted in terms of reward and punishment morality, approval and disapproval morality, fairness morality, law and order morality, and values and principles morality?

Discussion

After learning about moral development in this chapter, break into small groups and brainstorm examples of each of the types of morality described. Remember that once we learn a certain kind of morality, we can always practice it, no matter how old we are. Give examples from home life, school life, or television shows about how people exhibit different types of moral judgment. What examples can you give of people who seem to live according to their own ethical principles?

Sin *in Scripture is described as "missing the mark."*

Reconversion Implies Reconciliation

Both the early practice of public repentance and the later practice of monastic confession show clearly that reconversion implies reconciliation, not only with God and with our own conscience, but also with the Church and with anyone with whom we are emotionally at odds. A look within our own lives also shows why this has to be so.

At the root of every sin, there is only one fault: the absence of love. This isn't love in the sense of a warm feeling, but love in the New Testament sense of *agape*, which means "active caring." Whether we sin by hate or apathy, we are not caring for others. Whether we sin by stealing or not sharing, we are not caring for their welfare. When we sin, we are neither caring nor concerned that we are not caring.

The New Testament word for sin is *hamartia:* missing the mark, the absence of something that should be there. What should be in our hearts and lives always, if we claim to be followers of Jesus, is caring love. That is what he taught, and that is what he did. That is what he died for, and that is what he made possible by his resurrection. Without love in the sense of active caring, we may be many things, but we are missing the one thing that we ought to be. Paul tells us this in no uncertain terms:

> *If I speak in tongues of mortals and of angels, but do not have love, I am a noisy gong or a clashing cymbal. And if I have prophetic powers, and understand all mysteries and all knowledge, and if I have all faith, so as to remove mountains, but do not have love, I am nothing. If I give away all my possessions, and if I hand over my body so that I may boast, but have not love, I gain nothing.*
>
> 1 Corinthians 13:1–3

May the Lord guide your hearts in the way of his love. . . .

—*Rite of Penance, #58.*

Love is the essential ingredient in the Christian moral life. When we are not loving, we are missing something crucial. When we are not loving, there is only one way back: through reconversion. And reconversion always implies reconciliation. It implies reconciliation with ourselves: caring about ourselves enough to let go of our stubbornness and pride. Reconciliation also helps us let go of our guilt about what we may or may not have done in the past. Reconversion implies reconciliation with others: caring about them enough to let go of our self-image and our self-interest to forgive and ask forgiveness, and then to do what they need us to do for them. Reconversion implies reconciliation with the Church, our faith community.

Authentic Christian life is a converted life. This converted life begins with an interior repentance and a new heart made contrite by the grace of God. It is a life converted to loving with God's love, *agape.* It is the life that Jesus lived, and the life that he still lives in us when we love and care for one another.

True Christian community is a reconciling community, a community dedicated to reuniting people with God, and to reuniting people with one another. The Sacrament of Reconciliation is one important way that reunion is available in our community, but it is not the only way. Reconversion and reconciliation need to go on all the time in our lives.

WHAT THE CATECHISM SAYS

The Catechism summarizes the effects of the Sacrament of Reconciliation along these lines:

- Reconciliation with God
- Grace
- Reconciliation with the Church
- Remission of the eternal punishment (hell) incurred by unrepented mortal sins
- Remission, at least in part, of temporal punishments (painful consequences and purgatory) (Indulgences are one way to obtain remission of all or some of the temporal punishment due to sin.)
- A peaceful conscience
- An increase of spiritual strength to live as a Christian

See the *Catechism of the Catholic Church, #1496.*

The good news is that it can. The very first words that Jesus spoke in his public ministry were, "The time of waiting is over! God's reign is here! Turn around and believe the good news!" (see Mark 1:15). Turn around, repent, convert, change—they all mean the same thing. The good news proclaimed by Jesus is that anyone can turn around and find God if we're only willing to change.

✝ Activities

1. Read the following Scripture passages and write an essay explaining what the apostle James says is needed to be a morally good Christian.

   James 1:26–27
   James 2:8–13
   James 2:14–17

2. Read the *Catechism of the Catholic Church*, #s 1471–1473, explain what an indulgence is, and give examples of what must be done to obtain an indulgence.

inteRview

With the advice and direction of your teacher, talk with someone who is in a Twelve-Step program (Alcoholics Anonymous, Narcotics Anonymous, and so on) and admits that he or she had to go through an experience of conversion in order to get his or her life back in order. Listen to that person's story and learn what you can about the process of conversion. Report to your teacher or your class about what you have learned, relating it to what is said in this book and the Catechism about the process of conversion.

DisCussioN

In the large group, discuss the following questions:

1. Before reading this chapter what was your understanding of sin?

2. In what ways, if any, is your understanding of sin different as a result of having read this chapter?

3. The Catechism (#s 1468–1469) says that the Sacrament of Penance brings about reconciliation with God and with the Church.

   • What are some ways that this is always true?
   • What are some circumstances in which it might not be true?

4. The Church is called to be a reconciling community.

   • In what ways does the Church help bring about reconciliation between people?
   • How might the Church be more actively engaged in reconciliation between people?

Review Questions

1. What was the purpose of the process of public repentance, an early form of the Sacrament of Reconciliation, in the early Church?

2. What is moral development? Explain some of its stages.

3. Why is love (in the sense of active caring) the essential ingredient in the Christian moral life?

Summary

The sacrament called Penance or Reconciliation has undergone many changes, some of them rather recent. Catholics too are different from the way they were a few generations ago: they are generally more educated and more familiar with the Scriptures, and they live with a Church and liturgy radically changed by Vatican II. All these changes can make the Sacrament of Reconciliation harder to understand and appreciate.

Many people think of Christian living as obeying a set of rules, such as the Ten Commandments, and not breaking any laws. This is certainly a minimum that every decent person should live up to, but people don't have to be Christians in order to be law-abiding citizens. It's quite possible to treat people unfairly or unjustly without breaking any laws. Jesus invited his listeners to follow him, to be like him, in the way he cared about and cared for people. Even when we try to follow him and ask for the strength to be like him, we sometimes stumble and fall.

If we look at Christian living in terms of living with God's Spirit within us, however, we can approach the Sacrament of Reconciliation as an opportunity for reconversion. Recognizing that we sometimes "get off track" or "miss the mark" in our Christian walk, Reconciliation gives us the chance to assess where we are and recommit ourselves to going where Jesus invites us to go.

Two others also, who were criminals, were led away to be put to death with [Jesus]. When they came to the place that is called The Skull, they crucified Jesus there with the criminals, one on his right and one on his left. Then Jesus said, "Father, forgive them; for they do not know what they are doing."

LUKE 23:32–34

Prayer

Deliver us, Father, from every evil
as we unite ourselves through penance
with the saving passion of your Son.
Grant us a share
in the joy of the resurrection of Jesus
who is Lord for ever and ever.
Amen.

RITE OF PENANCE, #19.

Scripture

[Jesus] left Galilee and went to the region of Judea beyond the Jordan. Large crowds followed him, and he cured them there.

MATTHEW 19:1–2

Prayer

Praise to you, God, the almighty Father.

You sent your Son to live among us

and bring us salvation.

All: Blessed be God who heals us in Christ.

Praise to you, God, the only-begotten Son.

You humbled yourself to share in our humanity

and you heal our infirmities.

All: Blessed be God who heals us in Christ.

Praise to you, God, the Holy Spirit.

Your unfailing power gives us strength

in our bodily weakness.

All: Blessed be God who heals us in Christ.

ANOINTING OUTSIDE OF MASS, #123.

8

Anointing of the Sick: Healing by God's Life

CHAPTER OVERVIEW

The Experience of Illness

Agape Gives Life

How It Might Have Been in the Second Century

Extreme Unction

Anointing of the Sick

Communal Anointing

Celebration of Salvation

The Church's Rituals After Death

Summary

The Experience of Illness

Have you ever been so sick you were forced to stay in bed? Actually welcomed the bed? Have you ever been down with a cold, in bed with the flu, or bandaged up with a cut or bruise? What did it feel like to be ill, to really not be yourself? Was it tiring? Frustrating? Scary? How did you feel when you were flat on your back and "out of it"? Did you feel you would never get well? Did you feel isolated? Alone?

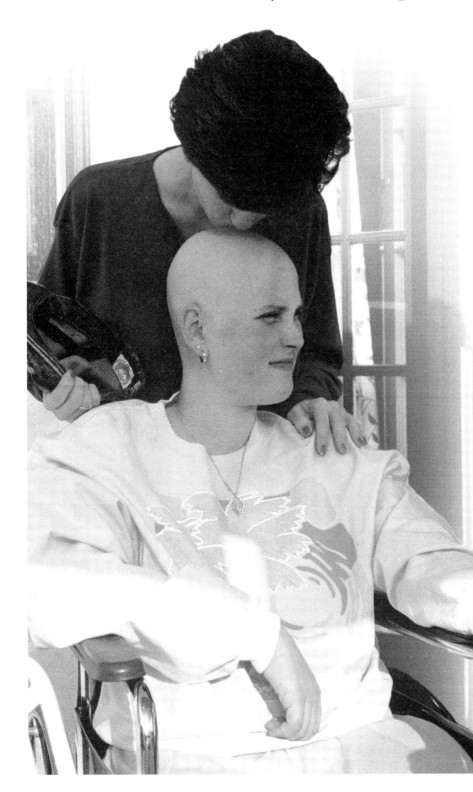

Wasn't it good to have someone around, taking care of you—someone who brought you your medicine or some food when you could bear to look at food? Remember Mom's chicken soup or Grandma's herbal tea, the loving hand on your head, feeling the fever, the concerned hand that held your wrist and took your pulse, the gentle hand that washed you, the strong hand that helped you out of bed and held you steady?

When we are sick, we are never just physically sick. It's not just our body that is sick, but we who are sick. Our head may be hot, our body aching, our leg hurting. But at the same time we are feeling out of sorts, our emotions are irritable, our spirit is sagging. We are always both physically and spiritually sick whenever there is something wrong with our body. We are a whole person, and the whole of us is sick, body and spirit. In serious illness we may be forced to face our fear of death and the loss of those we love.

Serious illness can be a crisis of faith or an opportunity for great growth.

When someone cares for us in our illness and ministers to our physical needs, they also touch something deeper in us. Even though our temperature hasn't gone down, something inside of us feels refreshed. Even though our body is aching, somewhere inside we have been soothed. Even though we still aren't well, somehow we feel better when someone cares for us and touches us with his or her presence.

Moments like those, so common in our lives, could be called **natural sacraments.** They are natural signs of a love that is like God's love. God's love is self-giving, caring, and healing. God's love is unconditional, not expecting anything in return. When we are sick and people give of themselves, even if we can't give anything back to them, we have a natural experience of what God's love is like.

It's no wonder, then, that the Church found a sacrament in this natural moment of grace. Whenever we are cared for and lovingly touched, we are also touched within by love—not any love, but that special, selfless, completely giving love: *agape.*

natural sacrament a natural sign of God, such as human caring being a sign of the way God cares for us

Journal

Think about a time when you were really sick or hurt. Write about the experience, and perhaps talk about it with someone.

1. What was it that had you down? How did you hurt?

2. How long did the illness last or the recovery take?

3. How did you feel about being "out of it"?

4. What helped you feel better?

Discussion

1. In the large group, discuss the questions in the first two paragraphs of this section, "The Experience of Illness."

2. Continue with these questions:
   - When you are feeling sad, depressed, lonely, sick, or hurt, what things help you feel better? (Maybe it's listening to music, engaging in some physical exercise, talking with a friend, getting away from it all, or doing something else.)
   - How does this help you get connected with what you need in order to feel better?

Research

1. Using the library or the Internet, find out what you can about spiritual healing. How can you separate what is probably genuine from what is probably phony? Report on your findings.

2. Using the library or the Internet, investigate Lourdes, Fatima, Medjugorje, and other places where Catholics pray for and receive healing. Report on your findings.

"Healing the Lame in the Temple" by James J. Tissot.

Agape Gives Life

salvation being saved from evil, whether physical or spiritual; in Christian terms, being saved from sin and evil through the power of the redemptive death and resurrection of Jesus

miracle an event, such as an unexpected cure or a rapid healing, that is attributed to God's power and that arouses admiration and wonder

God's love is the same as God's life. In a way, the only thing God ever does is love. And when God's love goes out to others, it gives life. God loved the world into creation. God's love keeps the universe in existence. God's love makes light out of darkness and turns death into life. God's love created each human person, body and spirit, in the divine image and likeness. Whenever we are touched by *agape*, we are touched by God's life.

The people who were touched by Jesus felt his love, and they felt God's life flooding into them. They were healed; they were made healthy. They were saved from the evil that was plaguing them. The word **salvation,** which means being saved, comes from the Latin word *salus*, which means health. The people who were healed by Jesus felt God's salvation in a very tangible way. Their healings were signs of the kingdom of God.

The only stories that the New Testament gives us about Jesus healing people are spectacular success stories. They are **miracles** in the root meaning of the word, *mirare,* to admire or marvel at. Certainly not all Jesus' miracles were healing miracles, but these are the most frequently mentioned. It's very likely too that there are hundreds of untold stories that never made it into the Bible, stories about Jesus touching people with love and about their feeling better, even though they were not spectacularly healed. God's love always gives life, even when it does not produce a miracle.

The early followers of Jesus understood the healing power of a loving touch. And they understood the power of God present in Jesus. The apostle James wrote to his community:

Are any among you sick? They should call for the elders of the church and have them pray over them, anointing them with oil in the name of the Lord. The prayer of faith will save the sick, and the Lord will raise them up; and anyone who has committed sins will be forgiven.

James 5:14–15

So the early Christians followed this advice and the example of Jesus, the one who healed. When someone in the community was sick, they came together and laid their hands on the person and prayed over him or her. They asked God to pour his life into the sick person and heal him or her. Sometimes they poured oil on the sick person to symbolize the outpouring of God's love on that person. In their own way, they were doing what Jesus had done, being sacraments of God's salvation to all who needed to be healed by God's life.

Journal

What do you think about the idea that God's life is love and the idea that God's love gives life? Explain the reasons behind your responses.

Discussion

Read one of the Gospel stories about Jesus healing someone (for example, Matthew 9:2–8, Mark 9:14–28, Luke 18:35–43). In a small group, discuss the following questions. Summarize the reading and your discussion, and report to the large group.

1. Do you think this actually happened the way it has been passed on to us? Why or why not?
2. What do you think the story teaches us?

Discussion

In the large group, discuss the following questions:

1. Have you ever been to a Catholic charismatic prayer service in which people were prayed over for healing, or a Pentecostal church service in which people asked for healing? Describe your experience.
2. What was and is your reaction to that experience?

Research

Write an essay in response to one of the following.

1. Look in the Gospels according to Matthew, Mark, Luke, and John for stories about Jesus healing people.
   - Which Gospel has the most healing stories and which the least?
   - Why do you think one writer put more emphasis on healing, while another put less emphasis on it?
2. Find the same healing story in two or more Gospels. (Use the cross-references to locate the parallel texts.)
   - How are the stories similar?
   - How are they different?
   - Why do you think the evangelists told the same story differently?

How It Might Have Been in the Second Century

For many centuries the touching and anointing of the sick for healing was a very informal sacrament among Christians. People did it for one another, the way that people who care for one another naturally do.

The joy of being a father quickly turned to anxiety when Dominic returned from the fields and saw the worried look on the midwife's face. His wife lay burning with fever on the cot where she had delivered their first son only days before.

"Why God allows this to happen I'll never understand," said the old woman when she had told him about the infection. "So many times I've seen women fall ill shortly after childbirth. Sometimes the little one has to grow up without. . . ." She could not bear to finish the sentence. "Maybe it's to test our faith."

"Is there nothing we can do?" the young man asked, wringing his hands.

"What can be done is being done," the midwife assured him. "Women from the community have been with Matilda all day. They take turns washing her with cool water, they anoint the inflamed area with holy oil, and they pray for deliverance from the evil spirit that has caused this."

Even as she spoke, other Christians arrived at the doorway of the room this little family called home. Some brought fresh baked bread and smoked fish for their neighbor's supper, but most just came to be with him in his hour of need. After a while, the elders arrived to lead the community in prayer.

"The letter from the apostle James recommends that we lay our hands on the sick while we pray," said the chief elder. Dominic welcomed them inside, and the cot was moved to the center of the floor so that as many as possible could touch Matilda while they asked the Lord to heal her.

Some prayed silently, while others recalled stories of how Jesus had cured many people who were sick and even brought the dead back to life. Dominic was wishing that Jesus could come again to work a miracle, when one of the elders reminded everyone of Jesus' words, "For where two or three are gathered in my name, I am there among them" (Matthew 18:20).

When all had departed, the young husband wondered in the silent darkness whether a miracle would really happen. The baby was sleeping peacefully, and his beloved wife seemed to be breathing easier. Sitting on the floor beside the cot, he touched Matilda's forehead and felt for the fever. It seemed to have gone down, but he could not be sure.

"Have faith," he said quietly, "Have faith, and the sickness will leave." He was not sure whether he was saying this to himself or to his wife beside him. He knew only that somehow, through the church that had come to minister to her that evening, Jesus had touched her.

 **Activity**

Write a poem or a song about being healed in response to prayer. Share your creation with the class and explain as needed.

Review Questions

1. What is meant by the phrase *natural sacraments?*

2. What is salvation?

3. What is a miracle?

4. What does the Scripture from James say about caring for those in the Christian community who are ill?

Extreme Unction

It was not until about the ninth century that the Church created a more formal liturgical sacrament of anointing. This Rite of Unction, as it was called, was fairly elaborate, and it could be done only in a church. All too often people did not ask for this church anointing until they were so sick that they were on the verge of dying. And all too often the people who were given the Sacrament of Unction died shortly afterward.

The prayers in this liturgical rite originally asked for God's healing and salvation, similar to the prayers in the earlier, less formal sacrament. However, when priests saw that the prayers for physical healing were not usually answered, they tended to drop these and just said the words that asked for salvation. Under the circumstances, then, the sacrament seemed to be only for salvation after death. Even the name that was attached to this sacrament reflected this: **Extreme Unction,** meaning "last anointing with oil."

In time, the rite was simplified so that it could be performed at the bedside or wherever the dying person happened to be—on a battlefield, in a hospital, or at the scene of an accident, for example. Even though this change made the sacrament more available to people, it was still associated with approaching death. It was not the sign of physical as well as spiritual healing that it had been originally.

This simplification of the rite of anointing also did not restore something that had been very important at the beginning of this sacrament, the loving touch of those who cared for the person who was dying. The priest performed the rite by himself, and he hardly touched the person except to put a dab of oil on various parts of the body. If others were present, they were only onlookers. They did not lay their own hands on the sick person and pray for him or her.

Extreme Unction
the former name for the Sacrament of the Anointing of the Sick, emphasizing the last anointing before death

"Cardinal Chigi Caring for Plague Victims," eighteenth century.

During the Middle Ages, experiences such as the bubonic plague forced many people, for their own safety, to avoid even the ordinary care of those who were sick. Known as the Black Death, this infectious disease caused the death of at least one-fourth of the population of Europe during the 1300s. The swiftness with which the plague killed people caused panic and hysterical fear of the dreadful process of dying for those who suffered the plague. Bodies were abandoned and burned.

The plague, combined with a general lack of medical knowledge, led to a fatalistic attitude toward illness. The practice of Extreme Unction being performed only when people were on their deathbeds only added to the pessimistic approach to sickness and dying. Certainly, the sacrament helped people face death with faith, and this spiritual healing was very important. But it did little to help people experience the physical healing that Jesus promised through his Church.

Discussion

Think about the possibility of a miraculous cure (sometimes also called *faith healing*). In the large group, discuss the following questions:

1. Is there anything to it? Is it all in the mind?

2. What does it prove?

3. What doesn't it prove?

Research

Prepare and present a report on one of the following topics.

1. Using the library or the Internet, read stories about Catholic saints who had the gift of healing.

2. Find some photographs of paintings about Jesus healing people. Look at the paintings carefully. What do you think the artists were saying about Jesus, about people, about illness, about God, about healing power? How did the time period in which the painting was made influence the artist?

3. Find out more about the bubonic plague and the response of individuals, governments, and the Church to this great challenge.

Anointing of the Sick

Twentieth-century scholarly research into the early history of the sacrament suggested that another change was needed, a change that would more clearly highlight the original meaning and purpose of the sacrament. At the Second Vatican Council, the sacrament's name was officially changed to **Anointing of the Sick,** and after the Council the rite was revised to reflect this original outlook.

The council document on the Church explained the sacrament in this way:

> *By the sacred anointing of the sick and the prayer of her priests, the whole Church commends those who are ill to the suffering and glorified Lord, asking that He may lighten their suffering and save them (cf. Jas. 5:14–16). She exhorts them, moreover, to contribute to the welfare of the whole People of God by associating themselves freely with the passion and death of Christ (cf. Rom. 8:17; Col. 1:24; 2 Tim. 2:11–12; 1 Pet. 4:13).*

The Documents of Vatican II,
"Dogmatic Constitution on the Church," #11.

The first thing this statement does is return us to an understanding of the sacrament as one of healing. And then it reminds us that Christ himself experienced the human condition, including suffering and death. Although Jesus may not have experienced every pain and loss that we ourselves feel, we can be sure that he felt suffering as keenly as we do. In this sacrament, we are united with Christ and with his death; we participate in the Paschal mystery.

Today the sacrament can be performed in a number of different settings, depending on the needs of the people who request it. Someone who is in danger of death can still, to be sure, ask to be anointed. The danger does not have to be so imminent, however, that the person is breathing his or her last gasps. Anyone who is seriously injured, or critically ill, or about to undergo an operation can ask to be anointed and prayed over. But people who are chronically ill with a sickness that could at any time become fatal, such as cancer, can also ask for the Anointing of the Sick. Each time a Christian is seriously ill, he or she may receive the Anointing of the Sick. The person may also be anointed again if an illness becomes worse. The sacrament is for all these people.

Anointing of the Sick
the Sacrament of Healing for those who are seriously ill or in danger of death due to sickness or old age, consisting of anointing with oil, imposition of hands, and prayers for physical and spiritual healing and the forgiveness of sins

Through this holy anointing
    may the Lord in his love
    and mercy help you
with the grace of the Holy
    Spirit.
Amen.

—Anointing of the Sick, #124.

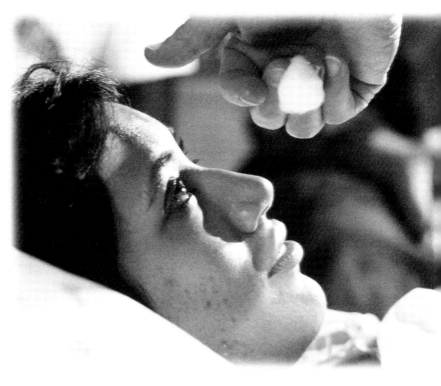

In situations like this, there may be some hope for a miraculous recovery, but the more usual expectation is for spiritual healing. And this healing is reflected in the sacramental encounter with the living God. People who are dying need to be assured that they are not alone in this final passage of their life. They want to hear again about the love of the God who is with them and waiting for them in the next life.

The Church distinguishes between the **Last Rites** and the Sacrament of Anointing. The Last Rites include the Sacraments of Reconciliation and Eucharist to help those who are dying experience God's forgiveness and closeness. (When Communion is given for the last time in a person's life, it is called *viaticum,* a Latin word for something to take "on the way with you.") The prayers and Scripture readings that can be selected for use in these circumstances speak of a hope and healing that are available from God, even when physical health is failing because of illness or age.

Even in situations like this, though, other people besides the priest can and should be present during the anointing and the giving of Communion. Their presence, their prayers, and their touch can intensify the sacramentality of the moment, speaking in their own way what the official rite says in a more formal fashion. All the more reason, then, for friends and family to be present when the priest is called to anoint someone who is seriously ill or injured, but not in immediate danger of dying. God's healing power that comes through them can be a strong assistance along with the grace that comes through the anointing by the priest. It can work with the grace of the sacrament and intensify it.

The prayers and Scripture readings that can be chosen for the Rite of Anointing in circumstances such as these can likewise give voice to the hope not just for spiritual healing but for physical recovery. Hearing of the ways that Jesus cured many who were blind and deaf and lame can give assurance that the Lord's willingness and power to heal are just as present now as they were two thousand years ago. Both the words of salvation and the action of anointing can be the channel through which God's healing grace, God's life and love, can flow.

Last Rites the Sacraments of Reconciliation, Eucharist (*viaticum*), and the Anointing of the Sick, when administered to someone who is dying

viaticum a traditional name for Communion that is given to a dying person, in the sense of "food for the journey" from this life to the next

The oil of the sick is one of these oils blessed during Holy Week.

Chapter Eight

After being blessed by the bishop, the oils are taken to each parish to be used in sacramental celebrations throughout the year.

holy oils oils used in the sacraments; chrism, the oil of catechumens, and the oil of the sick

The most remarkably different setting for the Anointing of the Sick, however, is when it is done for many people at the same time. Whether in a hospital or care center, or in a parish church, the sacrament can be celebrated wherever people are ill enough that they feel a need to be touched by God's grace in a special way. The rite today includes a communal Anointing of the Sick to celebrate together the healing love of God.

The bishop blesses the **holy oils** at the Chrism Mass during Holy Week. The holy oils include chrism, the oil of catechumens, and the oil of the sick. The Chrism Mass and blessing usually takes place at the cathedral on Holy Thursday, with most of the priests of the diocese in attendance. Representatives from all the parishes of a diocese take a small quantity of the oils back to their parishes, where they are kept in a special place in the church.

> ### WHAT THE CATECHISM SAYS
>
> Only priests are allowed to administer the Anointing of the Sick. They usually use oil that is blessed by the bishop, although priests may also bless the holy oils.
>
> See the *Catechism of the Catholic Church*, #1530.

DISCUSSION

In a small group, discuss the following questions:

1. Have you ever received the Anointing of the Sick?
   - What were the circumstances?
   - How did it feel?
   - What are your thoughts about that experience now?

2. Were you ever present when somebody you knew received the Anointing of the Sick?
   - What were the circumstances?
   - What happened?
   - What do you think about it?

Anointing of the Sick: Healing by God's Life

 **Activities**

1. Interview a priest about his experiences administering the Anointing of the Sick. Later, think and write about, or discuss, what you learned.

2. Create a short skit or mime about Jesus healing someone, and prepare a few discussion questions related to the story. Then present the skit or mime for the class and lead a discussion on it.

3. Make a drawing or sculpture about Jesus healing someone. Show your piece to the class, and explain what you were trying to say.

"Christ Healing the Paralytic at the Pool of Bethesda" by Bartolome Esteban Murillo, late 1600s.

interview

One of the Church's rules for this sacrament is that it can be administered only by a priest or bishop. At the same time, the number of priests in this country has declined significantly. In addition, many people admitted to a hospital do not stay long enough for the parish priest or chaplain priest to visit them. Talk with a Catholic pastoral minister in a hospital or care center (one who is not a priest) and find out how he or she helps people feel the loving presence and healing power of God. Share with the class what you learn.

Review Questions

1. What was the Rite of Unction?

2. What effect did the practice of Extreme Unction have on people's attitude toward the sacrament?

3. How does the name *Anointing of the Sick* change the perception of the sacrament from the name *Extreme Unction?*

4. What are the Last Rites?

5. What is *viaticum?*

6. Who may preside at the Anointing of the Sick?

7. What are holy oils?

Communal Anointing

At a communal anointing, people gather to thank God for the healing they have already received as well as to ask for further healing in their lives. The rite celebrates God's healing power that is always with us, whether we notice it or not. The sacrament is a chance to remember how God always loves us, how he has healed us in the past, and how he can touch our lives with health where we most need it.

Very often a communal Anointing is celebrated in a Mass for Healing. The readings and the homily speak to us of God's desire and power to heal us spiritually and physically. The presence of a supporting community reminds us that God's presence is most often felt in the people who love us and the care they give to us. The spirit of life that flows through such a community is the Spirit of God who animates the Church and makes it God's instrument of salvation in the world.

Presence and touch are the two most natural signs or sacraments of healing. In the liturgical Sacrament of the Anointing of the Sick, the presence of God's people symbolizes the presence of God, and their touch symbolizes God's healing touch. The rite calls for the priest, in silence, to lay his hands on, to touch, those who desire healing. He prays over them and anoints them with oil on their foreheads and hands. In the Eastern Rites, other parts of the body are also anointed. In a group setting, others too can touch those who are sick and add their personal prayers.

Anointing with holy oil is the central symbol in this sacrament because for many centuries olive oil or vegetable oil was one of the few healing agents known to everybody. Even today we can use oil to soothe burns and bruises; many medical creams actually have an oil base. Oil penetrates beneath the skin and carries healing to the source of our discomfort. In the same way, God's healing power does not just touch the surface of our lives but penetrates within us to heal us where we are hurting. At the time of the anointing, the priest prays,

> *Through this holy anointing*
> *may the Lord in his love and mercy help you*
> *with the grace of the Holy Spirit.*
> *May the Lord who frees you from sin*
> *save you and raise you up.*

RITE OF ANOINTING OF THE SICK, #124.

The presence of the community at the Anointing of the Sick reminds those who are ill of the community's prayers and support.

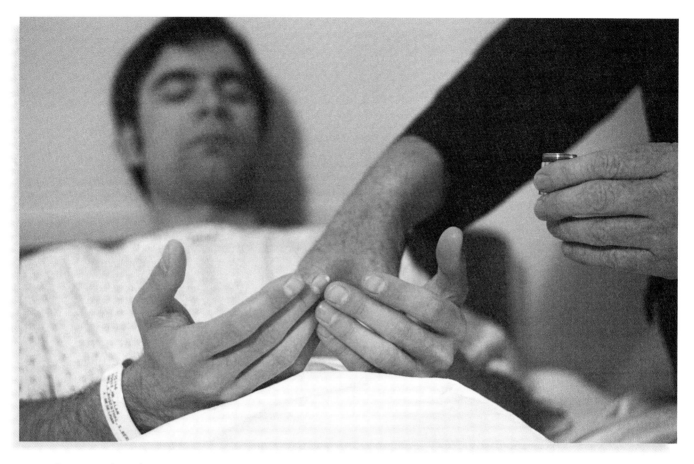

The healing that touches us in the sacrament may be physical, but it is always spiritual. That is, the symbolism of the sacrament always speaks to our mind and heart and enables us to know and feel how much God loves us and wants us to be well. Sometimes that spiritual experience becomes an experience of physical healing as well, and then we have all the more reason to rejoice that what we believe is real and true.

Depending upont the culture and traditions of the place, . . . the priest may also anoint additional parts of the body, for example, the areas of pain or injury.

—*Anointing of the Sick, #124.*

WHAT THE CATECHISM SAYS

The central parts of the sacrament are the laying on of hands and the anointing with oil with the priest's liturgical prayer. In the Roman or Latin Rite, the forehead and hands are anointed. In the Eastern Rites, other parts of the body are also anointed.

See the *Catechism of the Catholic Church*, #1531.

 ## Activity

Find a parish or health care facility where a communal Anointing of the Sick is going to be held. Attend the sacramental celebration. Talk with people before and after the anointing service. Think about what you saw and heard; then write or talk about it.

Celebration of Salvation

Then Peter, filled with the Holy Spirit, said to them, "Rulers of the people and elders, if we are questioned today because of a good deed done to someone who was sick and are asked how this man has been healed, let it be known to all of you, and to all the people of Israel, that this man is standing before you in good health by the name of Jesus Christ of Nazareth, whom you crucified, whom God raised from the dead. This Jesus is

> *'the stone that was rejected by you, the builders;*
> *it has become the cornerstone.'*

There is salvation in no one else, for there is no other name under heaven given among mortals by which we must be saved."

Acts 4:8–12

The first purpose of the Anointing of the Sick is not direct and permanent healing. It is not a magic formula for curing all that ails us. The purpose of this sacrament, as of all the sacraments, is celebration—the celebration of God's life in some special way. In the Anointing of the Sick, we rejoice in how God always desires our salvation and works to heal us, even when we are not aware of it. Sometimes, by heightening our awareness of God's saving power in us, we become more able to receive the healing grace that God is always offering us.

Whenever we are healed by God or remember how God has healed us in the past, we also learn more deeply what divine life is all about. God's life is the source of all physical and spiritual growth, the energy of all health and holiness, the power of life itself.

In this liturgical sacrament, we celebrate the healing power of God's life. But God's healing power is not just for the Church, and it is not just for liturgies. The good news is that it is for everyone, and it is for every day. Jesus knew this, and so he was able to be a living sacrament of God's salvation. If we know this and act on it, we too can be living sacraments for others. We can be the reason they and we would want to celebrate God's healing power liturgically, in the Anointing of the Sick.

DiSCUSSioN

In the large group, discuss the following questions:

1. What does salvation mean to you?
2. What is your reaction to the understanding of salvation presented in this chapter?

 ## Activity

With help from your teacher or another adult, design a prayer service during which people ask for the healing of some physical or emotional hurt. Make sure your service includes a way for these people to be touched (such as on the head, shoulder, the injured spot) by one or more of those who are praying for them. Afterward, discuss the experience.

The Church's Rituals After Death

Eventually, everyone dies. Sometimes people die young, with their deaths being unexpected. Sometimes they die when they are elderly or after a long illness. Either way death comes, we need to adjust mentally and emotionally to a departure and loss. This period of adjustment is known as the **grieving process.** Every culture and religion offers rituals to help people acknowledge their loss, accept the absence of their loved one, and affirm their beliefs about life and death. Christianity is no different.

The Catholic Church's rituals after death are the **vigil** for the deceased, the funeral liturgy, and the rite of committal. Similar to the natural sacraments discussed earlier, these are sacraments in a broad sense—the traditional word for them is *sacramentals.* That is, they are symbols that remind us and help us to get in touch with deeper meanings and spiritual realities.

The vigil for the deceased is a prayer service led by a priest or other pastoral leader. It normally takes place in the funeral home or mortuary, the place where the body is being kept during the **wake.** It is therefore sometimes called a wake service. This prayer service consists of prayers, Scripture readings, and symbolic actions such as making the Sign of the Cross over the deceased and sprinkling the casket with holy water.

During the wake, people come to pay their respects to the dead and offer their condolences to the family and close friends. Very often there is an informal or formal **eulogy** service, in which the deceased person is remembered and praised, perhaps with stories about the good things the person did and the effects he or she had on other people's lives. In the past, a common practice at Catholic wakes was the praying of the Rosary by all those present, and this is still sometimes done when families find it meaningful.

On the day of the funeral, the body of the deceased is brought into the church for a final ceremony of remembrance and farewell. It may be a funeral Mass celebrated by a priest, or it may be a Liturgy of the Word without a Eucharistic celebration, led by a deacon or lay person. In either case, the funeral liturgy contains Scripture readings and prayers that remind those assembled of the Paschal mystery, the mysterious passage through death to new life, exemplified by Christ's crucifixion and resurrection. Even while they are grieving a real loss, Christians are reminded that there is life after death and hope in the resurrection of the body at the second coming of Christ.

grieving process the normal process of psychologically adjusting to personal loss, involving denial, anger, bargaining, depression, and finally acceptance

vigil a gathering of people prior to an important event, such as the Easter Vigil on Holy Saturday or the vigil for the deceased prior to a funeral

wake the practice of "staying awake with the body" between the time of death and the time of burial

eulogy from the Greek, meaning "good word," hence, words of remembrance and praise for someone who has recently died

After the funeral liturgy, the body is taken from the church to the cemetery for burial. Family and friends again gather at the burial site, and the pastoral minister leads those who have assembled there in the rite of committal. This service commits or consigns the body to the ground, to wait in hope until the final resurrection from the dead. Mourners may be invited to touch the casket or to lay a flower on it in a gesture of farewell.

All three Catholic rituals—the vigil for the deceased, the funeral liturgy, and the rite of committal—recognize the sadness of loss while affirming the joy of God's life, life that continues even after death.

DisCuSsioN

In a small group, discuss the following questions:

1. Have you ever been to a wake? Describe what happened.

   - What were your feelings then?
   - What do you think about it now?

2. Have you ever been to a funeral? Describe what happened.

   - What were your feelings then?
   - What do you think about it now?

 ## Activities

Work in small groups to do one of the following activities:

1. Prepare a list of sacramentals that might be found in Catholic churches, homes, schools, and so on (for example, crucifix, statue).

2. Prepare a list of sacramental practices that are not sacraments in the strict sense (for example, making and praying the Sign of the Cross, praying the Rosary).

Research

1. Under the direction of your teacher, interview a funeral director on the process of planning and carrying out a funeral. Prepare a report to share with the class.

2. Use the Internet to explore the costs of funerals, caskets, cemetery plots, and so on. Why do you think funerals cost so much? What can be done to keep costs down?

 ## Activity

Search a parish hymnal for songs to use at wakes and funerals. Choose three of these hymns and summarize the message in them. Share with the class one of the hymns and its message.

CREMATION

cremation   the complete
incineration of a body,
turning it into ashes

atheist   someone who
denies the existence of God

The human body eventually turns into dust and ashes after death. In some religions and cultures (such as Hinduism in India) it is customary to hasten this process by burning it completely. This complete incineration of human remains is known as **cremation.**

For a variety of reasons, people in the United States today sometimes choose cremation rather than burial of the body. This, of course, needs to be done according to local government safety regulations. Ethically, they may be concerned about overpopulation and the overcrowding of cemeteries. Romantically, they may like the idea that their ashes will be scattered in some place that is special to them, although this is not approved by the Church. Economically, cremation is somewhat cheaper than burial. Also, when someone dies far from where he or she wants to be buried, it is less expensive to transport the ashes to the cemetery than to preserve and transport a body.

In the past, some **atheists** chose cremation to argue against the Christian belief in the resurrection of the body at the time of the last judgment. In a sense, they were defying God to find enough of their remains to raise them up on the last day! Because of these attacks by atheists, Catholics were for a time forbidden to choose cremation after death. Today this is no longer the case, and Catholics are once again free to choose cremation if they so desire. The Church asks only that the funeral or memorial service be held, followed by burial in a proper place, so that family and friends can begin the natural grieving process that follows upon the death of a loved one.

Burial of cremated remains is often in a mausoleum.

Discussion

In a small group, discuss the following questions:

1. What do you think about cremation?

2. Why might you prefer it—or not prefer it?

People who decide to donate their organs at the time of death have documentation and should make their wishes known to their families.

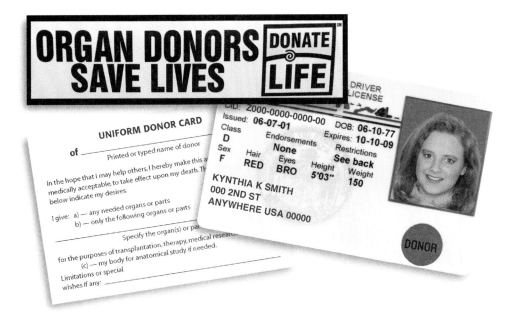

Research

Research the Catholic Church's teaching on organ donation (see, for example, the Catechism, #2296). Some people arrange to have their organs donated to people who are awaiting organ transplants. Usually they carry a card saying that, if they die suddenly in an accident, their body may be taken to a hospital for the removal of vital organs such as the liver and kidneys. After doing your research, respond in an essay to these questions:

1. What do you think about this practice?

2. Would you be willing to be an organ donor? Why or why not?

Research

Read each of the following Scripture passages. Explain how each passage relates to the topics of this chapter.

John 11:21–26a	Revelation 20:11–12	1 Corinthians 15:20–26
John 6:51	Romans 5:17–21	1 Corinthians 15:51–57
Matthew 25:31–46		

Review Questions

1. When and where is a communal celebration of the Anointing of the Sick usually celebrated?

2. What are the central parts of the Sacrament of the Anointing of the Sick?

3. How does this sacrament help us understand salvation?

4. What is the purpose of the Church's rituals after death?

5. What is the Catholic Church's teaching on cremation?

Summary

We all experience times when we need additional strength to go on. Sickness is one of those times, and Christians have always brought healing strength to those who were sick by caring for them and showing their care through prayer and touch. Following the example of Jesus, who communicated the healing power of God through words and actions, the Church celebrates the Sacrament of the Anointing of the Sick. This sacrament celebrates God's comforting and strengthening presence for those who are sick and dying.

In a special way those who are anointed come into deeper contact with the Paschal mystery, exemplified by the suffering, death, and resurrection of Jesus. Sickness brings to mind the fact of our mortality. When faced with death more directly, we may be tempted to give in to fear and despair; we may want to turn away from God. With the grace of the Anointing of the Sick, we can instead turn once more to God with the confidence of children who are loved and cared for by a compassionate parent. God is that loving, forgiving, compassionate Father who, even at the time of death, draws us ever closer to him. We can be good witnesses to that belief by the way we suffer in union with Christ.

The communal celebration of the Anointing of the Sick within the parish community reminds us that everyone is an important member of the community. Even those who are ill and dying build up the Body of Christ. In the rituals following death, we gather to celebrate God's love and mercy in the life and the sufferings and the death of a Christian who has contributed and is contributing to our well-being and that of the entire Church.

Scripture

Then Jesus called the twelve together and gave them power and authority over all demons and to cure diseases, and he sent them out to proclaim the kingdom of God and to heal.

LUKE 8:29

Prayer

All-powerful and ever-living God,
the lasting health of all who believe in you,
hear us as we ask your loving help for the sick;
restore their health,
that they may again offer joyful thanks in your Church.
Grant this through Christ our Lord.
Amen.

VISITS TO THE SICK, #60B.

Scripture

Then the LORD God said, "It is not good that the man should be alone; I will make him a helper as his partner." . . .
Then the man said,
"This at last is bone of my bones
and flesh of my flesh;
this one shall be called Woman,
for out of Man this one was taken."
Therefore a man leaves his father and his mother and clings to his wife, and they become one flesh.

GENESIS 2:18, 23–24

Prayer

Father, by your power you have made everything out of nothing.
In the beginning you created the universe
and made mankind in your own likeness.
You gave man the constant help of woman
so that man and woman should no longer be two, but one flesh,
and you teach us that what you have united
may never be divided. . . .

Keep [married couples] always true to your commandments.
Keep them faithful in marriage
and let them be living examples of Christian life. . . .
Amen.

RITE OF MARRIAGE, #33.

Marriage: Union in God's Life

CHAPTER OVERVIEW

Weddings

Do you expect to see your name on a wedding invitation at some point in the future? Or is matrimony too far ahead to even think about?

By this time in your life, there's a good chance that you have already attended a wedding or two. Whether they were Catholic or Protestant weddings—and most marriage ceremonies in the United States are one or the other—they were probably very similar. If there was any noticeable difference, it was that the Catholic wedding may have been accompanied by a Mass, which made the church service considerably longer. Church weddings by themselves, though, have many similarities.

There are, of course, the bride and groom. The bride most likely wears a formal or culturally traditional gown, possibly white. She may wear a veil, and it might hide her face as she walks down the aisle for the last time as a single woman. In her hand she carries a bouquet of flowers. The groom is also formally dressed, probably in a tuxedo, the perfect picture of the dashing suitor.

In many places it is customary for the bride to be accompanied down the aisle by her father or by both of her parents. According to a newer custom, the groom may be the first to walk down the aisle, and he may also be accompanied by his parents. If he precedes the bride down the aisle, he waits for her at the foot of the altar.

The wedding party includes the maid (or matron) of honor, the best man, and other bridesmaids and their escorts. There are others, too: the presiding minister, altar servers, and perhaps a little flower girl and ring bearer. Members of the family and friends of the couple are there. And these days there is the ever-present photographer and maybe even a video technician.

At a certain point in the ceremony, the minister turns to the bride and groom and asks them to take each other's hand. He calls on them to pledge their lives to one another in the state of holy matrimony. Whether they recite the wedding vows themselves or say "I do" to the presider's questions, this is the turning point in the ceremony and in their lives. Before this, they were single; now they are married.

The honor of your presence

is requested at the

Nuptial Mass uniting

_____

and

_____

in the Sacrament

of Holy Matrimony.

All actual life
is encounter.

—Martin Buber

As a sign of their belonging to each other, the groom slips a wedding ring on the third finger of the bride's left hand, and most times (but not always) she does the same for him. At the end of the church service, they kiss and turn to receive the congregation's approval of their decision. They stand before their applauding relatives and friends, who are congratulating them for the important step they have taken.

Why do most wedding ceremonies have so many similarities? Where do these customs come from? We need to spend some time looking back at our roots.

Discussion

In the large group, discuss the following questions:

1. Have you attended a wedding in the last few years? Was it a Catholic ceremony or a different one? Describe what you remember of the wedding.

2. What are some of your thoughts about that ceremony?

3. Weddings and the things that go along with them (reception, honeymoon) are becoming increasingly expensive, sometimes costing tens of thousands of dollars. What do you think about all the expenses connected with weddings?

Research

1. Almost every parish has a few weddings every month, usually on Saturdays. With the help of your teacher, call your parish office, inquire about the wedding schedule, and ask if, for a class project, it would be all right to attend the church service. Be sure to dress up for the occasion, so that you are not conspicuous because of your clothing. Observe the wedding ceremony and take notes about what goes on. Write a report on what you observed, and present it in written or oral form.

2. Find a source (book, encyclopedia, Internet site) that gives information about marriage and wedding customs (veil, ring, and so on). Make a written or oral report about what you learned. If possible, include pictures.

3. Look in the library or on the Internet for information about planning weddings, receptions, and honeymoons. Make a written or oral report about what you learned.

JUMPING THE BROOM

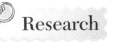

Research

Investigate other ethnic wedding customs, along with their meanings. Present your findings to the class.

Jumping the broom is an African American custom that may have roots in Africa. It certainly has roots in slavery. Shortly after slavery was established in the United States and its territories, the marriage of slaves was forbidden by law. There were probably several reasons for this. Slaves were not considered human; marriage would promote strength in numbers and lead to revolt; marriage would interfere with the buying and selling of individual slaves.

Being a spiritual people, enslaved Africans created their own ceremonies to celebrate marriages, even though they could not be married legally. One such custom was "jumping the broom." As it was practiced by enslaved people, this was a simple ceremony. The couple held hands as they jumped over a broom as a sign that they were entering a marriage relationship with each other. In some places they jumped forward, in others, they jumped backwards.

It's hard to figure out the original meaning of this practice. The broom may have represented the threshold of a new home, the passing over of which indicated that the couple was going from single life to the responsibilities of marriage. Another interpretation is that the broom symbolized the sweeping away of the old and the welcoming of the new. Some places developed a tradition of having the couple compete to see who could jump higher over the broom, with the idea that the one who jumped higher would be the decision-maker in the marriage.

Today the custom of jumping the broom is returning to many African American weddings. The short ceremony may take place during the wedding itself, or it may be part of the wedding reception. The broom is generally decorated with flowers and ribbons that coordinate with the wedding colors. After the broom is placed on the floor, the couple hold hands and jump over the broom. If the ceremony takes place at the wedding reception, the guests may gather in a circle around the couple as a sign of their community support and the coming together of two families.

The Baltimore archdiocese includes the following in a reflection on the topic:

Jump, children, and as you jump, climb up in the arms of all those who have laid the groundwork, climb onto their backs and let their spirit carry you over all the rough places.

Alexander the Great's marriage feast. Undated engraving from original painting by Andreas Muller.

Roots of the Marriage Ceremony

Obviously, marriage was around for a long time before Jesus and the apostles. Mary and Joseph were married, as was Peter (whose mother-in-law is mentioned in the Gospels), and they certainly weren't married in a Catholic church! Part of their Jewish heritage was a wedding ceremony that was already hundreds of years old at the time of Jesus.

Surprisingly, however, this was not a religious ceremony. Nowhere in the religious laws of the Old Testament do we find the description of a wedding. In Jewish society, as in many ancient cultures, marriage was a family affair. Fathers arranged marriages of their children, often years in advance (although mothers also had a voice in the selection of suitable **spouses**) and presided at the wedding ceremony. Each family did it in its own way, following its traditional customs.

This was also true in most European cultures, which explains why traditionally the father of the bride "gave" her to her husband-to-be. For many centuries, marriages were not for love, but to carry on the family line and to increase its wealth. To compensate the family of the bride for the loss of a worker, her family was given a "bride price" agreed on by the parents of the groom. Later on, this payment was replaced by a gold ring given at the wedding ceremony.

When Rome became an empire spread around the Mediterranean Sea, fathers were often away from home in military service, and children began to marry for their own reasons, with or without their parents' approval. Roman law in early Christian times recognized the mutual consent of the partners to the marriage as the element that made it legal. Christians too recognized this moment as the point at which a marriage came into being.

spouse generic term for male or female marriage partner; half of a married couple

1. In the days of the Roman Empire, people could marry just by giving their consent to one another, without any public ceremony and without any witnesses. What do you think were the advantages and the disadvantages of this custom?

2. In some cultures, and in many parts of the world today, parents choose marriage partners for their children, or, at the very least, young adults cannot get married without the consent of their parents. What do you think about these cultural practices?

monogamy   having only one spouse at a time

polygamy   having more than one spouse at a time

indissoluble   not able to be dissolved or broken apart

For many centuries, Christians entered into marriage according to their own local customs. It was either a marriage arranged by the parents or an agreement between the couple, depending on the locality. If a priest happened to be invited to a wedding it was only as a guest (although, of course, he was usually asked for his blessing).

Even when weddings were secular in nature, marriage itself has been seen as a holy union that came from God. Many of the stories and other writings in the Old Testament speak of the sacredness of marriage. Jesus affirmed this and stressed the lifelong nature of matrimony. Christianity built on that foundation and developed an understanding of marriage as an intimate communion of life and love. As such, it was subject to special laws that came from God. In other words, it was seen as much more than a legal contract—it came to be seen as a sacrament.

MONOGAMY AND INDISSOLUBILITY

The Catechism tells us that when the first humans were created, God wanted marriage to be **monogamous** (no **polygamy**) and **indissoluble** (no divorce or remarriage). Experience tells us that when people marry, they desire a happy, faithful, lifelong marriage; people naturally understand that this is what marriage is all about. Because of the first couple's fall from grace, however, selfishness and weakness frequently led to a disordered understanding of marriage. As a result, domination, polygamy, and divorce became common. At the time of Jesus, domination within marriage, polygamy, and divorce were still practiced, and those practices have continued to this day.

While the Catholic Church does not accept a literal interpretation of Genesis, the religious message behind the stories is understood to be God's revelation. Catholics can certainly believe in biological and cultural evolution regarding the origins of the human race and marriage. However, the religious truth of the creation story in the Book of Genesis is that God wanted marriage to be monogamous and indissoluble.

DiSCuSSioN

In the large group, discuss the following questions:

1. Why was and is polygamy practiced?

2. What are the disadvantages of polygamy?

3. What are the advantages of monogamy?

4. What are the advantages of indissolubility in marriage?

Origins of the Nuptial Mass

Let's return to the development of the marriage ceremony. In some localities, a marriage that had taken place in a civil setting was celebrated later at a Sunday Eucharist. The whole community was invited to this church celebration. In the course of time, special prayers were composed and Scripture readings were chosen to accent the Christian meaning of marriage. These attempts to stress the sanctity of marriage within the context of the Eucharist became the origins of the **Nuptial** Mass, although the ceremony itself was not made a part of this Mass until the Middle Ages. It is the Nuptial or Wedding Mass that is frequently the setting for the Catholic Sacrament of Marriage, or to use the more traditional word, *Matrimony.*

At this point in history, a specifically Christian wedding ceremony began to develop. When the Roman Empire collapsed, there were no longer civil magistrates to decide matters in the ancient equivalent of domestic relations court. Often bishops were called on as neutral third parties to decide marriage cases. Sometimes young people pleaded that they should not have to marry spouses that their parents had picked out for them. Private marriages with no public ceremony were considered legal in those days, and it sometimes happened that a woman found herself abandoned by a man who claimed that they had only been "living together." She would then appeal to the bishop, saying that they had indeed been married by mutual consent, even though there had been no witnesses to their exchange of vows.

To head off problems such as these, bishops passed Church laws decreeing that a marriage between Catholics was legal only when the partners gave their free consent in a public ceremony in the presence of a priest (who represented the Church) and witnesses (who represented the civil society). Hence the presence of a priest and two witnesses (usually maid or matron of honor and best man) are normally required at any Catholic wedding, even today. Because it is a public celebration, however, the wedding usually includes others—the families and friends of the couple, and sometimes the parish community as well.

nuptial from a Latin word meaning related to or pertaining to marriage

Matrimony the Sacrament of Marriage, a covenant relationship between a man and a woman that is oriented toward their loving unity and the procreation, raising, and education of children

The fifteenth-century marriage of Philip II and Isabelle was captured by Jacques de Guise.

Marriage is indeed a public state of life. The celebration of a marriage in a public liturgy points to the importance of this vocation for the individuals, their families, and society as a whole. In some countries today, such as France, a civil marriage ceremony is required; the Church wedding usually takes place a few days later. In most other countries, including the United States, priests and other ministers are licensed by the state government to perform marriage ceremonies, so church weddings fulfill the civil legal requirement to have the marriage witnessed and recorded.

WHAT THE CATECHISM SAYS

Catholic weddings should take place in the context of a Nuptial Mass whenever possible. This practice emphasizes the connection of marriage with the Paschal mystery, which the newly married couple enter more deeply in their covenant relationship. The Eucharist, among other things, is a memorial of the covenant between Christ and the Church, which is reflected in the Sacrament of Matrimony. Moreover, by receiving Communion together, the couple symbolize their unity in Christ. Because of this, it is appropriate that the couple prepare for their marriage with the Sacrament of Reconciliation some time before the wedding day.

See the *Catechism of the Catholic Church*, #s 1621–1622.

At this point it might be well to emphasize that, in the Church in the West, the priest or deacon does not marry the bride and groom: the bride and groom marry each other! Very often couples say, "Father Smith married us," but this is a misconception. In the understanding of the Catholic Church in the West, it is the giving and receiving of consent by the couple to each other that makes them married. In traditional theological language, the couple are said to confer the sacrament on one another.

Now, back to our history. Since the presence of a priest was required in the Middle Ages for a Catholic wedding, more and more marriages began to be celebrated in a church. This encouraged the celebration of the Nuptial Mass in conjunction with the wedding ceremony rather than after it. In the wedding ceremony, the parents' role diminished, and the priest took over as the "master of ceremonies." By the twelfth century in Catholic Europe, all legal weddings were not only witnessed by a priest but also presided over by a priest. The Rite of Matrimony had at last become an official church service!

The Sacrament of Marriage is celebrated in the community of family and friends.

Chapter Nine

Discussion

Where it is possible, the Church encourages Catholics to celebrate the rite of matrimony (wedding ceremony) within a Nuptial Mass. In a small group, discuss the following questions:

1. What are its reasons for doing this?

2. What do you think about having a Nuptial Mass if you marry?

You might ask, isn't there anything else besides the presence of a priest and lay people as witnesses that is a distinctively Catholic addition to the wedding ceremony? There is. Believe it or not, it is the kissing of the bride and groom! Originally this was the kiss of peace, which, since Vatican II, has been restored to the Eucharistic liturgy as the sign of peace. In the Middle Ages, after the exchange of vows, the priest gave the kiss of peace to the bridegroom, who in turn passed it on to his new wife. In the United States, this symbolic gesture, between the Lord's Prayer and the Lamb of God of every Mass, may be a handshake or a hug or a kiss, depending on the relationship between the two exchanging the sign of peace.

Thus the Christian wedding ceremony in all its essentials was complete, although it took about twelve centuries to put it all together!

There are some reasons why a Nuptial Mass may not be the best choice. If one of the couple is not Catholic (or if his or her family is not Catholic), it may be a wise decision to have a Catholic wedding celebration without a Mass. Communion is especially difficult if half or most of the assembly cannot participate. With Catholic Church permission, the marriage may take place in the religious building of the non-Catholic with the ceremony presided over by the non-Catholic religious leader. This may be especially appropriate if one of the couple is not Christian—for example, Jewish or Muslim. Some dioceses, due to a shortage of priests, encourage couples to either celebrate their marriage at a parish liturgy (the way infant Baptisms are often done) or have a deacon preside at their wedding without a Mass. A Catholic wedding outside of Mass includes the Liturgy of the Word, the marriage rite itself, and the nuptial blessing.

 Activity

Tape two or three wedding clips from TV programs or choose two or three from movie videos. Family members may also have videos of their own weddings; include one or two of these if you wish. Show the video clips to the class and lead a discussion on these questions:

1. What overall impression did you receive from each video clip?

2. What religious elements did you notice in the church weddings?

3. What religious elements did you notice were missing from these weddings?

4. What might have even detracted from the religious nature of the celebration?

Review Questions

1. What is the point in a wedding when a marriage takes place?

2. Why did the ritual of "jumping the broom" develop in the United States?

3. Before there was an official church ceremony for weddings between Christians, what is the evidence that marriage was considered sacred?

4. What is monogamy? Polygamy?

5. What does it mean to say that marriage is indissoluble?

6. How did the Nuptial Mass originate?

Marriage: A Sacrament

Our brief historical review raises the question: What makes marriage a sacrament? Aren't all the sacraments supposed to go back to the time of Jesus and the apostles?

The answer to that question depends on what you mean by the word *sacrament*. If by sacrament you mean a Catholic religious ritual, then it is clear that church weddings came in only during the Middle Ages. If, on the other hand, by sacrament you mean a visible sign of a sacred mystery, then it is equally clear that Christian marriage has been sacramental from the earliest days of the Church. While the institution of the Sacrament of Matrimony is not explicit in Scripture, the nuptial theme permeates Scripture from the beginning as an analogy to the relationship between God and the people of God. In the Old Testament, for example, Israel is sometimes regarded as the "bride" of God, for God's union with Israel is like a marriage bond.

Jesus performed his first miracle at a wedding in Cana (see John 2:1–11). The Church sees this event as significant. By his presence, Jesus proclaimed the goodness and dignity of marriage, which for the baptized is sacramental. The relationship between a husband and a wife in the Sacrament of Marriage is that of **covenant**—a sacred, binding agreement that reflects God's covenant relationship with his people as well as the union between Christ and his Church.

covenant a solemn agreement between humans or between God and humans involving mutual commitments or guarantees

vocation from the Latin word for a call or invitation, a state of life or work to which one feels called, in contrast to work that would be considered simply a job

Commitment and love are the keystone of the vocation of marriage.

[Marriage] is rooted in the conjugal covenant or irrevocable personal consent. Hence, by that human act whereby spouses mutually bestow and accept each other, a relationship arises which by divine will and in the eyes of society too is a lasting one. For the good of the spouses and their offspring as well as of society, the existence of this sacred bond no longer depends on human decisions alone.

Documents of Vatican II, "The Church in the Modern World," #48.

The Catechism refers to the Sacraments of Matrimony and Holy Orders as "sacraments at the service of communion and the mission of the faithful." Perhaps, in order to understand this better, it would be easier to refer to them as Sacraments of **Vocation.** Marriage is indeed a vocation, and one that requires a great deal of commitment and love. The grace of the sacrament is like the glue that binds two things together; it is the self-giving love that binds the couple in a growing relationship that is a foretaste of the joy of heaven. Marriage is also a participation in the Paschal mystery, for in it a man and a woman die to themselves and become one with the other, giving rise to new life in themselves and their children.

✝ Activity

Search a parish hymnal for songs designated or suggested for weddings. Choose three of these and jot down the main idea of each. Share the songs and your main ideas with the class. If possible, play a recording. Discuss other possible hymns that you know of which might be appropriate for a church wedding.

Marriage reflects the relationship of love between Christ and the Church.

The New Testament Letters and Marriage

In the New Testament the Letter to the Ephesians says the following:

Wives should be submissive to their husbands as if to the Lord because the husband is head of his wife just as Christ is head of his body the church, as well as its savior. As the church submits to Christ, so wives should submit to their husbands in everything.

Husbands, love your wives, as Christ loved the church. He gave himself up for her to make her holy, purifying her in the bath of water by the power of the word, to present to himself a glorious church, holy and immaculate, without stain or wrinkle or anything of that sort. Husbands should love their wives as they do their own bodies. He who loves his wife loves himself.

Observe that no one ever hates his own flesh; no, he nourishes it and takes care of it as Christ cares for the church for we are members of his body. "For this reason a man shall leave his father and mother, and shall cling to his wife, and the two shall be made into one." This is a great foreshadowing: I mean that it refers to Christ and the church.

See Ephesians 5:22–32.

What the writer is saying here to the Christians of the first century is that the relationship between a husband and wife who love each other is a visible sign of the loving relationship between Christ and the Church. The logic works in both directions: from the marriage relationship to the divine relationship, and from the divine to the human relationship.

Since Christ loves his own body (the Church) in a totally self-giving way ("gave himself up for her"), and since the Church is totally obedient to the Lord ("the church submits to Christ"), husbands and wives should love each other in the same way. And when husbands and wives love each other so deeply that they are united in love ("the two shall be made into one"), then their unity is a visible sign of a mysterious reality ("it refers to Christ and the church").

Much has been written through the centuries about the quality of the human relationship described in this passage from the Letter to the Ephesians. It appears that the wife is supposed to be submissive to her husband, but the husband is not asked to be submissive to his wife. Scripture scholars tell us, however, that this way of describing the marriage relationship simply reflects the way marriage was lived at the time the passage was written. It is not meant to be the norm for all times.

In ancient societies, the man was always the head of the household and the woman was practically his servant. The writer is simply taking this style of marriage for granted, just as slavery was taken for granted in those days. But he is also announcing something radically new: that the husband should be totally dedicated to the welfare of his wife. Men had not been told to look at marriage that way before! It was as if the writer was looking for the words to say that in marriages between Christians both partners should be completely caring and self-giving.

As a matter of fact, this passage begins with a sentence that was intentionally left out until now, in order to make a point: "Be subordinate to one another out of reverence for Christ" (Ephesians 5:21). This opening sentence puts the whole passage in its proper context.

We can't ignore, however, the fact that patriarchal views of the husband-wife relationship do show up in Scripture. The following is from another New Testament letter. In reading such passages, we have to remember the times and adapt the message to our situation today.

Wives, in the same way, accept the authority of your husbands, so that, even if some of them do not obey the word, they may be won over without a word by their wives' conduct, when they see the purity and reverence of your lives. Do not adorn yourselves outwardly by braiding your hair, and by wearing gold ornaments or fine clothing; rather, let your adornment be the inner self with the lasting beauty of a gentle and quiet spirit, which is very precious in God's sight. It was in this way long ago that the holy women who hoped in God used to adorn themselves by accepting the authority of their husbands. Thus Sarah obeyed Abraham and called him lord. You have become her daughters as long as you do what is good and never let fears alarm you.

Husbands, in the same way, show consideration for your wives in your life together, paying honor to the woman as the weaker sex, since they too are also heirs of the gracious gift of life—so that nothing may hinder your prayers.

1 Peter 3:1–7

Lord, may they both praise you
    when they are happy
and turn to you in their sorrows.

—*Rite of Marriage, #121.*

Research

Some Protestant churches teach that since there are Scripture passages that teach that wives should be submissive to their husbands, the man should always have headship in the marriage. Find an article, a book, or an Internet site that promotes this view. Summarize it in your own words, and explain what you think about it.

Today only a foolish man would refer to women as the weaker sex. Even biblical literalists (people who take every sentence in the Bible as literally true) usually don't insist that women avoid braids, gold jewelry, or good clothes. Despite the differences in culture between that time and ours, however, we can glimpse some important truths in this passage. It is still true that many men become serious about their relationship with God and their membership in the Church only because their wives gently lead them in that direction. And true beauty certainly comes from within rather than from clothes and jewelry. Finally, all of us, men and women, are indeed "heirs of the gracious gift of life."

Discussion

In a small group, discuss the following questions:

1. Some people take Ephesians 5:21–33 and 1 Peter 3:1–7 literally to mean that God wants the husband to be the head of the household and that God wants the wife to be submissive to her husband in everything. What do you think? Give reasons to support your answer.

2. Explain in your own words the teaching of the Letter to the Ephesians, explaining how the relationship between a Christian husband and wife reflects the relationship between Christ and the Church.

The Christian Ideal of Marriage

In one family the husband has "the final word"; in another the wife makes the important decisions; in a third the couple always hash things out until they reach a compromise. This is a lifestyle choice that each couple makes for itself. Still, the ideal is that, regardless of their marriage lifestyle, both the husband and the wife should work in harmony and give the other's welfare top priority. And that's a distinctively Christian ideal, going all the way back to the New Testament.

Jesus himself taught this ideal, and he quoted the same Old Testament text cited in the Ephesians passage, that in marriage "the two shall be made into one." The people of Jesus' day took this simply to mean sexual union, but Jesus gave it a deeper interpretation, saying, ". . . what God has joined together, let no one separate" (Matthew 19:6; see also Mark 10:9).

How does God join people together? Isn't it through the love that they have for one another? John tells us that God is love, and that if we love one another, God's own love becomes real in our lives (see 1 John 4:8, 12). In his own way, then, Jesus is telling his followers that they ought to love one another so deeply that separation is impossible for them. That deep, self-giving love is divine love, *agape,* God's love in us, uniting us in caring for one another.

The Catholic teaching on marriage is another way of putting this New Testament revelation into modern words. The Church teaches that true Christian marriage is a "partnership of the whole of life." This intimate partnership is made possible only by openness and sharing, care and dedication, unconditional and self-sacrificing love, God's love lived in a human way. Such intimacy of life is sacramental because, when we see this kind of unity in a loving marriage, we catch a glimpse of the mysterious intense unity between the heavenly Christ and the whole body of the Church.

Love is not a deal, it is a sacrafice.

—Thomas Merton

This then is why the Catholic marriage ritual is a sacrament, for a sacrament is a symbolic way of expressing a divine mystery. The prayers and Scripture readings remind us of how God has always loved the people of God and called them to share in divine life. And in every wedding ceremony, the visible love of the bride and groom for one another is a sign of God's invisible but totally real love for all of us. Moreover, the Sacrament of Marriage itself, as a living reality in the relationship of husband and wife, is a special meeting with God. God reaches into the life of this couple and promises again to be faithful; it is a renewal of the covenant God has with us.

The sacramental dimension of the marriage relationship is continually renewed in the daily life the couple experiences together. The sacrament energizes, sustains, and sanctifies the daily commitment of the couple to one another and to God. It is a reflection of the intimate love of Christ for the Church. It is this reflection of the total commitment of God that makes **fidelity** and the indissolubility of marriage such important aspects of the Catholic vision of marriage. The ideal becomes a reality in a sacramental marriage.

fidelity faithfulness; in the context of marriage, not having a sexual relationship with anyone but one's spouse; in addition, commitment to growing in love for one another

Journal

Catholics these days are just as likely to marry someone who is not Catholic as they are to marry a Catholic.

1. How important is it to you to marry someone with a faith similar to yours? Explain your answer.

2. What values do you see yourself as bringing to a marriage from the fact that you are Catholic? (If you are not Catholic, respond in terms of your own religious background.)

WHAT THE CATECHISM SAYS

A valid marriage creates a special sacramental bond between the spouses. By its nature this bond is exclusive and lasts as long as both partners live. The marriage bond is established and sealed by God and reflects the covenant between God and his people. When a true marriage bond exists, it cannot be dissolved, for the covenant established is guaranteed by God's own faithfulness.

See the *Catechism of the Catholic Church*, #s 1638–1640.

DiSCUSSioN

In the large group, discuss the following questions:

1. The Catholic Church teaches that a marriage between Christians (with few exceptions) is a sacrament, even if the Christians are Protestants who not believe that marriage is a sacrament. What do you think about this?

2. The Catholic Church proclaims that Christian marriage is different from ordinary human marriage. What are some of the ways that it is different? Do you find evidence of this difference in real life? Explain.

3. Catholics believe that the Bible clearly teaches the Catholic understanding of marriage, yet Jews and Protestants, who also derive their theology of marriage from the Bible, have different understandings of marriage and its indissolubility. How do you account for this?

Chapter Nine

The Purposes of Marriage

As was suggested above, marriage in different cultures and in different periods of history has had a variety of purposes. In tribal societies, for example, one of the important purposes of marriage was to increase the size of the extended family. In the Middle Ages, rulers arranged the marriages of their children in order to strengthen treaties with other rulers. In all traditional societies and cultures, having children was an important purpose of marriage. In ancient Judaism, children were regarded as a blessing, and an inability to produce children was sometimes interpreted as a sign that God was not pleased with the marriage or with one of the partners.

Concern for the child . . . is the primary and fundamental test of the relationship of one human being to another.

—*Pope John Paul II*

The Church today recognizes that marriage is primarily for the benefit of the husband and wife—something not always recognized in the Middle Ages, when marriages could be arranged for the benefit of the parents of the husband and wife. The Church also continues to affirm the tradition that children are both a blessing from God and a purpose of marriage. According to the Catechism, marriage "is by its nature ordered toward the good of the spouses and the procreation and education of offspring." (See the *Catechism of the Catholic Church*, #1601.)

First of all, the love a husband and wife have for each other is meant to sustain them as they journey together through life. Sharing everything, including sexual intimacy, is a joyful challenge to form a relationship with one heart and soul, as it were. Husband and wife are called to be truly helpmates to each other. Through their intimacy and their caring for each other, they experience God's presence and love. Likewise, in their fidelity to each other they find a reflection of God's faithfulness.

Second, marriage is supposed to be life-giving, that is, "ordained for the procreation and education of children." Not all couples who marry are able to have children, but the Church asks those who can to be open to having, raising, and educating children. In deciding how many children to have, a couple must weigh their physical, emotional, and economic situation. And when they do have children, they need to be good parents, trusting that God will help them to raise them properly.

Openness to children has some practical responsibilities. The Church teaches that artificial means of contraception and birth control, as well as sterilization for the sake of ending fertility, are morally wrong. Nevertheless, abstinence from sexual intercourse and **natural family planning** are permitted for the spacing of children. Natural family planning, which involves both partners in planning when to have children and thus when not to have sexual intercourse, is permitted if the couple is not motivated by purely selfish reasons such as simply having a life with fewer hassles or more disposable income.

The promise of the Sacrament of Matrimony is that God offers husbands and wives the real possibility of a lasting and fruitful marriage. This gift, known theologically as the grace of the sacrament, remains throughout the years of the marriage to help the couple grow in holiness and raise their family as good Christians. Faithful and caring husbands and wives love each other with the love Christ has for the Church, and in that love they experience God's love. In partnership with each other and in cooperation with God's gift, their love grows stronger through good times and difficult times.

Children are a great responsibility and an awesome blessing.

May they reach old age in the company of their friends, and come at last to the kingdom of heaven.

—*Rite of Marriage, #121.*

WHAT THE CATECHISM SAYS

Jesus himself grew up in a family, one we call the *Holy Family.* A Christian family is called to be another holy family; it is a domestic Church. Within such a family, children first learn to live as good persons and good Christians. Sound parenting, good example, and participation in the sacramental and prayer life of the Church are essential for the success of the domestic Church.

See the *Catechism of the Catholic Church, #s 1655–1657.*

inteRVieW

Interview an older couple who you know are happily married or who others say are happily married. Find out from them why they think people marry and what the purpose of marriage really is. Then ask them what they think are the three most important things in creating and maintaining a happy, long-lasting marriage. Report your findings on paper or in an oral presentation.

DiSCuSSioN

In a small group, discuss the following questions:

1. What are some practical ways that love, in the sense of caring, is given and shown in a marriage?

2. What do you think would be most difficult about raising children?

3. What are some of the joys of raising children?

4. Name some characteristics of a family that would truly be a domestic Church.

Love in marriage is lived out in the ordinary events of family life.

Abiding Love

Unfortunately, some people prepare more seriously for their wedding than they do for marriage. They may have studied harder for a driver's test than they do for the marriage license. The Church believes preparation is essential for such a serious commitment and wants its members to understand and appreciate the sacramentality and permanence of marriage. For this reason parishes and dioceses today have marriage preparation programs. Such programs cover every aspect of married life from personal communication to child rearing, from sex to sacramentality. The Church wants to make as sure as possible that every Catholic has the best possible chance of entering into a marriage that will be emotionally and spiritually rewarding, founded on abiding love and able to last forever.

Pope John Paul II expressed the Church's vision and hope in his encyclical on the family:

> *God is love and in himself he lives a mystery of personal loving communion. Creating the human race in his own image and continually keeping it in being, God inscribed in the humanity of man and woman the vocation, and thus the capacity and responsibility, of love and communion. Love is therefore the fundamental and innate vocation of every human. . . .*
>
> *By virtue of the sacramentality of their marriage, spouses are bound to one another in the most profoundly indissoluble manner. Their belonging to each other is the real representation, by means of the sacramental sign, of the very relationship of Christ with the church.*

On the Family, 11, 13.

Every newly married couple wants a marriage that lasts forever. Not all of them get their wish because, sadly, they do not have or are not willing to work at a relationship based on the *agape* love that makes it indissoluble. The Catholic Church teaches that at the heart of every truly loving marriage, there is God's love and that the marriage relationship itself, visible to others in the way the couple care for one another, is a sign, a symbol, a sacrament of God's love for all of us.

Research

Write an essay or give a presentation to your class on one of the following.

1. Marriage preparation programs available to Catholics in your parish or diocese

2. Other marriage preparation programs available to people in your area, through churches and counseling centers, and so on

3. Marriage preparation information that is available in books, magazines, and the Internet

Journal

1. Do you see yourself getting married some day? If so, what do you hope your marriage will be like?

2. Do you have any brothers or sisters who are married? How has marriage affected their lives?

3. How does thinking about other marriage relationships affect your thinking about marriage?

Declaration of Nullity

divorce declaration by a civil court that a legal marriage has ended and that the parties are free to remarry

Jesus' teaching on **divorce** is well known to people who read the Bible:

> Some Pharisees came, and to test him they asked, "Is it lawful for a man to divorce his wife?" He answered them, "What did Moses command you?" They said, "Moses allowed a man to write a certificate of dismissal and to divorce her." But Jesus said to them, "Because of your hardness of heart he wrote this commandment for you. But from the beginning of creation, 'God made them male and female.' 'For this reason a man shall leave his father and mother and be joined to his wife, and the two shall become one flesh.' So they are no longer two, but one flesh. Therefore what God has joined together, let no one separate."
>
> Then in the house the disciples asked him again about this matter. He said to them, "Whoever divorces his wife and marries another commits adultery against her; and if she divorces her husband and marries another, she commits adultery."

declaration of nullity declaration by a Church court that a failed marriage was never really a sacramental marriage, even though people may have thought it was; commonly referred to as an annulment

tribunal a Church court that examines and decides cases with regard to Church law, especially marriage cases

No one plans to fail at marriage. Counseling can help couples in trouble and those whose marriage has ended.

Mark 10:2–12

Based in part on this teaching of Jesus, the Catholic Church teaches that a sacramental marriage is for life and cannot be dissolved, which is why the Church does not grant divorces. The Church does, however, look at a marriage that has failed and is willing to grant a **declaration of nullity** if it finds that the marriage was not truly sacramental. In fact, in every diocese there is an ecclesiastical court or **tribunal** whose judges are trained to examine and decide marriage cases.

People often think that a declaration of nullity (an annulment) is some sort of Catholic divorce, but it isn't. It is a judgment made by a diocesan tribunal that what appeared on the surface to be a sacramental Catholic marriage really wasn't. Because of the seriousness of this decision, the Church will not even consider beginning an annulment investigation until after a marriage has already been dissolved by a civil divorce. At this point, it is apparent that the couple will not or cannot make the effort to begin again in creating a truly sacramental marriage.

In times gone by, the reasons for seeking an annulment were fairly simple. Marriage was considered to be a contract between two persons, so if one of the persons was actually incapable of entering into the agreement, the contract was nullified. For example, if a man married a woman and later discovered that she was already married and, therefore, not legally able to be his wife, he could ask for an annulment to show that he was still free to marry.

Another example would be the case of a couple who married and then found out that the man was impotent (unable to have an erection) and therefore incapable of the sexual intercourse needed to produce children. The woman could seek an annulment because he could not live up to his side of the marriage contract, and she would be free to marry again.

While these reasons are still valid, the picture has gotten more complicated in recent times. Psychologists tell us that the emotional demands of modern marriage are greater than they were in simpler times. At the same time, the understanding of marriage has been expanded to included new dimensions of partnership and intimacy. In other words, today we understand that it takes more to be capable of marriage, especially a truly Christian marriage, than was understood in the past to be required.

The Church has recognized this by declaring that marriage is a covenant relationship and a "partnership of the whole of life." A covenant is a deeper and more intimate personal relationship than a contract. We can enter into contracts even with strangers (in business, for instance), but we enter into covenants only with people we know personally. The bond between parents and children is like a covenant because there is nothing that can break it. In the Old Testament we read that God made a covenant with Israel, and that God remained faithful to that covenant with the chosen people even when they sinned and tried to run away from their relationship with God.

If marriage is a covenant between two persons, then both of them have to be capable of living at the deeper interpersonal level that a covenant relationship requires. It may turn out, however, that even though a couple was legally married, one of the spouses was actually incapable of entering into the deep relationship of the Christian marriage covenant (and perhaps both were incapable of this). To find out if a covenant relationship, a sacramental marriage, existed in the eyes of the Church, one or both of them could ask for an annulment investigation.

If the investigation does not find evidence of nullity, the assumption of the tribunal is that the marriage was sacramental from the beginning and remains such, even though a civil divorce has been granted. In the Catholic Church it is not a sin to be divorced, but it is against Church law to remarry without a declaration of nullity with regard to a prior marriage. This is why divorced Catholics who do not receive an annulment are not allowed to have a church wedding if they want to marry again. In the Church's eyes, the prior marriage is still sacramental and therefore still in existence. At the same time, the Church recognizes that divorced people can be morally innocent victims of their partner's decision.

Divorced Catholics who remarry in a Protestant or civil ceremony are invited to participate in the life of the Church, but Catholic law does not allow them to receive Communion. From an institutional perspective, the reception of Communion is a sign of unity with the universal Church, and such Catholics are not in full unity with the Church.

It can happen, however, that a Church tribunal rules that at the time that they were married at least one of the couple was incapable of a true covenant relationship. Then a declaration of nullity is issued, stating that the marriage lacked something essential to be a sacramental marriage. Once the Church declares that the couple were not sacramentally married, they are free to ask for a Catholic wedding if they want to marry again. Sometimes, though, they may be asked to go for counseling first to make sure that what destroyed their first marriage does not hurt their second relationship as well.

Paradoxically, the deeper appreciation for sacramental marriage as a covenant relationship has made it possible for many more annulments to be granted than in the past. People sometimes see this and think that the Church is getting more lenient about marriage, but actually it is getting stricter. By pointing out how hard it is to achieve a truly sacramental marriage, the Church has raised the ideal of Catholic marriage even higher.

 **Research**

In the New Testament, Mark 10:2–12 (quoted in this section) and Matthew 19:3–11 tell the same story with some small differences. Use a Bible commentary or other reference book to learn what scholars have said about these passages.

1. In which ways are the stories similar?

2. In which ways are they different?

DisCussioN

In the large group, discuss the following:

1. Describe in your own words what a declaration of nullity is.

2. How does the fact that more Catholic marriages than in the past are being annulled (being declared not to be sacramental marriages) show that the Church has a very high standard for Christian marriage?

Review Questions

1. What is the relationship between marriage and the love Christ has for his Church?

2. Why is fidelity essential for a marriage?

3. What are the two purposes of the Sacrament of Marriage?

4. What is the difference between a divorce and a declaration of nullity?

5. When is a declaration of nullity given?

6. When is it permissible for a Catholic to remarry?

Summary

Marriage is very familiar yet very mysterious. People all around us are married, yet the relationship we call marriage is not easy to understand—or to live. From the time of Jesus, Christians have been invited to live in the same kind of loving and caring relationship that God has for all people, and indeed for all of creation. That relationship is called sacramental because it is a visible expression of God's love.

A loving, sacramental marriage is also called indissoluble because it lasts forever, just as God's love lasts forever. The lasting commitment of husband and wife to one another is a special kind of faithfulness called fidelity. Such faithfulness is needed for the health of the relationship, and it is also a source of great joy.

A sacramental marriage gives love and life to others. The couple care about and for one another, and that caring enhances their life together. The sexual expression of their love also leads to new life in children, who grow physically and spiritually when they are loved. Their ability to give life and love also extends to the community around them; they are called to be signs to others of God's life and love.

Scripture

Once more Jesus spoke to them in parables, saying: "The kingdom of heaven may be compared to a king who gave a wedding banquet for his son. He sent his slaves to call those who had been invited to the wedding banquet, but they would not come. Again he sent other slaves, saying, 'Tell those who have been invited: Look, I have prepared my dinner, my oxen and my fat calves have been slaughtered, and everything is ready; come to the wedding banquet.'"

MATTHEW 22:1–4

Prayer

May God the eternal Father keep us in love,
so that the peace of Christ may stay with us
and be always in our homes.
Amen.

May we always bear witness to the love of God in this world
so that those who are afflicted and in need
will find in us generous friends,
and welcome us into the joys of heaven.
Amen.

ADAPTED FROM THE BLESSING AT THE END OF MASS,
RITE OF MARRIAGE #125.

Scripture

The spirit of the Lord GOD is upon me,
   because the LORD has anointed me;
he has sent me to bring good news to the oppressed,
   to bind up the brokenhearted,
to proclaim liberty to the captives,
   and release to the prisoners;
to proclaim the year of the LORD's favor,
   and the day of vengeance of our God;
   to comfort all who mourn;
to provide for those who mourn in Zion—
   to give them a garland instead of ashes,
the oil of gladness instead of mourning,
   the mantle of praise instead of a faint spirit.

ISAIAH 61:1–3

Prayer

Let us pray. . . .
for all bishops, priests, and deacons;
for all who have a special ministry in the Church
and for all God's people.
Almighty and eternal God,
your Spirit guides the Church
and makes it holy.
Listen to our prayers
and help each of us
in his [or her] own vocation
to do your work more faithfully.
We ask this through Christ our Lord.
Amen.

GENERAL INTERCESSIONS,
GOOD FRIDAY CELEBRATION
OF THE LORD'S PASSION.

Holy Orders: Ministering to God's Life

Jesus and Priestly Ministry

Jesus was a sacrament of God to people, a living sign of God's love and concern, embodying God's presence and power for good in the world. Jesus was also in a very real sense a priestly person, even though he never went through an ordination ceremony. A priest in the ancient world was a mediator between God and humans, and in this sense certainly Jesus was a priest.

Jesus gathered people around himself, immersing his followers in a community that gave them a taste of the kingdom of God. Jesus communicated his spirit to those who were open to receiving it, strengthening them and inviting them to care about others the way he did. Those who were willing to be taught by him were called his disciples or students. By word and example, Jesus taught them to minister to others, attending to their needs, curing their ills, forgiving their sins, healing their brokenness. Jesus as a priestly person did many of the things that we now associate with priestly **ministry.**

All Christians are called to be disciples of Jesus and a priestly people. Very early in Christian history, however, the call of some to minister like Jesus was marked by a special ceremony that we now call ordination. In the early Church a number of ministries (Would you believe seven?) were conferred through ordination, but other types of ministering were done by unordained Christians as well. Today there are three ordained ministries in the Church, and many ministries performed by people who are not ordained.

Ordination is something special in the Church. It is the only ceremony of passage into the service of God and the people of God that is recognized as one of the seven ecclesiastical (or official Church) sacraments and one of the Sacraments at the Service of Communion, one of the Sacraments of Vocation. As such, it is the primary example of what it means to be dedicated to a life of ministry in the Church.

ministry   service to others, derived from the Latin word for waiting at tables; generally designates service with a religious motivation

ordination   the act by which the bishop as a representative of the Church confers an order on a candidate, giving the candidate the power to perform the duties of that order

parish a local Catholic faith community, with a priest pastor or pastoral administrator appointed by the bishop

diocese a collection of parishes in a certain geographical area, headed by a bishop

archdiocese the principal diocese in a given region, headed by an archbishop

Discussion

In the large group, discuss the following questions:

1. What kind of ministry did Jesus engage? Give specific examples.

2. What qualities do you think Jesus looked for in the group of his followers?

3. What examples of ministry can you think of in the early Church? (Look at Acts, chapters 1–15, for stories, and at Romans 12 and 1 Corinthians 12 for lists.)

Other commitment ceremonies reflect the primary meaning that is found in ordination. When a man or woman becomes a member of a religious order such as the Benedictines, the Franciscans, the Dominicans, the Jesuits, or the Sisters of Charity, for example, he or she becomes first a postulant, then a novice, and finally a professed member of the community. Each of those rituals of consecration is similar to ordination in that it is a religious rite of passage into deeper commitment to God and further service to the Church. But they are not ordinations because they are not passages into priesthood. They are sacramentals, but they are not sacraments in the strict sense.

Likewise, lay people are sometimes called to serve or be affirmed in their ministry in a commissioning ceremony. In such a ceremony, locally designed and unique to each **parish** or **diocese** (or **archdiocese**), the pastor or bishop blesses those called to service in the local church, affirms their calling, and invests them with the authority to perform their ministry. Again, however, these ceremonies are not ordinations because they are not passages into priesthood. And they are sacramentals, but not sacraments.

JESUS THE HIGH PRIEST

Very early in the history of the Church, Christians came to understand the role of the risen Jesus as one of priestly mediation between people and God. Here is how the Letter to the Hebrews puts it.

Now the main point in what we are saying is this: we have such a high priest, one who is seated at the right hand of the throne of the Majesty in the heavens, a minister in the sanctuary and the true tent that the Lord, and not any mortal, has set up. For every high priest is appointed to offer gifts and sacrifices; hence it is necessary for this priest also to have something to offer. Now if he were on earth, he would not be a priest at all, since there are priests who offer gifts according to the law. They offer worship in a sanctuary that is a sketch and shadow of the heavenly one; for Moses, when he was about to erect the tent, was warned, "See that you make everything according to the pattern that was shown you on the mountain." But Jesus has now obtained a more excellent ministry, and to that degree he is the mediator of a better covenant, which has been enacted through better promises.

Hebrews 8:1–6

Discussion

In the large group, discuss the following questions:

1. In what ways is the author comparing Jesus to a high priest?

2. If you were to compare Jesus to an important type of person today, who would it be? Explain the comparison that you make.

THE PRIESTLY CHARACTER

The Catechism speaks about ordination in traditional theological language as conferring an "indelible spiritual character" similar to the seal of the Spirit associated with the Sacraments of Initiation. Because this character is permanent and indelible, it cannot be removed, and once the sacrament is received, it cannot be received again.

This language can be problematic because it suggests a magical change in the soul of the priest and because it seems to say that an invisible soul can have a mark on it that cannot be removed. This is fine for people who are comfortable with appealing to imagination, but it is not so good for people who ask what this means in real life or in terms of their experiences. In fact, neither the Catechism nor the Church documents from which this teaching is drawn explains how the character is to be understood. Theologically this is an open question.

Perhaps the character can be understood today in terms of the relationship between an ordained priest and the Christian community. This is similar to what happens in other sacraments. When people are baptized and confirmed, they become permanent members of the people of God, and these sacraments are not repeated even if a person leaves the Church and then comes back to it. When two people are married, they are permanently changed from being single to being married to each other. So also, when someone is ordained, his relationship to the Church is changed forever. Even if he leaves the priestly ministry, he is still an ordained priest, although one who is not practicing his priesthood.

Discussion

Think about examples of magical thinking in the following: children's fairy tales, classical myths and legends, cartoon superheroes, fantasy fiction, movies and television. In the large group, discuss the following questions:

- Do you think it is all right to understand sacraments in a magical way? Why or why not?
- How do you understand the priestly character? Explain your answer.

Review Questions

1. How was Jesus a priestly person?
2. What is ministry?
3. What is ordination?
4. What is a parish? A diocese? An archdiocese?
5. What is the priestly character received in ordination?

Ordination and Holy Orders

Holy Orders the sacrament of priestly ministry in the Church, conferred through the laying on of hands by a bishop

order a rank or level in a priestly ministry; a word derived from the Latin *ordo,* which designated a military rank or government administrative level in the Roman Empire

diaconate from the Greek word for one who serves; the first of the three ministerial orders in the Church

deacon one who has been ordained into the first of the three ministerial orders in the Church

presbyterate from the Greek word for an elder; the second of the three ministerial orders in the Church

priest one who has been ordained into the second of the three ministerial orders in the Church

episcopate from the Greek word for supervisor or overseer; the third of the three ministerial orders in the Church

bishop one who has been ordained into the third of the three ministerial orders in the Church

catechetics religious education and spiritual formation

Ordination to the priesthood means the beginning of a lifetime of service in and to the Church. Like Baptism and Confirmation, it is celebrated only once and is never repeated. At the same time, however, there are three different kinds of ordination ceremonies in the Church. This is why the official name of the sacrament is not singular but plural—**Holy Orders.**

In the distant past, young men worked their way through a series of **orders** in their training for the priesthood, sort of like the ranks in a military organization. These orders originated many centuries ago before there were seminaries for training priests. Candidates for the priesthood were somewhat like apprentices. They learned by practice, spending some time doing each of the things that clerics had to know for their ministry.

At each of these steps along the way, young men would be initiated more deeply into the priestly life by a special ordination ceremony. Today, however, that process has been greatly simplified, and there are only three rites of ordination: to the **diaconate** (for **deacons**), to the **presbyterate** (for **priests**), and to the **episcopate** (for **bishops**).

Let us begin with the last one first, since bishops are said to have "the fullness of the priesthood."

A bishop is the pastor of an entire diocese. He is ultimately responsible for the proper administration of a diocese, for all the parish churches and schools in the diocese, and for all of the diocesan offices and agencies (for example, Catholic Charities). He is also responsible for overseeing the **catechetics** and liturgy in the diocese. Realistically, however, a bishop doesn't do all of this himself; he appoints other people who do this administration for him. Bishops are appointed by the pope, but they are ordained by other bishops. They can thus perform all the sacramental functions in the Church, including ordinations.

Some priests work in schools as religion teachers or campus ministers.

A priest is ordinarily the pastor of a parish (although some priests do not do parish work, and some parishes do not have priest pastors). He is a co-worker with the bishop in a diocese, and so he is not allowed to minister in another diocese without permission from the other bishop. Priests are usually ordained by a single bishop, and the bishop of their diocese appoints them to their ministry. (It works a little differently for priests in religious orders.) Priests are the most visible sacramental ministers in the Church—they preside at Eucharist, they baptize, they preside at weddings, they hear confessions, and they anoint the sick. Priests cannot ordain, however, and they can perform Confirmations only if their bishop asks them to do so.

A deacon's sacramental ministry is somewhat more limited. As their name implies, deacons are ordained for service, and in fact deacons serve in many different capacities in parishes and dioceses. As liturgical ministers, deacons can preach but they cannot preside at Eucharist. They can preside at Baptisms, weddings, and funerals. *Transitional deacons* are in training for the presbyterate and will eventually be ordained as priests. *Permanent deacons* are called to the diaconate to fill a ministerial need that does not require that they be priests.

Research

The English word *deacon* derives from the Greek *diakonos,* the English word *priest* derives from the Greek *presbyter,* and the English word *bishop* derives from the Greek *episkopos.* Can you see how the shorter words evolved from the longer ones? Find ten more English words that are derived from Greek words. Give the meaning of the original words and the derived words. (You might try finding words that relate to Catholic practice or liturgy; begin with the glossary of this book.)

Discussion

In a small group, discuss the following questions:

1. What qualities do you think a good priest ought to have? Why?

2. What qualities do you think a good deacon ought to have? Why?

3. What qualities do you think a good bishop ought to have? Why?

Interview

With the help of your teacher, visit a seminary where priests are trained. Learn as much as you can about the course of study, the training in spirituality, and the preparation for ministry. Take photos of or videotape the places you see and the people you visit. Using these audiovisual aids, report back to your class about what you learned.

HONORARY TITLES IN THE CHURCH

Besides bishops, priests, and deacons in the Church, there are also cardinals and monsignors. And don't forget the pope! One difference between these positions and the others discussed in this chapter is that they are not conferred by ordination. Rather, they are titles of honor bestowed on priests and bishops who do special work or in recognition of special achievement.

A *monsignor* is a priest who holds a significant post in a diocese or who has served long and well as a pastor. The word itself derives from the French meaning "my lord," which is clearly a title of honor. Being a monsignor has few special privileges other than the title itself.

A *cardinal* is a priest, a bishop, or an archbishop who has served the Church long and well. Cardinals are special advisors to the pope, and they head most of the highest administrative offices in the Church. The word *cardinal* is derived from the Latin word meaning a door hinge. Since the cardinals in the Church elect the pope, the election "swings" on their decision.

The *pope* is a bishop who has been elected by his fellow bishops (actually, by those bishops who are also cardinals) to be the bishop of Rome and head of the Catholic Church. The word *pope* derives from the Latin *papa*, which is a familiar word for father. The pope is also called the Holy Father.

Pope John Paul II at the Easter Vigil in St. Peter's Basilica.

DISCUSSION

In the large group, discuss the following questions:

1. The Catechism (#1582) says that ordination "confers an indelible spiritual character" on those in Holy Orders. Yet there are men who leave the priestly ministry for one reason or another. How can one be ordained "a priest forever" and then "leave the priesthood"?

2. The Catechism (#1585) says that, through ordination, the Holy Spirit bestows grace that is proper to this sacrament. However, we may have heard or read about priests who did a bad job or who even committed crimes. How is God's grace to be understood, if it is not something that automatically guarantees success or good behavior?

The vast majority of priests are involved in parish work. They preside at the sacraments, preach, teach, and lead the community in service.

 **Research**

1. Look up each of the following Scripture passages and relate them to the ministerial orders in the Church or to various aspects of priestly ministry: Matthew 18:18; Matthew 28:19–20; Luke 22:17–20; John 20:21–23; Acts 15:1–6; 1 Timothy 3:1–13.

2. Find five other passages in the New Testament that relate to ministry. In an essay, summarize the passages and explain what they say to you about ministry.

 **Journal**

1. Have you ever thought about being a priest?

2. What kinds of factors did you consider?

3. Where are you now in your thinking?

Review Questions

1. What is the Sacrament of Holy Orders?

2. Name the three orders of priestly ministry in the Church today.

3. Describe the role or work of bishops, priests, and deacons.

4. What is a monsignor? A cardinal? The pope?

Ministry Means Service

The meaning of ministry, whether ordained or not, is intimately connected to service. The Rite of Ordination to Holy Orders spells this out clearly and dramatically—both symbolically and liturgically. The candidates approach the bishop and ask to be allowed to serve the people of God in an official capacity. After being questioned by the bishop about their intention and resolve to perform their duties, they promise to respect and obey him and his successors, for by entering the service of the Church they are willing to put the needs of others ahead of their own personal desires.

At one point in the ceremony, the candidates lie face down on the floor while everyone prays that they will be strengthened by God for the work that they are about to undertake. When they get up, they kneel before the bishop who lays his hands on their heads as a gesture of approval and appointment. Then the bishop prays for an outpouring of the Holy Spirit and his gifts, asking that God will be with them, bless their work, and make it fruitful. The laying on of hands and the prayer of consecration are the essential elements of the Sacrament of Holy Orders. This prayer of consecration is different for the ordination of deacons, priests, and bishops, for it spells out the different ministries to which the candidates are being dedicated.

Ordination is a call to service.

The prayer for a bishop shows the ministry of service to which he is consecrated:

Father, you know all hearts.
You have chosen your servant for the office of bishop.
May he be a shepherd to your holy flock,
and a high priest blameless in your sight,
ministering to you night and day;
may he always gain the blessing of your favor
and offer the gifts of your holy Church.
Through the Spirit who gives the grace of high priesthood
grant him the power
to forgive sins as you have commanded,
to assign ministries as you have decreed,
and to loose every bond by the authority
which you gave to your apostles. . . .

So now pour out upon this chosen one
that power which is from you, the governing Spirit
whom you gave to your beloved Son, Jesus Christ,
the Spirit given by him to the holy apostles,
who founded the Church in every place to be your temple
for the unceasing glory and praise of your name.

Prayer of Consecration, *Ordination of Bishops,* #26.

WHAT THE CATECHISM SAYS

The grace of the Holy Spirit in each order of the Sacrament of Holy Orders is configuration to Christ, who is Priest, Teacher, and Pastor. Bishops receive especially the grace of strength to guide and defend the Church. Priests are given the grace to fulfill the ministry of word and sacrament. And deacons are strengthened for the ministry of service and works of charity and for liturgy and the proclamation of the gospel.

See the *Catechism of the Catholic Church,* #s 1585–1588.

Research

1. Borrow a copy of the *Rite of Ordination of Priests.* Find the places that speak of service and summarize what they say.

2. Borrow a copy of the *Rite of Ordination of Deacons.* Find the places that speak of service and summarize what they say.

Activity

If a deacon, priest, or bishop is invited to talk with your class about ordination and ministry in the Church, work as a class to write up a list of questions that you would like to ask the speaker. After the event, discuss with your class what you have learned.

The miter and crozier are signs of the bishop's authority and mission.

Signs of Ministry

In each ordination rite, the candidates are also invested with signs of their official ministry in the Church. Deacons are dressed in the stole that is worn diagonally like a sash, and the dalmatic, which is a simple liturgical garment worn over the alb (white robe). They also receive the Book of the Gospels as a sign that they may now proclaim the gospel and preach at Mass.

Priests are vested in the stole, which they wear over both shoulders, and the chasuble, which is the large outer vestment worn at Mass. They are also anointed on the hands with chrism as a sign of the anointing of the Holy Spirit who will make their ministry fruitful. They are presented with a chalice and paten, as they are now empowered to consecrate the Eucharist.

A bishop is anointed on the head with chrism and given the Book of the Gospels, a ring, a miter (hat), and a crozier (staff) as a sign of his teaching authority and mission to proclaim the gospel, faithful to the Church and his office as shepherd. He wears the miter and carries the crozier in official ceremonial functions of the Church.

One other sign usually associated with Holy Orders in Western Catholicism is celibacy, or the promise to not marry or have sexual intercourse. In the ordination ceremony for deacons who are headed for the priesthood (transitional deacons), the bishop addresses the candidates and asks, "In the presence of God and the Church, are you resolved, as a sign of your interior dedication to Christ, to remain celibate for the sake of the kingdom and in lifelong service to God and mankind?" To which the candidates each answer, "I am."

Activity

With help from your teacher or pastor, attend an ordination ceremony by yourself or with other members of your class. If possible, meet with one of those who participated in the ceremony, either by ordaining or by being ordained.

1. Discuss with others in your class what you felt and learned.

2. Reflecting on your experience, how do you think it feels to be a priest?

Research

Using print and electronic media, research:

1. The origins of clerical clothing (such as the black suit and Roman collar) and priestly vestments (the special clothing worn during liturgy). Using photocopies, slides, or other audiovisual aids, report to your class what you learned.

2. The ordained ministry and ordination in other Churches besides the Catholic Church.
   - What did you learn?
   - What do you think about what you learned?

Celibacy as a Sign

Celibacy is a sign of total dedication to a life of service. It is a lifestyle that is connected not only with Holy Orders but also with communities of men and women religious. Men who become brothers or monks in monasteries and women who become cloistered nuns or active sisters have vocations to a committed religious life that leaves no room for marriage. Religious life involves living and working together in a ministry of dedication to God and service to others. Although men and women religious are not ordained (with the exception of religious order priests), they are expected to be so completely devoted to their religious vocation that for the sake of the kingdom of God they give up their right to marry, have sexual intercourse, and raise a family of their own.

Actually, in the history of the Church, celibacy was first practiced by lay people. Beginning in the fourth century, men and women who wanted to live a more perfect life of prayer left the busy towns and cities for the countryside where they could pray and meditate in solitude. By the next century, most of the people who did this were gathering into small communities that lived, worked, and worshiped together. In the course of time, these initial foundations grew into the great monasteries and abbeys of the first religious orders. If an order had priests, it was only as many as were needed to celebrate the Eucharist and the other sacraments in the community.

During these centuries of Christianity, priests generally married; if they did not, it was not by law that they remained single. Eventually, however, more and more bishops were persuaded by the symbolic value of celibacy to demand celibacy of themselves and the young men whom they ordained. In the Middle Ages, too, many of those who volunteered for the priesthood came from the monastic communities that were already living a celibate life. There were practical reasons to promote celibacy as well, such as being able to transfer men from one post to another and avoiding the problems connected with Church property and inheritance. By the twelfth century, the growing practice of celibacy among the clergy was written into Church (canon) law, and it became the normal practice of the Church in the West. Priests in the East (covering modern-day Greece, Turkey, the Middle East, and Egypt) continued to marry and raise families. Today the Eastern Rite in most countries and Orthodox Churches everywhere allow parish priests to marry.

Celibacy is meant to help an ordained minister be of greater service to God and the people of God.

The effect of priestly celibacy on the Church was both positive and negative. The positive effect was that, freed from the concerns of marriage, priests could devote all their time and energy to the service of God's people. The negative effect was really the other side of the same coin, in that priests took over virtually all ministerial functions in the Church, except for the service rendered by religious sisters and brothers (mainly in schools and hospitals). Although they were ordained primarily to carry out pastoral and sacramental ministries, priests took on many of the ministries that in the early days of the Church had been performed by lay people. These included the administration of programs, the management of institutions, the evangelization of non-Christians, the teaching of theology, and the visiting of those who were sick, to name a few.

At a time when the clergy were the only educated people in society (We still refer to work that involves reading and writing as "clerical work."), it was natural for the Church to expect its priests to provide everything that was needed for people's spiritual welfare. Also, to the degree that marriages were arranged by parents for their children and when career options were very few, a life of self-chosen celibacy and dedication to God was a positive value for men who were attracted by the rewards of personal development and service to others. As long as the benefits remained very positive, young men continued to swell the ranks of the priesthood, and the Church continued to rely primarily on priests to meet all its ministerial needs.

Discussion

In the large group, discuss the following questions:

1. In the Catholic Church in the West, most priests and all bishops are not allowed to marry, but in other Churches (including Eastern Rite Catholic Churches in some countries) priests can be married if they marry before ordination. What do you think might have been some of the reasons for this difference in Church policies?

2. Catholic men who want to be priests cannot be married, but ministers from other Churches who want to convert and be priests in the Catholic Church can sometimes get permission to be ordained and to remain married.
   - What problems are created by these two different Church policies about priesthood and marriage?
   - What different perspectives do married priests bring to their ministry?

Review Questions

1. What are some things that happen during the ordination of a priest?

2. What signs of ministry are presented to the candidates in the ordination rite of deacons? Of priests? Of bishops?

3. Explain the meaning of celibacy as a sign.

A Priestly People

Since the 1960s, the Church's understanding of ministry has been changing. The Second Vatican Council affirmed that all people in the Church, not just priests and religious, because of their Baptism and Confirmation are called by God to lives of personal holiness and service to others. The people of God, said the council, are a "priestly people," bringing God's life into their families and their communities. Their priesthood is referred to as the *priesthood of the faithful* or the *common priesthood of all believers.*

Something that the bishops at the council did not foresee was a great decline in the number of priests that took place from the late sixties to the late seventies in many countries. Even though this decline in the United States has now leveled off, there are not enough priests to replace those who are aging and dying. Some seminaries have closed; others have been consolidated. Parishes that once had two or three priests now have to make do with one, and some parishes share a priest with one or two other parishes. In parts of the world where vocations are on the rise, the population is increasing faster than the priests who are available to serve them.

Motivated in part by the council's affirmation of the common priesthood of all believers, lay people began to envision themselves as truly able to participate in ministry, and those in religious orders began to look beyond teaching and nursing in Catholic institutions. The numbers of lay people serving in parishes and dioceses went up, as did the numbers of those who sought professional training for such work in Catholic colleges and universities.

As a result, lay people today are involved in the liturgy, most visibly by proclaiming the Scriptures, leading prayers and music, and distributing Communion. They are also involved behind the scenes by preparing the music, creating the environment, and coordinating the entire liturgical team. Large parishes have hired lay or religious professionals to work in liturgical planning, religious education, and parish administration, and smaller parishes have encouraged volunteers to help with these tasks. Most of the teaching done in Catholic schools is done by lay people, and most parish programs, both social and educational, are lay staffed. In many parishes, lay people and religious are also involved in counseling and other types of social services available to parishioners.

Research

In recent decades many books and articles have been written about the Catholic priesthood. Using books, articles, and Internet resources, investigate why the number of priests in the United States declined after Vatican II, or learn about vocations to the priesthood in more recent years. Summarize your findings in an oral presentation or a written report.

A Center of Ministry

In the course of a single generation there was a veritable revolution in the role of priests in the Church, and it is still going on. From being the only minister or one of several priests in a parish, the priest has become a coordinator of ministries at the parish level. His role as pastor enables him to be a community builder and spiritual counselor, and his role as the primary liturgical minister and preacher empowers him to be a community energizer and motivator. The priest is still at the center of ministry, even though he is no longer the whole of ministry.

This shift in the role of the priest has raised new questions that were hardly heard a few generations ago. Some people question whether priests, given their ministerial work today, really have to be celibate. Protestant congregations seem to do well with married clergy, so why not Catholic parishes? At the present time, the Catholic Church does allow married men to be ordained to the permanent diaconate. The Church also occasionally ordains married men as priests, if they were, for example, Episcopalian priests or Lutheran ministers who become Catholic and want to serve the Church as priests.

Perhaps the most sensitive question is the ordination of women. The Church teaches that God has not given the Church the power to ordain women now or ever. Because of this, only men can be called to the ministerial priesthood and be ordained as deacons, priests, or bishops. Nevertheless, the role of women in the Church will continue to be a topic of discussion, especially since so many of the lay ministers in the Church are women, and there will continue to be new ministries and new responsibilities for women in the Church's future.

In the meanwhile, priesthood is still the paradigm of ministry in the Church. The ancient definition of a priest was "a mediator between God and humankind." And insofar as any minister in the Church makes God more real for people and brings people closer to God, he or she is performing a priestly role.

When and where do you encounter priests?

Vatican II reminded us of the important fact that, as the people of God, all of us in the Church are a priestly people, and, therefore, all of us have a Christian vocation to bring the life of God to others. In this sense, husbands and wives should be like priests to one another, as should parents to their children, and as all Catholics should be to the people with whom they live and work. We are all mediators of God's grace to others whenever we help them increase the goodness in their lives.

Professional and volunteer ministers in the Church perform this priestly role in a more visible way. This is why, as mentioned earlier, not only those who enter religious communities, but also lay people who serve the parish or the diocese are sometimes received into their ministry through a ceremony which draws its inspiration from Holy Orders. Today it is not uncommon to hear of catechists and teachers, Eucharistic and music ministers, and even parish council members being commissioned by their pastor to exercise their ministry with devotion to God and dedication to the people whom they serve.

The basic meaning of ordination is being ordered or directed toward service. In the ordination ceremony, we see the Church's understanding of what such service ultimately entails. The homily for the ordination of deacons (for *diakonia* literally means ministry or service) expresses this most clearly:

> *Like the men the apostles chose for works of charity, you should be men of good reputation, filled with wisdom and the Holy Spirit. Show before God and mankind that you are above every suspicion and blame, true ministers of Christ and of God's mysteries, men firmly rooted in faith. Never turn away from the hope that the gospel offers; now you must not only listen to God's word but also preach it. Hold the mystery of faith with a clear conscience. Express in action what you proclaim by word of mouth. Then the people of Christ, brought to life by the Spirit, will be an offering God accepts. Finally, on the last day, when you go to meet the Lord, you will hear him say: "Well done, good and faithful servant, enter into the joy of your Lord."*

Rite of Ordination of Deacons, # 14.

Research

Make an appointment with someone who works in your parish office, and find out the following.

1. In your parish, what are the major parts of the priest's ministry?

2. If there is a permanent deacon, what is his ministry?

3. Who are the other people on the parish staff? What are their ministries?

4. In your parish, what do volunteers do?

WHY CAN'T WOMEN BE ORDAINED?

In the Catholic Church (and in other Churches as well), only men are allowed to be ordained to the priesthood. Some reasons given for this are:

- Jesus was a man, and at Mass the priest represents Jesus.

- Jesus did not select women to be apostles, even though there were women among his followers, and even though Jesus treated women more fairly than they were often treated in his day. In this, the Church must respect the will and example of Jesus.

- The constant practice of the Church has been to ordain only men, and the Church must respect the force of tradition.

- Priesthood is a vocation from God that comes through the call of a bishop. No one has a right to be ordained a priest.

DISCUSSION

In the large group, discuss the following questions:

1. Summarize the arguments against women priests in your own words.

2. What does it mean to say that ordination is not a right?

3. Why are Catholics expected to accept this teaching?

Journal

1. What gifts for ministry do you have?

2. How might you use these gifts?

interview

1. Interview a deacon or someone in the permanent deacon preparation program (the man to be ordained or his wife). Ask questions such as the following, and report back to the class.

   - Why did you (or your husband) want to be a permanent deacon?
   - What did you (or your husband) have to do to be accepted into the program?
   - What is the preparation like? How long does it take? What do you study?
   - What happens at the ordination of a deacon?

2. With help and direction from your teacher and pastor, talk with a woman minister from a Protestant denomination about her work. Among other things, ask her about the advantages and difficulties of being a woman minister. Write an essay or make an oral presentation about your discussion.

A Day in the Life of Father Jones

While the role of full-time housekeeper for priests isn't as common an occupation as it was in the past, there are many places where it is still common.

Working as a housekeeper in a rectory, I've seen a lot of priests come and go. In years gone by, some of them didn't seem overly busy (if you want to know the truth!), but that's all changed now with the shortage of priests. If they don't keep busy by themselves, something's always coming up to keep them hopping!

Take Father Jones, for example. After saying the eight o'clock Mass every morning, he goes over to the school to spend some time with the children—unless, of course, he's got a funeral, which pretty well takes the whole morning (and he's often at the wake the night before). Then he makes his Communion calls, visiting people who are homebound or in the hospital. He usually gets those done by lunch time, but sometimes he doesn't even get back in time for lunch. I just put it in the refrigerator, and he gets to it when he can.

A couple of afternoons every week he's running to meetings for the diocese or some social agency here in the city. He's on a number different advisory boards and planning councils, and they're always calling him. In the afternoon he also makes his phone calls. And then there are his appointments, people coming to see him about personal problems or for spiritual direction, or because they do business with the parish and they have to talk to him. And he gets his paperwork done. A lot of it is done now by various parish committees, but he still has to read the reports and he still has to sign the checks. And he has to keep up with what's going on in the area. I think we must get a dozen different newsletters at the rectory!

Evenings start with supper, of course. I like Father Jones because shortly after he moved in he made it a point to invite people from the parish to have supper with him almost every night. It's more like cooking for a family that way, and I like to cook! By seven-thirty or so, though, he's usually out again. I don't think there's a day that goes by without some evening meeting at the school or at the parish center that he has to go to! There's the liturgy commission, the peace and justice group, the RCIA gathering, the religious education program, the parish council, the finance committee—well, the list just goes on and on!

When he gets in, it's usually after ten, and he relaxes a bit, probably by reading a book or newspaper or watching the news on television. That's about the only time he gets to himself, except for his one day off each week. People sometimes forget that priests have to work on Sunday! Saturdays he's busy, too, spending time with the youth group or supporting one of the parish sports teams or presiding at a wedding. In between all of this, he spends a great deal of time writing his homilies. I suppose he hardly ever gets to sleep before midnight, but by then I'm long gone to sleep. Tomorrow will be another busy day in the parish!

The life of a parish priest is busy, demanding, and very rewarding.

Discussion

Imagine that you are a parish priest. In a small group, discuss the following questions:

1. How would you feel about being a priest? What might you like about it, and what might you not like about it?
2. What would you spend most of your time doing?
3. What would you try to do differently in your parish?

interview

Do one of the following interviews, and write a written report or make an oral presentation to your class about what you learned.

1. Talk with a priest about the meaning that ordination has for him and about his work as a priest.
   - What does he like best about the priesthood?
   - What does he wish might be different?
2. Talk with a permanent deacon about the meaning that ordination has for him, and about his work as a deacon.
   - What does he like best about the diaconate?
   - What does he wish might be different?

Review Questions

1. What is meant by the priesthood of all believers?
2. How is this different from the ordained priesthood? How is it similar?
3. How can the ordained be a center of ministry?
4. Describe some lay ministries in the Church today.

Summary

Ordination is a special ceremony of empowerment for ministry in the Church. Only deacons, priests, and bishops are ordained for their particular ministries. People can be inducted into religious orders and lay ministers can be commissioned for service, but these ceremonies are not the same as ordination. They can be regarded as sacramentals, or sacraments in a broad sense, but they are not one of the seven ecclesiastical sacraments.

The official name for this sacrament is Holy Orders, referring to the three degrees of the ministerial priesthood. Whereas in the past, priests performed most of the ministries in the Church, today that situation is changing. The priest who is a resident pastor is the coordinator of parish ministries performed by lay people and people in religious orders. A priest may also be the sacramental minister for more than one parish where he presides at the Eucharistic liturgy and other sacramental rites.

While not everyone who serves in the Church today is in Holy Orders, the Rite of Ordination can be understood as a model for the true meaning of ministering to others for the sake of God's kingdom.

Scripture

The gifts he gave were that some would be apostles, some prophets, some evangelists, some pastors and teachers, to equip the saints for the work of ministry, for building up the body of Christ, until all of us come to the unity of the faith and of the knowledge of the Son of God, to maturity, to the measure of the full stature of Christ . . . [S]peaking the truth in love, we must grow up in every way into him who is the head, into Christ, from whom the whole body, joined and knit together by every ligament with which it is equipped, as each part is working properly, promotes the body's growth in building itself up in love.

EPHESIANS 4:11–13, 15–16

Prayer

All powerful and ever-living God,
fill this church with your love
and give your help to all who call on you in faith,
May the power of your word and sacraments . . .
bring strength to the people gathered here.
We ask this through our Lord Jesus Christ, your Son,
who lives and reigns with you and the Holy Spirit,
one lives and reigns with you and the Holy Spirit,
one God, for ever and ever.

OPENING PRAYER, COMMON OF THE
DEDICATION OF A CHURCH.

Glossary

agape—(a–GA–pay) the Greek word for love that is used in the New Testament, sometimes called *self-giving love* or *unconditional love;* an action word that can also be translated as *care* or *caring* (page 41)

anoint—from the Latin word for oil or salve, originally a pouring of perfumed oil on the head or a smearing of scented salve over the upper body (page 114)

Anointing of the Sick—the Sacrament of Healing for those who are seriously ill or in danger of death due to sickness or old age, consisting of anointing with oil, imposition of hands, and prayers for physical and spiritual healing and the forgiveness of sins (pages 48, 179)

archdiocese—the principal diocese in a given region, headed by an archbishop (page 221)

atheist—someone who denies the existence of God (page 188)

Baptism—from the Greek word for immersion, the name of the first of the three Sacraments of Initiation; the sacrament of new life in God and of incorporation into the Church performed by full or partial immersion in water, or by pouring water over the head of the candidate, while the presider proclaims, "I baptize you in the name of the Father, and of the Son, and of the Holy Spirit." (pages 43, 66)

baptismal vows—promises made at Baptism by the person baptized, or by the parents, godparents, and assembly, to reject sin and confess the Christian faith (page 76)

Beatitudes—what Jeus taught his followers about what to do in order to be really happy and fulfilled (page 159)

bishop—one who has been ordained into the third of the three ministerial orders in the Church (page 223)

Blessed Sacrament—the consecrated Bread or Wine, especially the consecrated hosts or wafers considered apart from the Eucharistic liturgy, reserved in the tabernacle for special worship services (such as Benediction of the Blessed Sacrament) and for distribution to those who are sick (page 122)

canon law—the Church's code of laws (page 12)

catechetics—religious education and spiritual formation (page 223)

catechumen—an unbaptized person who has celebrated the rite of entrance into the catechumenate and who is preparing for full membership in the Christian community (page 45)

catechumenate—the first formal stage; a time of formation and education in the Rite of Christian Initiation of Adults when people are preparing for Baptism through a process of learning and faith sharing, and solemnized in the rituals of the RCIA (pages 45, 71)

celibacy—remaining deliberately unmarried and not have sexual intercourse for a purpose, such as service to others; in the Catholic Church, choosing to remain unmarried and not have sexual intercourse in order to be of greater service to God and the people of God (page 230)

charism—a spiritual gift; today the term usually refers to special abilities in ministry (page 106)

chrism—blessed oil used in the Sacraments of Baptism, Confirmation, and Holy Orders (pages 77, 114)

Church—the community of the people of God that draws its life from Christ (page 31)

Communion—the consecrated Bread and Wine, perceived in faith to be the Body and Blood of Christ; also, the act of receiving the consecrated Bread or Wine (page 122)

confession—the act of honestly telling one's sins to another—God, another person, or in the sacrament, to a priest (page 240)

Confirmation—the Sacrament of Initiation that completes Baptism and celebrates the gifts of the Holy Spirit; performed ordinarily by a bishop who anoints the forehead of the candidate while saying, "Be sealed with the Gift of the Holy Spirit." (pages 44, 100)

conscience—the human ability to judge what is right and wrong, sometimes thought of as the voice of reason or the voice of God (page 162)

consecration—Jesus' words of institution of the Eucharist at the Last Supper recited by the priest at Mass, changing the bread and wine into the Body and Blood of Christ (page 122)

conversion—also called repentance; changing one's thoughts, feelings, and behavior; turning one's life around, at least with regard to some parts of it that are either bad or not as good as they could be (page 150)

covenant—a solemn agreement between humans or between God and humans involving mutual commitments or guarantees (page 202)

deacon—one who has been ordained into the first of the three ministerial orders in the Church (page 223)

declaration of nullity—declaration by a Church court that a failed marriage was never really a sacramental marriage, even though people may have thought it was; commonly referred to as an annulment (page 213)

diaconate—from the Greek word for one who serves; the first of the three ministerial orders in the Church (page 223)

diocese—a collection of parishes in a certain geographical area, headed by a bishop (page 221)

disciple—someone who is willing to learn from a specific teacher; more generally, a follower; derived from a Latin word that refers to a student. For Christians, a disciple is one who accepts Jesus' message, follows him, and lives according to his teachings. (page 43)

divorce—declaration by a civil court that a legal marriage has ended and that the parties are free to remarry (page 213)

Eastern Rite—a Catholic Church whose liturgical traditions are very ancient and different from the Roman or Latin Rite and whose origins are in Eastern Europe or the Middle East (page 10)

empowered—strengthened, energized, given the ability to do something (page 95)

episcopate—from the Greek word for supervisor or overseer; the third of the three ministerial orders in the Church (page 223)

ethical, moral—pertaining to the goodness or badness of human acts (page 163)

Eucharist—from the Greek, meaning an act of thanksgiving, an ancient name for the Christian celebration of the Paschal mystery that includes remembrance of the Last Supper and distribution of Communion; the sacrament of thanksgiving that celebrates the Paschal mystery—Jesus' suffering, death, and resurrection; also the name given to the consecrated Bread and Wine, the Body and Blood of Christ (pages 41, 123)

Extreme Unction—the former name for the Sacrament of the Anointing of the Sick, emphasizing the last anointing before death (page 177)

fidelity—faithfulness; in the context of marriage, not having a sexual relationship with anyone but one's spouse; in addition, commitment to growing in love for one another (page 208)

gifts of the Spirit— capabilities or dispositions (sometimes called strengths or virtues) that help us follow the promptings of the Holy Spirit and grow in our relationship with God and others (page 102)

godparent—Baptism sponsor who takes on the responsibility to help the newly baptized person to live a Christian life (page 76)

gospel—the good news of God's mercy and forgiveness revealed by Jesus in his life, death, and resurrection, and proclaimed by the Church to the whole world (page 31)

grace—from the Greek word for gift, used in Christian theology to mean any gift from God, including the spiritual gifts symbolized and received through the sacraments; the free and undeserved gift of God's life and help that enables us to respond to God's call to be his children and to act by his love (pages 55, 68)

grieving process—the normal process of psychologically adjusting to personal loss, involving denial, anger, bargaining, depression, and finally acceptance (page 186)

holy oils—oils used in the sacraments; chrism, the oil of catechumens, and the oil of the sick (page 181)

Holy Orders—the sacrament of priestly ministry in the Church, conferred through the laying on of hands by a bishop; the three degrees of orders of the sacrament are deacon, priest, and bishop (pages 52, 223)

Holy Spirit, God's Spirit, Spirit of God, Spirit of the Lord, Holy Ghost—different ways that Scripture and Christian tradition name the invisible spiritual reality that is God; the third Person of the Holy Trinity; the personal love of the Father and the Son for each other (page 92)

homilist—ordained minister who "breaks open the word,"—explains the Scripture readings at liturgy and calls the assembly to live according to those readings (page 128)

incarnation—literally, enfleshment; used to describe how the Son of God, the second Person of the Blessed Trinity, became human in order to bring about the salvation of all people (page 29)

indissoluble—not able to be dissolved or broken apart (page 198)

initiation—the process of becoming a member of a group; the process by which an unbaptized person prepares for entrance into the Christian community and membership in the Church (page 43)

Last Rites—the Sacraments of Reconciliation, Eucharist (*viaticum*), and the Anointing of the Sick, when administered to someone who is dying (page 180)

laying on of hands—an ancient ritual gesture of approval, blessing, and acceptance, in which one or both hands are placed on the head of the one receiving the gesture (page 113)

liturgy—from the Greek, meaning a public work or service done in the name of or on behalf of the people; in general, any formal Christian worship, especially one that follows a prescribed pattern such as a sacramental rite; a religious ceremony or ritual; a church service; the Church's celebration of the Paschal mystery; sometimes used exclusively to refer to the Eucharistic liturgy (pages 5, 123)

Liturgy of the Eucharist—the second major part of the Mass that includes the presentation and preparation of the gifts, the Eucharistic Prayer, and the Communion rite (page 123)

Liturgy of the Word—the first major part of the Mass that includes the readings, homily, profession of faith, and general intercessions (page 123)

Lord's Supper—a name for Eucharistic worship that is found in the New Testament; the name often given by Protestant Churches to their communion service (page 141)

Mass—from the Latin word for dismissed or sent, in this case, sent on the mission of proclaiming the good news of salvation and the kingdom of God; since the Middle Ages, a common Catholic name for the Eucharistic liturgy (page 123)

Matrimony—the Sacrament of Marriage, a covenant relationship between a man and a woman expressed in faithful love for each other and the care of children (pages 49, 199)

Messiah—Hebrew term for the anointed one; *Christ* is the Greek term (It is related to chrism, a type of oil used for anointing.) (page 29)

ministry—service to others, derived from the Latin word for waiting at tables; generally designates service with a religious motivation (page 220)

miracle—an event, such as an unexpected cure or rapid healing, that is attributed to God's power and that arouses admiration and wonder (page 174)

missal—book containing the ritual of the Mass (page 12)

monogamy—having only one spouse at a time (page 198)

mystery—something that is real but hidden from view; a spiritual or intangible reality known through experience but only partially understood (page 8)

natural family planning—a method of planning the conception of children that is based on natural signs of fertility and infertility in a woman's menstrual cycle (page 210)

natural sacrament—a natural sign of God, such as human caring being a sign of the way God cares for us (page 173)

nuptial—from a Latin word meaning related to or pertaining to marriage (page 199)

order—a rank or level in a priestly ministry; a word derived from the Latin *ordo*, which designated a military rank or government administrative level in the Roman Empire (page 223)

ordination—the act by which the bishop as a representative of the Church confers an order on a candidate, giving the candidate the power to perform the duties of that order (page 220)

original sin—the sin of the first man and woman and the fallen state of human nature into which every person is born, with the exception of Mary and Jesus (page 72)

Orthodox Church—a Church whose liturgical traditions are very ancient, but which is not in full unity with the Catholic Church (The Catholic and Orthodox Churches split from each other in the eleventh century.) (page 10)

parish—a local Catholic faith community, with a priest pastor or pastoral administrator appointed by the bishop (page 221)

Paschal mystery—Christ's work of salvation accomplished through his passion and death, leading to his resurrection and ascension; the mysterious way that goodness comes out of self-sacrifice or dying to self (page 68)

penance—originally another word for repentance or conversion; later, acts of prayer and other good works (page 150)

Penance—one of the official names for the Sacrament of Healing that is also known as the *Sacrament of Reconciliation;* the sacrament of repentance or conversion (page 150)

polygamy—having more than one spouse at a time (page 198)

presbyter—the term used in the early Church for an elder or community leader; still used today in reference to the second of the Holy Orders; the word *priest* is derived from this word (page 52)

presbyterate—from the Greek word for an elder; the second of the three ministerial orders in the Church (page 223)

priest—one who has been ordained into the second of the three ministerial orders in the Church (page 223)

prodigal—wasteful, spendthrift (page 149)

Real Presence—the name for Christ's presence in the Eucharistic liturgy, and especially in the Blessed Sacrament, which is believed in faith but can also be experienced by those who are open to it (page 141)

reconciliation—overcoming emotional separation, usually through some process in which one party admits wrongdoing and another party grants forgiveness; can be between two people, between a person and God, or between a person and a community (page 149)

Reconciliation—the Sacrament of Penance in which we seek assurance of God's love and receive forgiveness for our sins through the ministry of a priest and special words of absolution; the repentant person confesses serious sins and makes reparation (pages 47, 148)

reconversion—converting again, if it needs to be done, as is often the case when one is trying to change one's life for the better (page 150)

repentance—also called conversion or internal penance; changing one's thoughts, feelings, and behavior away from sin; turning one's life around, at least with regard to the parts of it that are sinful (page 162)

revelation—anything that is revealed or disclosed; also, the act of revealing or disclosing; for Christians, God's self-communication, realized by words and actions over time, and fully in Jesus (page 27)

Rite of Baptism for Children—the ritual of Baptism specifically for infants and children; Christian formation follows Baptism as the children grow (page 76)

Rite of Christian Initiation of Adults—the process of gradual initiation into the Christian community and the rites that celebrate the various stages of that process, culminating in the Sacraments of Initiation (pages 45, 71)

sacrament—broadly, any sign or symbol of a sacred reality; a Christian ritual that celebrates or signifies a sacred mystery; as defined by the Catechism: an efficacious sign of grace, instituted by Christ and entrusted to the Church, by which we receive the life of God through the work of the Holy Spirit (pages 5, 22)

sacramental—a sacred sign that is similar to the sacraments in some ways, by which spiritual meanings and realities are signified or by which spiritual blessings are able to be obtained by God's grace through the prayers of the Church (page 23)

sacramentary—a book of rules and prayers for the proper performance of Church rituals (page 12)

Sacraments of Initiation—the three liturgical rites through which a person is received into full membership in the Catholic Church: Baptism, Confirmation, and Eucharist; the sacraments that are at the foundation of the Christian Life (pages 45, 71)

sacrifice—a ritual offering made to God by a priest on behalf of the people, as a sign of adoration, thanksgiving, entreaty, and communion; originally, an act of offering, or the gift that is offered, very often accompanied by a ritual meal for the purpose of communion with the divine (page 139)

salvation—being saved from evil, whether physical or spiritual; in Christian terms, being saved from sin and evil through the power of the redemptive death and resurrection of Jesus (page 174)

scrutinies—rites of repentance celebrated with the elect during Lent (page 45)

sin—originally understood as falling short or missing the mark; can be understood legalistically as breaking a law or commandment; can be understood relationally as weakening (venial) or breaking (mortal) a relationship (page 159) spirit of Jesus, spirit of Christ, spirit of the Lord, Holy Spirit, Holy Ghost—different ways that Scripture and Christian tradition name the invisible spiritual reality that motivated and empowered Jesus, and that motivates and empowers those who commit themselves to following him (page 94)

spiritual direction—also called pastoral counseling; the practice of seeking and receiving spiritual and moral guidance (page 156)

sponsor—an active Catholic who accompanies a catechumen during his or her journey toward Baptism, offering spiritual support and participating in the Rite of Christian Initiation of Adults (page 76)

spouse—generic term for male or female marriage partner; half of a married couple (page 197)

supernatural—above and beyond what is natural, usual, ordinary (page 27)

symbol—something visible or tangible that reminds us of and is able to put us in touch with a reality that is invisible and intangible but still real; something that communicates effective emotional or spiritual meaning (page 20)

symbolic action—an action that says more than words can express, that communicates what is in the heart and what we want someone to know (page 20)

theological virtues—faith, hope, and love; spiritual gifts that enable us to act as children of God and followers of Jesus (page 103)

Tradition—the passing on of beliefs and customs from generation to generation; the living transmission of the gospel message in the Church (page 5)

tribunal—a Church court that examines and decides cases with regard to Church law, especially marriage cases (page 213)

viaticum—a traditional name for Communion that is given to a dying person, in the sense of "food for the journey" from this life to the next (page 180)

vigil—a gathering of people prior to an important event, such as the Easter Vigil on Holy Saturday or the vigil for the deceased prior to a funeral (page 186)

vocation—from the Latin word for a call or invitation, a state of life or work to which one feels called, in contrast to work that would be considered simply a job (page 203)

wake—the practice of "staying awake with the body" between the time of death and the time of burial (page 186)

Index

(° defined in margin)